Information Technology For All

Information Technology For All

(Volume – One)

Editor-in-Chief
Arvind Kumar

INSTITUTE FOR SUSTAINABLE DEVELOPMENT
LUCKNOW
&
ANMOL PUBLICATIONS PVT. LTD.
NEW DELHI - 110 002 (INDIA)

ANMOL PUBLICATIONS PVT. LTD.
4374/4B, Ansari Road, Daryaganj
New Delhi - 110 002
Ph.: 23261597, 23278000
Visit us: www.anmolpublications.com

Information Technology for All

First Edition, 2004

ISBN 81-261-2016-9 (Set)

PRINTED IN INDIA

Published by J.L. Kumar for Anmol Publications Pvt. Ltd., New Delhi and Printed at Mehra Offset Press, Delhi.

CONTENTS

PREFACE

All modern complex organizations deal with men, material, machinery and, of course, money. This was postulated long ago by Forrester who added information to the list. Information is as vital a component to an organization as the other four, and is as crucial to its continued viability as the others put together. The analogy is to the genetic code carried by our chromosomes in a highly formal manner, — the sheer regularity and carrying forward is essential for the organism to survive. Any departure can only lead to a cancerous decay process.

The long talked about growth of computers and the "information explosion" are today's realities in our social and economic institutions. The purpose of this work is to provide the fundamental knowledge to enable one to participate in the development and use of information systems in modern organizations.

The Internet is *not* owned or funded by any one institution, organization, or government. It does not have a CEO and is not a commercial service. The Internet is, however, directed by the Internet Society (ISOC), composed of volunteers. The ISOC appoints a sub-council, the Internet Architecture Board (IAB), which works out issues of standards, network resources, network addresses, and so on. Another volunteer group, the Internet Engineering Task Force (IETF), handles day-to-day issues of Internet operation. Practically speaking, the Internet is composed of people, hardware, and software. With the proper equipment on both ends, you can sit at your computer and communicate with someone any place in the world. You can also use the Internet to access vast amounts of information, including text, graphics, sound, and video. From your computer, you can send e-mail, "chat" with others on another continent, work with others on an electronic whiteboard, and, with the appropriate equipment, video-conference. The Internet grew out of a series of developments in the academic, governmental, and information technology communities. In 1969, ARP Anet, an experimental 4-computer network, was established by the Advanced Research Projects Agency (ARPA) of the U.S. Department of Defense so that research scientists could communicate.

'Informational Technology for All', as is obvious from the name of the title, this work contains very judiciously selected succinct information on Information technology, meant for one and all. The beginners as well as experts will find the contents of utmost use. The entire information is covered under twenty two chapters, followed by appendices and bibliography.

To make the information reliable, we have borrowed the matter from various authoritative sources. Expert opinions are also consulted. We owe a deep sense of gratitude to all those whose works are cited and substantially reproduced.

Finally, we will be failing in our duty if we do not acknowledge the kind of assistance we receive from our colleagues at the Institute in completion of this work. We are equally indebted to Shri J.L. Kumar, Managing Director, and Mr. Kripal D. Joshi, Editor, Anmol Publications Pvt. Ltd., New Delhi for publishing this manuscript in a very limited time.

Arvind Kumar

1

INFORMATION SYSTEMS CONCEPTS

As a nation we are fond of using labels to characterise a significant aspect, event, or emotion for a given time period. Examples of these labels are, "The Dark Ages," "The Stone Age," "The Age of Chivalry," "The Roaring 20's," and "The Depression." A survey of current literature is likely to find references to "The Computer Age," "The Information Age," and "The Systems Age." Whether these labels are fads or of historical importance is not known nor necessarily important to know at this time. However, to more than half of the persons employed today, developing and operating computer-based information systems are what they do for a livelihood.

The long talked about growth of computers and the "information explosion" are today's realities in our social and economic institutions. The purpose of this text is to provide the fundamental knowledge to enable one to participate in the development and use of information systems in modern organisations. Before we discuss the variety of information requirements and the sophisticated ways in which these requirements are satisfied in modern organisations, we first examine the basic concepts underlying information systems. The specific objectives of this chapter are:

1. To develop a descriptive and functional definition of data and information.
2. To analyse systems and their use in developing the information systems concept.
3. To present an overview of the information systems development methodology.

DATA AND INFORMATION

Our analysis of information systems begins with functional definitions of data and information and a discussion of their relationship. This initial understanding is enhanced by distinguishing between formal and informal information, discussing the attributes which give value to specific information, and analysing how information is produced from data.

Basic Definitions

The terms data and information are often used interchangeably, but they refer to two distinct concepts. *Data* are language, mathematical, and other symbolic surrogates which are generally agreed upon to represent people, objects, events, and concepts. Simply stated, data are raw facts. While *Information* is data placed into a meaningful context for its recipient. The following examples illustrate these concepts and their relationship:

> . . . let's consider the implications to various people of a train whistle penetrating the evening dusk. To the saboteur crouching in a culvert, it might signify the failure of his mission because the whistle indicates that the train has already passed over his detonating charge without causing an explosion. To the playboy, it might presage the imminent arrival of the transgressed husband ... To the lonely wife it means the return of her traveling husband. To the man with his foot caught in the switch down the track, it preshadows doom . . .[1]

It is also likely that others who hear the train whistle associate nothing of value to its sound. Perhaps, some within range of the whistle do not even hear it!

The single most important transaction to any company is the receipt of a customer order. The information value of a specific customer order, however, will vary among the employees of the company. Those individuals most directly responsible for processing customer orders (e.g., credit clerks, inventory pickers, packagers, shipping clerks, etc.) will value the contents of a specific order as necessary information to perform their respective jobs. Individual salespersons will likely be interested in only those orders pertaining to their customers and, perhaps, only the aggregate of all orders received in a given time period (i.e., daily, weekly, monthly). The sales manager may be interested in all customer orders but only values these data when reported or presented in reference to quotas, forecasts, or budgets. Accountants view customer orders as data until such time as they represent or are processed into billable shipments, accounts receivables, monthly revenues, and so forth. Others in the company such as employee relations, research, and engineering personnel routinely are not interested in customer order data.

The sound of a train whistle and a customer order are two examples of data. Whether or not these data are to be valued as information, as the above examples illustrate, depends upon each recipient's specific situation, which includes their particular set of attitudes, emotions, and goals. The amount of data available at any time to each of us, whether it be in our classroom endeavors, recreational pursuits, or job responsibilities is virtually unlimited. Unless we have identified information requirements to satisfy, the sheer volume of available data represents a time and economic burden impossible to overcome. Therefore, if we want to provide information rather than data to individuals, it is necessary to have analysed their specific situation and determined their specific information requirements.

Formal Versus Informal Information

Formal information systems are based on the supposition that we can identify individuals' information requirements and that we can also determine the methods of producing information from data to satisfy these requirements. The distinction between formal and informal information is a third important concept.

Examples of *formal information* include: legal requirements, government legislation, union contracts, accounting procedures, planning requirements, organisational budgets, job demands, communication requirements, control needs, stockholders and creditor demands, problem situations, and general decision-making processes. Pay-checks, invoices, purchase orders, and receiving tickets are all examples of structured forms of formal information. Status reports, variances, probabilities, return on investment, reorder points, contribution margins, and traditional accounting statements are highly formalised forms of information. In contrast, *informal information* includes opinions, judgments, hunches, intuition, hearsay, personal experiences, "grapevines," "rules of thumb," gossip, assumptions, and so forth.

From the examples presented, the difference between formal and informal information should be clear. Formal information allows us to extract from the recipient the processing or conversion procedures for producing information from data. On the other hand, the value of informal information is arbitrarily assessed by its recipient. The form and content of informal information are both subjective and unstructured, and the process which converts data to information cannot be separated from the recipient.

Both types of information may be essential to the management and operation of an organisation, but formal information is the only valid output of a formal information system, and the only valid information discussed in this text. It should be noted, however, that advances in accounting, operations research, finance, and statistics have resulted in formalising some of what was previously regarded as informal information (e.g., human resource accounting, management forecasts, probability theory).

Information Attributes

Many attributes or qualities associated with the concept of information assist us in identifying and describing specific information requirements. Figure 1 illustrates several attributes of information.

As we move from the concept of providing generalised information to providing specific information to an individual, determining the values for the various information attributes illustrated in Figure 1 is necessary. This is not an easy task. Some of the attributes are difficult to state and almost impossible to measure objectively. For example, assume you are responsible for scheduling ships in a large shipping company. It is likely that one of your major responsibilities would be to know where each ship is at any given time. It is also likely that you would be routinely asked the location of a given ship by a variety of people. Your response could be any of the following: "At sea," "In the Atlantic," "On her way to Gibraltar," "Three days out of New York," "Latitude 38°N, longitude 51°W."

While each response is accurate and timely, it may or may not satisfy the information requirements of the individual because it fails to satisfy other attributes. The nature of each response presupposes that you have determined each individual's "meaningful context" and that you have determined the relevance of each attribute to that context. To the extent your judgment is correct, you have provided information. To the extent you have misunderstood the individuals' needs or failed to consider correctly the importance of the attributes, you have provided data and are likely to hear the following: "Can you be more precise?," "Will you clarify that?," "May I have the exact location," "When did she last report?," or "Is that in the Atlantic or Pacific?"

As we identify and define specific information requirements, it is essential that we describe these requirements in terms of information attributes as best we can. Properly analysed, information attributes which are related to specific information requirements, begin to formulate a demand on the overall design of an information system. A demand, simply put, means to get the right information to the right person at the right time!

Producing Information from Data

To the extent that we can identify an individual's information requirements, it is possible to provide the information necessary to satisfy these requirements. The ways in which data become or are converted into information are almost as numerous as the specific situations we can identify. Our emphasis here, however, is on organisations and the information requirements of members of these organisations. Even with this qualification it would appear that the ways to convert data into information are almost endless. For example, examine the variety and number of

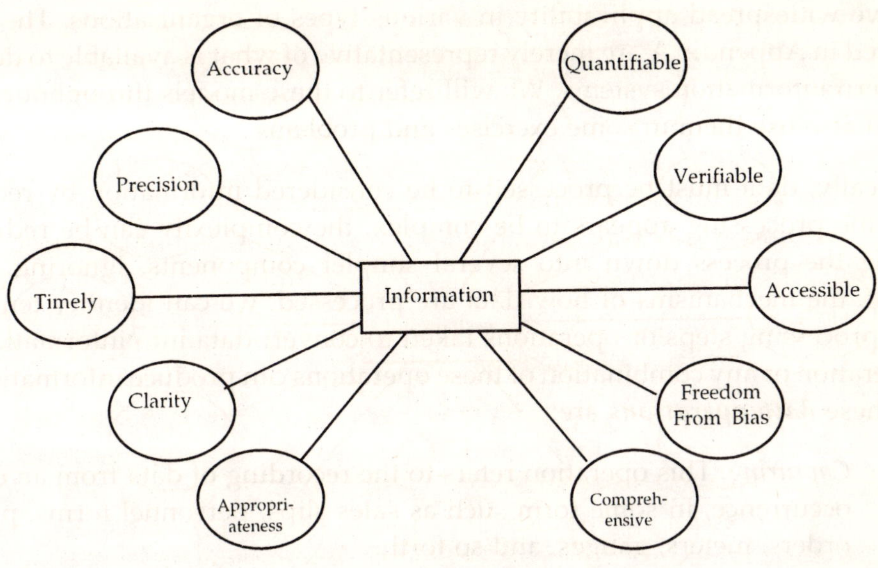

Timely— The receipt of information within the time frame it is needed by the recipient.	Accessible— The ease and speed with which information can be obtained.
Precision— The measurement detail used in providing information.	Freedom From Bias— The absence of intent to alter or modify information in order to influence recipients.
Accuracy—The agree of the absence of error in information.	Comprehensive— The completeness of the information.
Quantifiable—The ability to state information numerically.	Appropriateness— How well the information relates to a user's requirement.
Verifiable— The degree of consensus arrived at among various users examining the same information.	Clarity—The degree to which information is free from ambiguity.

Fig. 1: Information attributes.

course offerings in your business or management curriculum that are intended to provide information on how organisations operate. We can reduce this apparent variety by using a different conceptual approach to describe information and the ways it is produced. Producing information involves concepts and techniques as simple as communicating previously received data in a timely fashion or as complex as the development of a linear program. In Appendix A we provide brief descriptions of a variety of logico-mathematical models which produce information from data and have widespread applicability in various types of organisations. The models presented in Appendix A are merely representative of what is available to designers of modern information systems. We will refer to these models throughout the text and will also use them in some exercises and problems.

Basically, data must be processed to be considered information by recipients. Where the processing appears to be complex, the complexity can be reduced by breaking the process down into several simpler components. Ignoring, for the moment, the mechanisms of how data are processed, we can identify ten unique logical processing steps or operations taken to convert data into information. Any one operation or any combination of these operations can produce information from data. These ***data operations*** are:

1. *Capturing.* This operation refers to the recording of data from an event or occurrence, in some form such as sales slips, personnel forms, purchase orders, meters, gauges, and so forth.
2. *Verifying.* This operation refers to the checking or validating of data to ensure that it was captured and recorded correctly. Examples of verification might be one person reviewing another's work, the use of check digits in coding structures, or cross-footing.
3. *Classifying.* This operation places data elements into specific categories which provide meaning for the user. For example, sales data can be classified by inventory type, size, customer, salesperson, warehouse shipped from, or any other classification that will give the sales data more meaning.
4. *Arranging* (Sorting). This operation places data elements in a specified or predetermined sequence. An inventory file, for example, can be arranged by product code, activity level, dollar value, or by whatever other attribute is coded in the file and deemed desirable by a user.
5. *Summarising.* This operation combines or aggregates data elements in either of two ways. First, it accumulates data in a mathematical sense. For example, when a balance sheet is prepared, the aggregate figure of the category current assets represents a number of specific and more detailed accounts. Second, it reduces data in the logical sense, as in the example where the personnel manager wants a list of names of employees assigned to Department 23.
6. *Calculating.* This operation entails the arithmetic and/or logical manipulation of data. For example, computations must be performed to derive employees' pay, customers' bills, students' grade point averages, and so forth. In

many instances, very sophisticated calculations must be performed to manipulate the data in management science models such as PERT, linear programming, forecasting, and so on.

7. *Storing.* This operation places data onto some storage media such as paper, microfilm, or magnetic tape, where the data can be retrieved when needed.
8. *Retrieving.* This operation entails searching out and gaining access to specific data elements from the medium where it is stored.
9. *Reproducing.* This operation duplicates data from one medium to another, or into another position in the same medium. For example, a file of data stored on a magnetic disk may be reproduced onto another magnetic disk or onto a magnetic tape for further processing or for security reasons.
10. *Disseminating/Communicating.* This operation transfers data from one place to another. It can take place at a number of junctures in the data processing cycle. For example, data can be transferred from a device to a user in the form of a report or a display on the screen of a computer-controlled terminal. The ultimate aim of all information systems is to disseminate information to the final user.

The role of these ten data operations in an information system is similar to the role of the six simple machines identified by the physical scientist. Just as all larger, more complex machines are composed of the lever, pulley, screw, incline plane, wheel and axle, and wedge in a variety of combinations, all complex information systems are composed of some combination of the ten simple data operations.

THE SYSTEMS CONCEPT

The term system has become quite popular in recent years. It has been used to describe many different things, particularly those activities required for data processing. Early attempts to apply technology to data processing centered around the development of machines which were capable of performing a single data operation more efficiently (e.g., typewriters, calculators, mechanical files, microfilm, and copy machines). The introduction of the punched card as a recording medium resulted in the development of various machines (e.g., keypunch, sorter, collator, printer) which perceived the conversion of data into information as a process (hence the term data processing). The development of the digital computer and its related technology popularised the use of the word systems and a methodology for the development of "systems" to satisfy the information requirements of modern organisations. We begin this section with a brief explanation of systems. We then use a systems context to analyse organisations. Finally, we conclude this section with a discussion of the information systems concept.

Systems

A *system* can be defined as any set of objects and ideas, and their interrelationships which are ordered to a common goal or purpose. Figure 2 illustrates a conceptual model of a system. In this illustration the various symbols *A* through *I* represent the components of the system. The lines connecting the symbols represent the relationships among components. Identical symbols represent a unique relationship among one or more components, which can be termed a ***subsystem.*** The use of the term subsystem facilitates analysis or communication. For example, we can describe the system by its components *A, B, C, . . ., I* or by its subsystems *ABC, DEFG, HI,* whichever serves our purposes better. With complex systems, we can divide the analysis and design of the system into subsystems for control and implementation purposes.

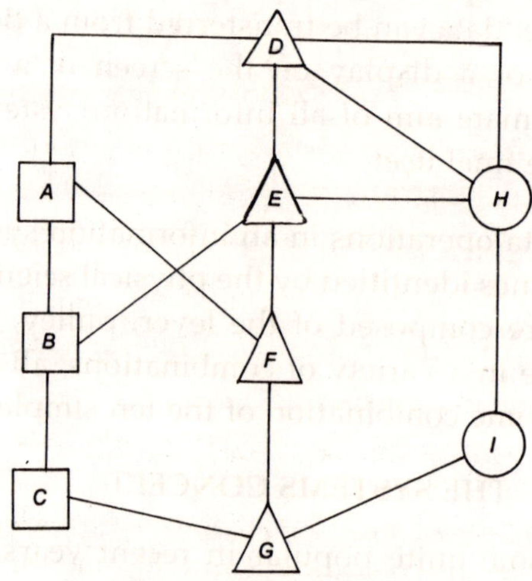

Fig. 2: Conceptual model of a system.

A system and any of its components and subsystems may be found as such in reality or they may be purely logical in nature. For example, a person can be viewed as a system. We might begin to describe or analyse a person by identifying and listing physical components (e.g., toe, eye, ear, heart). On the other hand, if this is too cumbersome or represents unwanted detail, we might identify major subsystems (e.g., respiratory, reproductive, endocrine). Another description of a person as a system might perceive the physical, intellectual, moral, and emotional aspects as either components or subsystems.

The first way of describing a person coincides fairly directly with what we find in reality: a set of physical organs. The second way implies the existence of physical organs and adds an awareness of specific relationships among these organs. The third perception represents logical entities. Each way would have value depending on our analytical or communication goals.

The value of approaching reality from a system's perspective can be as simple as just another technique to analyse or design complex machines, projects, or theories; or, on another level, we could argue that the true value of this perception of reality lies in the fact that the "Whole is greater than the sum of its parts." In other words, the effectiveness of components considered collectively as a system may be greater than the sum of the effectiveness of each component considered separately. The added measure of value or effectiveness is called the *synergistic effect*.

Organisations Perceived as Systems

Any organisation can be viewed as a system composed of three subsystems, namely, the operations subsystem, the management subsystem, and the information subsystem. For the local corner drugstore all of the subsystems may reside within one person plus several filing cabinets and a typewriter. In a large drug manufacturing and distribution organisation these three systems are separate and well-defined, but highly related. This relationship is depicted in Figure 3.

The *management subsystem* includes all the people and activities directly related to determining the planning, controlling, and decision-making aspects of the operations subsystem. For example, determining what services to market, deciding how many warehouses to have and the location of each, outlining the responsibilities and composition of a steering committee, and the like, are functions of the management subsystem.

The *operations subsystem* includes all of the activities, material flow, and people directly related to performing the primary functions of the organisation. For example, selling the finished product or service, producing finished goods, warehousing inventory, delivering health care services, designing products, purchasing raw materials, engineering, and so forth, are functions of the operations subsystem.

The *information subsystem* is an assemblage or collection of people, machines, ideas, and activities that gather and process data in a manner that will meet the formal information requirements of an organisation. Its purpose is to satisfy information requirements including accounting and routine operational needs; planning, controlling, and decision-making needs of all levels of management; and the needs of concerned parties external to the organisation.

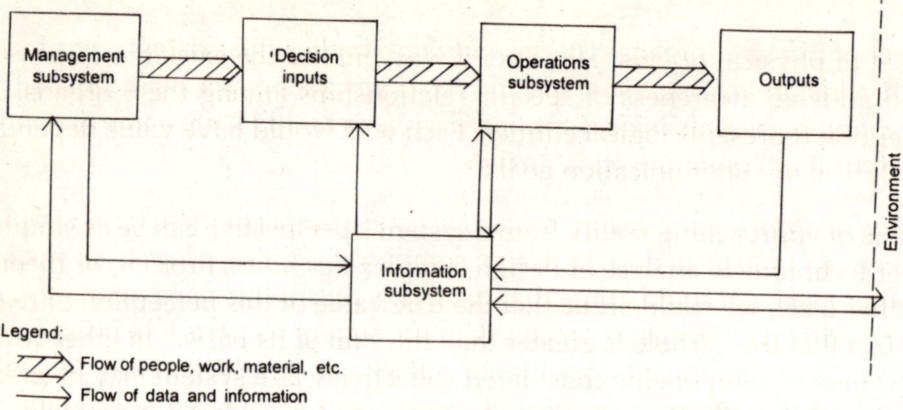

Fig. 3: Example of the relationship between the management, operations, and information subsystems of an organisation.

Analysing the interactions of these three subsystems allows us to make several key observations. First, the actual performance of the operations subsystem is represented by a variety of data input to the information subsystem. The information subsystem processes these data and produces information for the management subsystems (e.g., all forms of performance reporting), other segments of the operations subsystem (e.g., a customer order is input and processed or is converted to a production order or inventory withdrawal notice), or external users (e.g., a vendor purchase order, a customer invoice, a government report, or the financial statements). Second, the needs and requirements of external users in the environment within which the organisation exists, interface with the information subsystem as a series of data inputs (e.g., customer order, governmental reporting requirements, industry statistics). These inputs are also processed and provide information either for the operations or the management subsystems. Finally, the management subsystem provides a variety of data inputs to the information subsystem which will affect the operations subsystem, external users, and other levels of management. These inputs might be objectives, budgets, forecasts, schedules, work orders, and so forth.

Viewed as a system, both the organisation and its information subsystem are highly integrated. The information subsystem serves all departments or functions (i.e., horizontal integration) and all levels of management (i.e., vertical integration).

In most organisations, for example, inventories of finished goods, raw materials, in-process goods, supplies, etc., must be maintained. Depending on several management or organisational factors, the responsibility for maintaining physical inventories can reside in the marketing, purchasing, production, or materials department. Regardless of the department responsible for maintaining inventory, the need for information concerning inventory levels exists throughout the organisation. Using product inventory and the information concerning inventory levels, we can demonstrate the integrated nature of the information system. Figure 4 illustrates the horizontal or interdepartmental integration.

Clearly, inventory planners need to know current inventory levels. Accountants need inventory level information for reporting purposes. A purchasing agent may need to know what is currently available to replenish the stock of raw material. A salesperson needs to know current inventory levels to commit to a delivery schedule for a customer. A production scheduler must know what inventory is available at various levels before assigning or scheduling other resources such as direct labor and machines. The finance department, when determining an organisation's short-term cash requirements, includes the value of present inventories in their analysis. To arrange for proper warehouse space or freight schedules, other departments also must know current inventory levels. This integration does not mean that all departments or all levels of management use the resources of the information system in the same way. From department to department and from level to level, differences, as expressed by the information attributes, result in a multiplicity of information requirements.

The Information Systems Concept

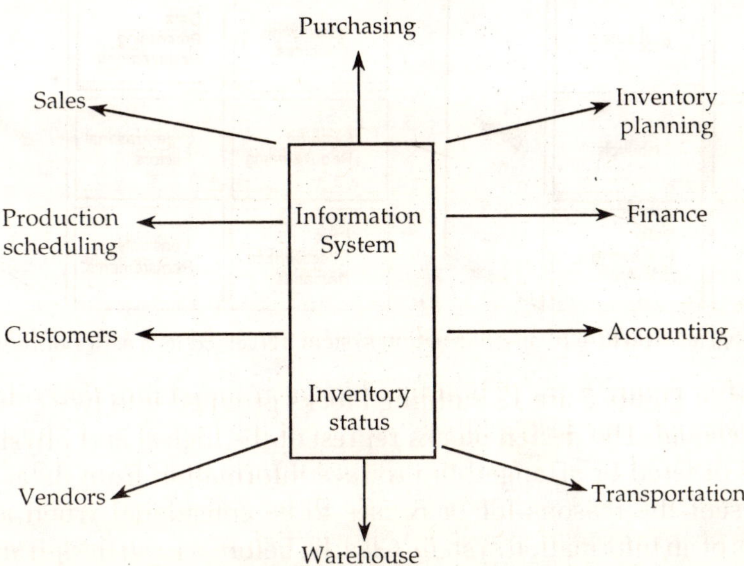

Fig. 4: Integrated nature of the information system as it relates to the functional-units of the organisation.

All organisations have an information system. This information system is a formal entity composed of a variety of logical and physical resources. From organisation to organisation, these resources are arranged or structured in an infinite number of ways. Moreover, because organisation and information systems are dynamic resources, a structure we construct one day may not necessarily reflect the actual arrangement of these resources the next day. Thus we need a concept that logically portrays the structure of an information system, reflects all of its physical resources, is appropriate for any size information system in any type of organisation, and remains relatively constant. Figure 5 illustrates such a logical structure for information systems in terms of a series of building blocks.

Understanding the concepts represented by each of the building blocks shown in Figure 5 and their interrelationships, provides the basic knowledge for describing or developing the information system in all organisations. The material discussed in this text will expand your understanding of the logical content of each building block, its relationship with the other building blocks, and provide you with a methodology for applying this knowledge on a practical level.

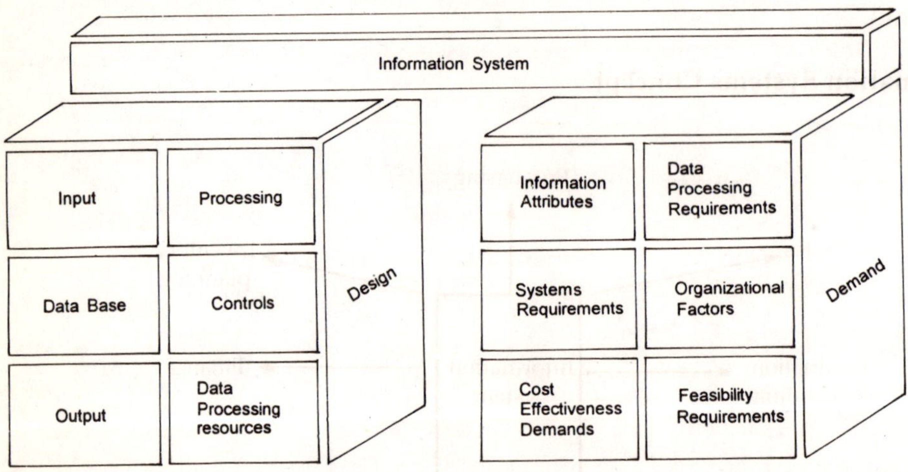

Fig. 5: The logical structure of an information system perceived as a series of building blocks.

Illustrated in Figure 5 are 12 building blocks grouped into two columns labeled ***design*** and ***demand***. The design blocks represent the logical and physical resources that must be ordered or arranged to produce information from data. The demand blocks represent the reasons for or causes to be considered when arranging the design blocks of an information system. Clearly, before we can design an information system (i.e., arrange the design blocks), we must ascertain the needs and requirements of the organisation (i.e., the specific values of the demand blocks). The specific values that each building block contains in a given information system, is the result of a specific study performed within and for an organisation. In Part III we provide a methodology for determining the specific values of both the design and demand building blocks.

Figure 6 expands the concepts of the design blocks with more detail or examples of the entities which they represent.

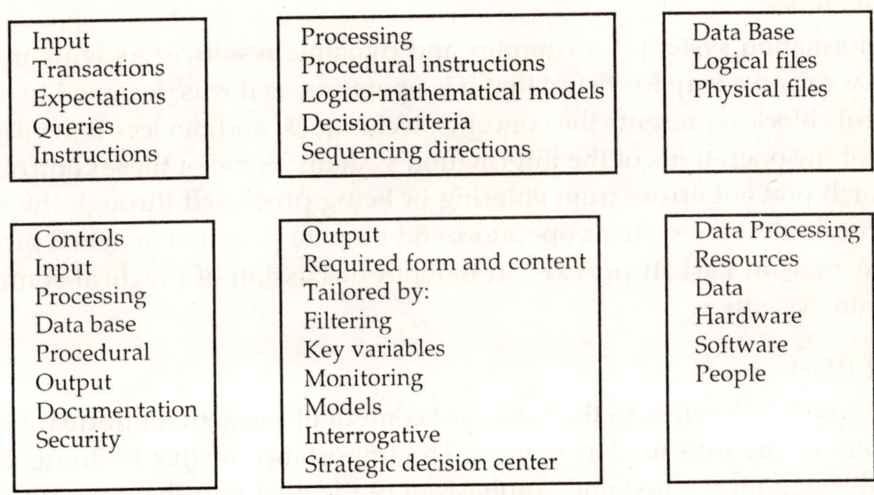

Fig. 6: Detail components of the design building blocks.

1. *Input Block*

The input block illustrates the variety of data which are input into an information system. Generally, the required data to be input into a system are derived from specific information requirements. Throughout the text, and particularly in solving the exercises and problems at the end of each chapter, we will become more familiar with determining input data.

2. *Processing Block*

In the previous section we discussed the processing block in terms of data operations. We also referred to Appendix A, where a variety of logico-mathematical models are discussed. As with the input block, the specific values of the processing block are derived from specific information requirements and considerable opportunities will be given throughout the text for you to become adept at developing specific values for this block.

3. *Data Base Block*

A broad all-encompassing definition is that a data base is a repository of all data of interest and value to the users of the information system. As noted in Figure 6, its two important dimensions are logical and physical files. Files are a concept of structuring data contained within the data base. Logical files refer to the inherent or implied relationships among the data, while physical files are associated with the way in which data are organised physically on specific storage devices or media. Part II in the text is dedicated to analysing and illustrating the data base block.

4. Controls Block

An information system is a complex and dynamic resource. As with any other resource, we need a way to ensure that it is operating as it was designed to operate. The controls block represents the concepts, techniques, and devices that ensure the integrity of the operations of the information systems. Some of these controls act as filters which prevent errors from entering or being processed through the system. Other controls alert the systems operators and users to potential or actual problems. Several sections in Part III provide an indepth discussion of practical controls for information systems.

5. Output Block

The output block refers to the form and content of the actual information given to the users of the information system. The importance of this building block is stressed throughout the text and emphasised in the next two chapters. We discuss a variety of techniques listed in Figure 6, which can be used to tailor information outputs to specific information requirements.

6. Data Processing Resources Block

The final design block is labeled data processing resources. The physical implementation of the other design blocks is expressed in terms of a particular set and arrangement of data, hardware, software, and people. Appendix B provides brief descriptions of major components of the hardware resource. Aspects of data base hardware and software are discussed in Part II.

Figure 7 expands the concepts of the demand blocks with more detail (or examples of the entities which they represent). As noted previously, the demand blocks determine the form and substance of the design blocks.

1. *Information attributed.* The foremost demand on the information system is derived from the specific information requirements of the users. As we discussed previously, these requirements are stated in terms of information attributes listed in Figure 7.

2. *Data processing requirements.* This demand summarises the impact of providing

specific information requirements for one or more users of a system. Furthermore, an assessment of data processing requirements implies alternatives to satisfy more efficiently or effectively these requirements for both the individual user and the organisation.

3. *Systems requirements.* This demand is somewhat similar to data processing requirements. Systems requirements recognise the dynamic nature of the organisation and its information system, and the costs of the data processing resources with which the logical aspects of the system are implemented. Systems requirements are defined and referenced throughout the text.

4. *Organisational factors.* Every organisation develops and operates an information system to satisfy its specific information requirements. The quantity and quality of user requirements are often dictated by broader organisational theories and practices. We analyse the organisational factors noted in Figure 7 and assess their impact on the design and development of information systems.

5. *Cost/effectiveness demands.* Information and the information system are resources. The acquisition or building of resources in organisations is normally done with an idea to make or to save money. Thus it is necessary to identify the costs and benefits to be derived before expending significant funds for developing information systems. In Part III we analyse how this justification process is conducted.

Information Attributes	Data Processing Requirements	Systems Requirements
Timely	Volume	Reliability
Precision	Complexity	Cost
Accuracy	Time	Installation schedule
Quantifiable	Computational	Life expectancy
Verifiable		Flexibility
Accessible		Growth potential
Freedom from bias		Maintainability
Comprehensive		
Appropriateness		
Clarity		

Organisational Factors	Cost/Effectiveness Demands	Feasibility Requirements
Nature	Direct costs	Technical
Size	Indirect costs	Economic
Structure	Direct benefits	Legal
Management style	Indirect benefits	Operational
		Schedule

Fig. 7: Detail components of the demand building blocks.

6. *Feasibility requirements.* All of the specific values of the other demand blocks are expressed in terms of feasibility requirements. As previously noted, compromises among demands and among their implementation in the design blocks must be achieved from various points of view before a system can be designed and implemented. Feasibility requirements are defined and discussed in Part III.

In summary, when we make a judgment that an information system is good or bad, effective or ineffective, efficient or inefficient, we are comparing the specific values of the design blocks to specific values of the demand blocks for that system. This conceptual view of the information system and its development serves as our guide throughout the text.

An Analogy

At this point we have introduced the basic concepts of information systems, the foundation upon which any information system is developed regardless of size, orientation, or complexity. With these concepts, you have the framework and guidelines to keep you on track. In the final analysis, however, the specific system you design or implement depends on how well you determine and structure the specific values for each concept.

Architects design buildings to serve many purposes. Systems analysts design information systems to serve many organisations. The Roman Architect Vitruvius described the goals of architecture as use, strength, and beauty. These three goals continue to guide architects today.

The design of every building includes four components: (1) space, (2) materials, (3) light, and (4) style. The way these components or design blocks are arranged results in the kind of building that is constructed. The architect encloses space with walls and it flows through openings called doors and windows. The physical property of the building is made up of the materials used such as timber, steel, glass, concrete, and so forth. The architect must know the texture and structural properties of materials to use them properly. Light influences the appearance of a building's spaces and materials. Inside or outside, the architect uses materials to reflect or absorb light as it changes or to change the character of a room. There have been many architectural styles throughout history. Needs of people, their environment, and their tastes in fashion influence the development of styles. Some architects have broken with traditional styles stressing for example, organic architecture where a building, like a living organism, must "grow" out of its surroundings. No doubt there will be different styles in the future to accommodate structures such as ground homes designed to meet energy conservation demands. However, irrespective of the architectural styles, all buildings will still be designed and built using the basic concepts discussed here.

Many architects would say that there are form and function demands on the design components. They agree that form (the appearance of the building) and function (the purpose of the building) go hand in hand. Form is the way an architect puts together the design elements or design blocks. Function determines how well a building serves its purposes. Because of these two demands and their different levels of influence, the form design blocks of space, materials, light, and style can be arranged in different ways and take on different values.

The demands of form and function can be further subdivided. For example, a partial listing of demand blocks could be: aesthetics, shelter, efficient use of land, cost/effectiveness, safety, comfort, energy conservation, heat, ventilation, privacy, freedom of movement, single family dwelling, cooperative housing, building codes, zoning laws, permanent, mobile, temporary, environment planning, city planning, and so forth.

The building that is finally designed will be controlled by the specific values identified for the demand blocks listed above. For example, note that two demand blocks are aesthetics and efficient use of land. In cities, pleasing design and efficient use of land are strong demands. Architects have met this challenge by building impressive skyscrapers. Where land is more plentiful, architects design buildings with the land use demand less important compared to other demands. In this situation, architects normally design buildings with a pleasing horizontal look. In the development of buildings, architects have design and demand blocks which guide them in their work. So too, designers of information systems have design and demand concepts to guide them.

INFORMATION SYSTEMS DEVELOPMENT

The importance of information systems and their development can be seen in many different trends during the past 10 to 20 years. The emergence and growth of companies involved in the development of information technology is the most obvious. Within most other organisations, this growth is mirrored by the growth of data processing and information systems departments. The increased number of publications, both journals and textbooks, coupled with more course offerings in colleges and universities, represent added testimony to the increasing importance of information systems.

By providing specific values for each block, we are able to analyse or design any information system. How one goes about providing these specific values within an organisational setting is what is called the systems development methodology. Part III of this text, as we have alluded to before, describes such a methodology. Here we discuss the need for an information systems development methodology in modern organisations, provide an overview for the methodology presented, and examine the role of the systems analyst in this methodology.

A Project Perspective

Organisations are comprised of many resources. There are tangible resources such as land, machines, materials, tools, people, and money. There are also intangible resources such as trademarks, patents, copyrights, manufacturing processes, skill level of a work force, and information. Indeed, information and the information system, are valuable organisational resources.

Both tangible and intangible resources have value and costs associated with them. In general, when we acquire or develop resources, we prefer not to incur costs greater than the value we receive. To ensure that resources are acquired or developed efficiently and effectively, many organisations use a project concept.

Projects are logical entities having specific beginnings and ends. The project concept is a useful management technique or device. In addition to being an efficient and an effective way to manage change, many other benefits accrue to the users of the project concept when acquiring, modifying, or developing resources. The project concept allows all of the costs and benefits associated with the acquisition, modification, or development of a resource to be identified and described in monetary terms. This allows management to determine not only if that specific project is cost/effective, but it allows them to compare the cost/effectiveness of all proposed projects to determine organisational priorities. Thus, the project concept directly supports the classical responsibility of management to allocate scarce resources.

The use of the project concept permits and encourages the sharing of organisational resources which normally or routinely are responsible to different administrative units within the organisation. This is especially true in regards to personnel skills such as engineering, financial, technical, and management. Moreover, the project concept allows management to subdivide complex activities into smaller, simpler, and doable activities which can be planned and controlled effectively. The relatively short life of a project, as contrasted with the ongoing purpose of the organisation, provides achievable goals and objectives. In fact, the development and evaluation of projects can be described as an important task of any organisation's management.

While the original use of the project concept was popularised in the development of tangible resources (e.g., constructing new facilities) it has proven quite useful in the development of intangible resources (e.g., implementation of a new manufacturing process, revision of a marketing strategy, incorporation of a new employee fringe benefit) as well. The development and modification of information systems make good use of the project concept.

The Systems Development Life Cycle

Like any other resource, an information system must be developed and maintained to satisfy the requirements of the organisation it serves. Just as factories must be modernised, buildings must be renovated, and ships must be refitted, so must information systems be modified to meet continuously changing conditions. Examples of just a few of the many changes that impact an organisation and its information system are: New products being developed routinely; old production facilities replaced by new facilities; new management structures and philosophies introduced periodically; existing government requirements changed and new ones imposed; a renegotiated labor contract goes into effect; a new computer, reportedly faster and less expensive than the existing computer, is announced; sales volumes increase.

Required and desired modifications to an information system for whatever reasons are continuous. Where these modifications are minor they are regarded as maintenance to the system and routinely incorporated into the day-to-day activities of the organisation. However, proposed modifications or new enhancements to the system requiring large expenditures of time, effort, and money are often viewed as a project.

A five-phase project life cycle adapted to an information system development is illustrated in Figure 8. The activities included in the first four phases of the depicted life cycle are directed to providing the specific values for the design and demand blocks. Grouping these activities into phases is important. Each phase is associated with one or more communication points critical to the development cycle. The communication points are characterised in Part III by the preparation of formal reports. These reports have two significant roles. First, they allow the organisations' managements to direct and monitor the systems development project. Second, these reports provide a continuing opportunity for potential systems users to evaluate the systems goals and the proposed ways in which these goals will be accomplished. Thus, the needs and concerns of each person affected by the information system can be acknowledged and, if possible, accommodated.

It is widely accepted that the persons who have the title *systems analyst* are responsible for performing many of the activities in this methodology. The label **user** describes those individuals in the management and operations of the organisation for whom the information system is implemented. While the role of both the systems analyst and the user are important to the successful development of the information systems, we analyse the major activities of this life cycle from the perspective of the systems analyst.

The Role of the Systems Analyst

Let us again use the example of architects and their work to gain both a better understanding of the systems development life cycle and a perspective on the systems analyst's work. Systems analysts and architects go about their work using what is called a systems development methodology derived from Figure 8.

Let us assume that an architect has been commissioned to design a new university building. A meeting with university officials is scheduled. The architect interviews them to determine their needs and goals. Questions are asked such as: "How many classrooms are needed?," "What size classes will there be?," "What number of students are expected?" "How many faculty and staff?" "What special rooms and facilities are needed?" "For what purposes?"

Next, the architect does extensive research. Other buildings are observed and a preliminary visit is made to the proposed site. What the architect is trying to determine is the scope of the project and any constraints that might be imposed on the work to be done. Some assumptions must be made at this point because a final answer on several issues may be pending. After interviewing, researching, and observing, many study facts will be gathered. These facts will have to be analysed to define clear measurable objectives and performance requirements.

After completing the analysis phase, the architect's findings will be presented to officials of the university so that any misunderstandings or differences can be resolved. It is important to test the analysis and for the architect to receive feedback from all parties concerned so that a "Taj Mahal" is not designed when a functional structure is all that is wanted. The process of testing and feedback is done to see how demands (e.g., efficient use of land, safety, cost/effectiveness) impact upon design blocks (e.g., space, materials, light, style). Ideally, it should be done continuously; at the very least, it should be done at the end of each phase.

Assuming that the architect has completed the analysis phase successfully, work at the drawing board begins. *General design* alternatives are evolved that will meet objectives and various demands. The architect draws "plans" which shew how the rooms on each floor of the building will be arranged. A sketch is made of how the inside of the building will look and how it will appear from the outside. Even a three-dimensional model of each alternative plan may be constructed. These plans and

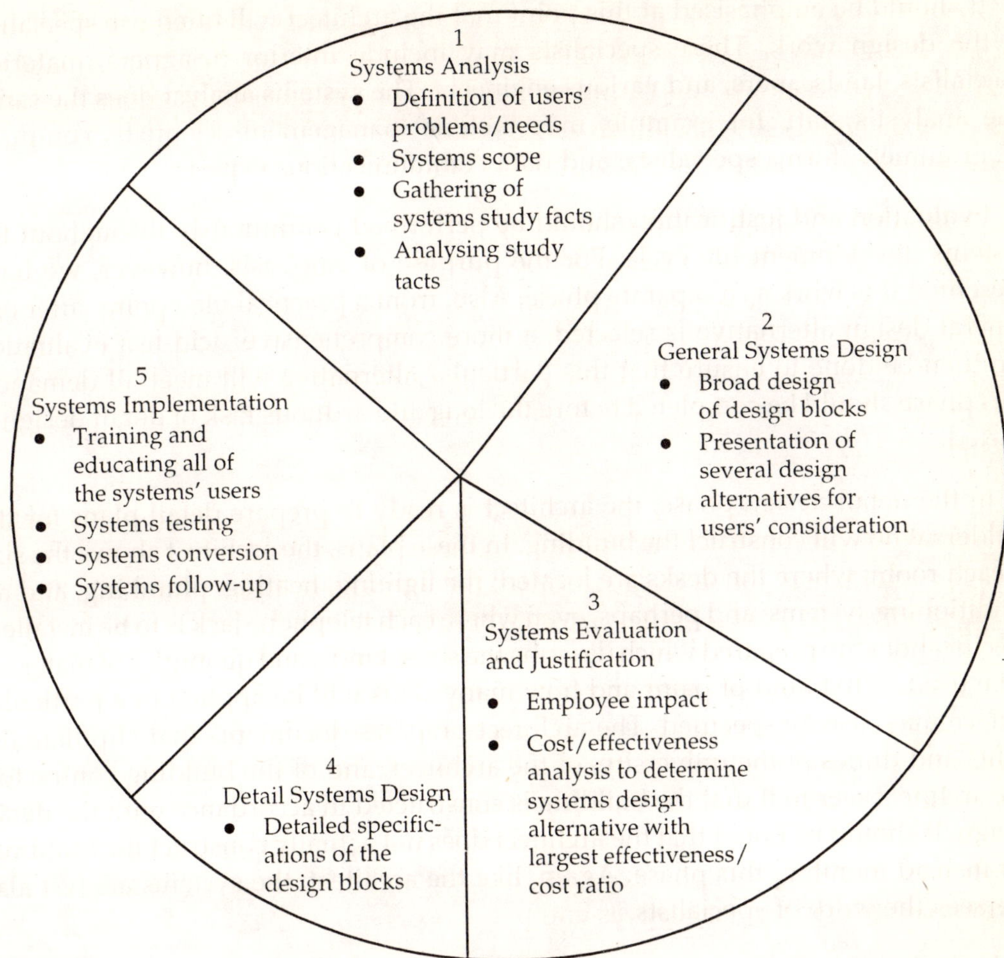

Fig. 8: The systems development life cycle showing five major phases and the major activities associated with each.

models are presented to university officials so that they may select the "best" design, or require the architect to "go back to the drawing board" to develop a better design. If a proper presentation is made in the analysis phase and the architect obtains sufficient and candid feedback, then the chance of having to go back to the analysis phase is reduced.

During the design phase and especially at its completion, strong consideration is given to the many *demand* blocks. After careful consideration, university officials will approve a design alternative or have the architect combine aspects of several alternatives into one. In any event, the architect comes out of the general design phase with a clear understanding of what is wanted in the detail design phase.

It should be emphasised at this point that the architect will often use specialists in the design work. These specialists may include interior designers, materials specialists, landscapers, and various engineers. The systems analyst does the same. The analyst's staff, for example, may include management scientists, computer programmers, forms specialists, and data communications experts.

Evaluation and justification should be performed continuously throughout the systems development life cycle. For the purpose of emphasis, however, we have presented this work as a separate phase. Also, from a practical viewpoint, after one general design alternative is selected, a more comprehensive, acid-test evaluation can then be done to ensure that this particular alternative will meet all demands. This phase should be completed before the long and arduous task of detail design is started.

In the detail design phase, the architect is ready to prepare detail plans for the builders who will construct the building. In these plans, the architect shows the size of each room; where the desks are located; the lighting, heating, plumbing, and air conditioning systems; and perhaps, even where each telephone jack is to be installed. Specifications are prepared which describe the sizes, kinds, and quantities of materials to be used. What kind of paint and how many coats will be applied to a particular surface may also be specified. The architect prepares documents that stipulate the rights and duties of the university, of the architect, and of the building contractor. The architect sees to it that the building is constructed in accordance with the detail design. It should be noted that the architect does not actually construct the building, but instead monitors this phase. Again, like the architect, the systems analyst also oversees the work of specialists.

In the implementation phase, the architect will make sure that skilled personnel are used. Certain tests are set up to see that proper materials are used and various systems, such as lighting, heating, and ventilation, work.

By following a well-defined methodology, the university building is finally constructed. After the building is completed, all components are tested together to see if the total system works. Assuming that all tests are passed, the new building may be moved into overnight. Or, the new building may be moved into in phases, such as one floor at a time. Or, it could be that both the old and new buildings are used in parallel.

After the new building has been in use for a short time, the architect performs a final inspection. If the development methodology described above has been followed, this final inspection should result in only minor adjustments being made.

Over time, because of increasing enrollment, additions must be made. An architect is hired, possibly the same one, to design an expansion. The systems development cycle is repeated. With very little effort we can substitute information systems terminology for the architect's work and have an accurate description of what the systems analyst does and how he or she goes about developing information systems, as shown in the following paragraphs:

During the ***systems analysis phase*** the systems analyst is involved with assisting the user in identifying what information is needed. This is often different from what users think they need, since frequently they have preconceived notions of what can be provided. The analyst is also concerned with identifying and quantifying the specific values of the other demand blocks.

In essence, the analyst is responsible for formalising the specific purpose and scope of the new system or of the proposed modification or addition to the old information system. At the completion of the systems analysis phase a formal report is prepared by the systems analyst detailing the identified user requirements. It is the responsibility of the user to understand and approve these requirements before general design alternatives are prepared.

During the ***general systems design phase,*** specifications are developed that capture the conceptualisations formed during the systems analysis phase. The main aspect of this phase is to equate the user's requirements with all of the design blocks that satisfy the demand blocks. In effect, the analyst has assigned specific values to each of the design blocks based on his or her understanding of the demand blocks. The analyst must formalise these values in such a way that each is a viable work assignment. Again, a formal report detailing the specific design proposals must be prepared by the analyst and approved by the users.

The systems analyst presents to the users several design alternatives for comparison, selection, and further analysis, especially concerning cost/effectiveness and the impact the new or modified system will have on the organisation as a whole. This work is performed in the ***systems evaluation*** and ***justification phase.*** One general systems design alternative is selected for detail design. In the ***detail design phase*** every design block is given precise specifications.

All of the analysis and design efforts come to a climax during the ***systems implementation phase.*** The analyst must identify cutoff dates, train and coordinate user personnel, instruct computer personnel, install new procedures and forms, test the new system, and be alert to significant oversights or omissions from earlier phases. Unfortunately, more than one well-designed information system has been scrapped due to poor conversion and implementation.

After conversion, the analyst should follow up to see that the system is operating as expected. The analyst should also monitor the system, seeking ways to improve its performance and to make modifications as users' needs change. Finally, at some point, the analyst will again review the system to recommend a new, greatly improved information system or subsystem for the organisation; and the life cycle is repeated.

The role of the information systems analyst just presented is, of course, a composite picture. In a large organisation the information system is a vast, complex entity, and many analysts are involved in designing and implementing even one subsystem of the organisation's overall information system. At a given point in time, an analyst might well be executing activities related to more than one phase of the system's development methodology and these activities must be properly coordinated.

To make the system more effective, the systems analyst will be engaged in a wide spectrum of activities ranging from formal to informal, quantitative to qualitative, structured to unstructured, specific to general, and traditional to revolutionary. In performing these activities, the analyst may use: flowcharts, data flow diagrams, decision tables, matrices, graphs, narrative reports, interviews, logico-mathematical models, and so forth. The application of these techniques reinforce one another and, when viewed in combination, provide the basic tools for systems work.

SUMMARY

Data and information are different but related concepts. Data are the raw material from which information is produced. Formal information, as distinguished from informal information, is the legitimate product of an information system. Specific information requirements are defined by identifying information attributes. Information is produced in a variety of ways ranging from very simple to complex processing procedures. Data operations are a way of analysing all information processing.

A system is a set of objects and their interrelationships which are ordered to a common goal. A synergestic effect results from a perception of a structure which emphasises the totality of entities when viewed as components of a whole. An organisation can be viewed as being comprised of three major subsystems. The information system is one major subsystem of an organisation. The components of an information system can be thought of as a series of building blocks which represent the resources to be structured or designed and the reasons or demands for this structure.

The development or modification of information systems is often termed a project. Projects can be viewed as having life cycles, which in the case of information systems, can be divided into five phases. These five phases provide a methodology for managing and developing information systems. The functional role of the systems analyst is the catalyst for implementing this methodology.

REVIEW QUESTIONS

1. Define the terms "data" and "information." If we want to supply information rather than data to individuals, what must be done?
2. How is informal information different from formal information? Why might information that is considered to be informal today, be considered formal tomorrow?
3. Why might your response to a question be information to one person but not to another?
4. Identify and describe the data processing operations.
5. What is a "system?" Why do we divide complex systems into subsystems? Why adopt a systems perspective?
6. List and explain the three major subsystems of an organisation. Provide an example that will help illustrate their overlapping nature.
7. What does "horizontal" and "vertical" integration imply in an information subsystem context?
8. Compare and contrast the two kinds of information systems building blocks.
9. List and define the design blocks. The demand blocks.
10. What are projects? Why is the project concept a useful management technique?
11. Why might "perfectly good" information systems be modified? When should modifications of the systems be viewed as a project? What phases are appropriate for describing the modification process?
12. What is a "systems analyst?" a "user?"
13. Describe the role of the systems analyst in each phase of the systems life cycle.

QUESTIONS FOR DISCUSSION

1. Discuss the statement: "Information is the cement that bonds an organisation together."

2. Overheard at a three martini lunch: "I get all my important information from Washington, D.C. and on the golf course." Discuss the type of information to which this statement refers.
3. Given the same job in two different organisations which are similar in nature, one is highly computerised and one is not; one involves a great deal of formal reporting and the other does not; and one emphasises the use of logico-mathematical models and the other does not. Discuss the probable reasons as to why this might be true.
4. Referencing the information attributes presented, evaluate the examples listed below. Identify the attribute(s) you would consider particularly significant, important, or most difficult to ascertain for each example.
   (a) Testimony to Congress on proposed social legislation.
   (b) Landing instructions to the pilot of a 747.
   (c) Job instructions to each worker on a mass production line.
   (d) Brochure for a proposed two-week trip to Europe next summer.
   (e) Directions for driving from New York to Los Angeles.
   (f) Advice on buying/selling stocks and bonds.
5. "In today's hectic environment, we cannot manage effectively if we depend solely on intuition and personal judgment." Would the author of this statement support or protest the usefulness of formal information systems? Would the author consider such systems as necessary or optional?
6. Assume that a particular data processing configuration is obtained to satisfy the data processing requirements of an organisation. Does it follow that all the information needs for the organisation have also been met?
7. "Data processing projects are not unique. These projects must compete with other large capital projects proposed within the organisation." Discuss.
8. "Systems analysts are programmers who do not or cannot code." "Systems analysis requires a great deal of creativity and, as such, a person cannot be taught how to conduct systems analysis." "Systems Analysis is a new term for an old activity." Discuss these statements.
9. Using accounts payable information, discuss the dimensions of horizontal and vertical integration.
10. "Traditional organisational concepts (e.g., assigning responsibility and accountability, delegating authority, span of control) are time proven concepts. However, these concepts when implemented in an organisation prohibit the effective use of the systems concept on a practical level." Discuss.

EXERCISES

1. Review the information attributes illustrated in Figure 3.1 and attempt to describe a system of measurement for each attribute. It may be helpful to use specific information to explain your answer.
2. From the library, obtain financial reports from *Standard and Poors* or *Moodys* on a particular company of your choice and decide whether or not you would invest in this company based on the information furnished by the financial reports. Using a scale of 1-10 (1 = poor, 10 = excellent), evaluate these reports in terms of the information attributes discussed in this chapter.
3. List and discuss the data processing operations required: (a) to prepare a payroll check, (b) to prepare a financial statement, and (c) to prepare an inventory status report.
4. Selecting several logico-mathematical models from Appendix A, describe how they produce information for organisational users.
5. Investigate an organisation of your choice and describe its information system in terms of the design and demand building blocks.
6. Interview a variety of individuals (e.g., a businesswoman, a blue-collar worker, a professor of accounting, a military officer) and ask them to describe an information system. Prepare a presentation which compares and contrasts their descriptions with one another, and with that provided in this chapter.
7. Using the systems requirements illustrated in Figure 7, prepare a presentation for the head of a monastery as though you were selling typewriters and copy machines to replace pen and ink.
8. Many information systems are intended to provide an organisation with a competitive edge in the market place. Select an organisation and ascertain the way in which its information system helps to achieve a competitive edge.

PROBLEMS

1. Visit the local government office(s) responsible for issuing licenses for operating motor vehicles and registering motor vehicles. Evaluate the literature you obtain there and answer the following questions:

   (a) Are these two functions administered separately or as a single department?

(b) How many information systems operate to perform both functions?

(c) To what degree are the systems integrated if there are more than one?

(d) If more than one system exists, what difficulties might prevent the designing of an integrated system?

(e) From your point of view, what commonalities exist between the data collected for each function?

2. The purpose of a city government is to provide public services desired or demanded by its citizens. These services include such things as law enforcement, fire protection, garbage pickup, gas and electric utilities, recreational facilities, and so forth. As cities grow, services often expand in terms of size and variety. This growth is often unplanned (e.g., neighborhood development) and responsibility is often achieved by adding new departments, or adding to existing departments for political reasons rather than based on efficient organisational principles. Using a hypothetical city with a population of 250,000 or more, list the kinds of services these cities are likely to offer. Then using the systems concept, reorder these services as you view their natural relationships for effective and efficient administration.

3. You have been asked by your boss to respond to a recent intracompany memo indicating your department would be billed $240 for keypunching of a 16,000-card job. A friend on your bowling team has supplied you with the following cost data on the last ten jobs performed by the keypunch section:

Job Size (In Thousands of Cards)	*Cost*
15	$180
30	320
12	140
18	240
20	230
9	110
17	190
22	270
12	160
25	300

Required: Prepare an appropriate response. (Hint: The least-squares model, illustrated in Appendix A, may be useful.)

4. Prepare a diagram illustrating the flow of data and information from and to the following components of the organisation's information system[2]:

   1. An order entry component that accepts sales orders.
   2. A finished goods inventory componenet that processes the orders to determine if the ordered items are available for shipment.
   3. A production scheduling component that schedules the resources of the manufacturing process to produce the items that the finished goods inventory system identifies as being unavailable.
   4. A raw materials inventory component that is consulted by the production scheduling component to determine if adequate raw materials are on hand for input to the manufacturing processes.
   5. A purchasing component that creates purchase orders for mailing to vendors requesting shipment of any raw materials found to be unavailable by the raw materials inventory system. The accounts payable component is notified of the financial obligations incurred by the firm.
   6. A receiving component that receives the raw materials into raw material inventory when they arrive from the vendor and that notifies the accounts payable component so that the vendor might be reimbursed.
   7. A production control component that monitors the manufacturing process to ensure that standards for time and cost are met. The manufacturing process is not begun until all of the needed raw materials are available and production scheduling has finalised the production schedule. When the production process is complete, the finished goods inventory component is notified of the availability of the finished goods. The production control component also enters information into the general accounting component so that production cost and inventory information from the manufacturing processes can be summarised.
   8. A personnel component that advises payroll of any changes (additions, deletions, or other changes) to the personnel resources of the firm.
   9. A billing component that prepares invoices for mailing to customers when items are identified by the finished goods inventory component as being available. Copies of the invoices are used by the warehouse stock clerks to select the items for shipment.
   10. An accounts receivable component that has the responsibility of following up on the outstanding amounts owed the company, as established by the billing component. The output of the accounts receivable component becomes input to the consolidated financial records of the firm.

11. An accounts payable component that makes payments to vendors for the raw materials received, and that enters a summary of these transactions into the general accounting component.
12. A payroll component that pays employees for their services and enters information into the general accounting component.
13. A general accounting component that consolidates that data from the various input sources and prepares the financial reports for the firm.

NOTES

1. Edward D. Dwyer, "Some Observations on Management Information Systems," in *Advocates in EDP and Information Systems* (New York: American Management Association, 1961), pp. 16 and 17. Used with permission of the American Management Association.
2. Adopted from Irvine Forkner and Raymond McLeod. Jr. (*Computerised Business Systems*, John Wiley & Sons, New York, 1973), Chaper 17.

REFERENCES

Davis, *Computer Data Processing*, Second Edition, New York: McGraw-Hill Book Company, 1973.

Davis, *Management Information Systems: Conceptual Foundations, Structure, and Development*, New York: McGraw-Hill Book Company, 1974.

Dwyer, "Some Observations on Management Information Systems," *Advances in EDP and Information Systems*, New York: American Management Association, 1961.

Forkner and McLeod, Jr., *Computerised Business Systems*, New York: John Wiley & Sons, Inc., 1973.

Hudson, "Determining Organisational Information Requirements," *Journal of Systems Management*, January 1981.

Kirk, *Total System Development for Information Systems*, New York: John Wiley & Sons, Inc., 1973.

Langefors & Samuelson, *Information and Data in Systems*, New York: Petrocelli Charter, 1976.

Lasden, "Overcoming Obstacles to Project Success," *Computer Decisions*, December 1981.

Lucas, *The Analysis, Design, and Implementation of Information Systems*, New York: McGraw-Hill Book Company, 1976.

Miller, "Problem Avoidance in the User/Analyst Relationship—Part 1," *Journal of Systems Management*, May 1981.

Murdick and Ross, *Information Systems for Modern Management*, Second Edition, Englewood Cliffs, NJ: Prentice-Hall, Inc., 1975.

Murdick and Ross, *Introduction to Management Information Systems*, Englewood Cliffs, NJ: Prentice-Hall, Inc., 1977.

Sadek and Tomeski, "Different Approaches to Information Systems," *Journal of Systems Management*, April 1981.

Sutherland, *Systems—Analysis, Administrations and Architecture*, New York: Van Nostrand Reinhold, 1975.

Weinberg, *An Introduction to General Systems Thinking*, New York: John Wiley & Sons, Inc., 1975.

2

PATTERNS OF INFORMATION MANAGEMENT

All modern complex organisations deal with men, material, machinery and, of course, money. This was postulated long ago by Forrester who added information to the list Information is as vital a component to an organisation as the other four, and is as crucial to its continued viability as the others put together.·The analogy is to the genetic code carried by our chromosomes in a highly formal manner, — the sheer regularity and carrying forward is essential for the Organism to survive. Any departure can only lead to a cancerous decay process.

Human Analogy

Before we look at our complex organisations managing their information, let us see the human being managing his. An average human being has a fairly healthy system working and maintaining itself with the help of food, drinks and respiratory inputs changing and metabolising their content into matter and energy, and segregating and eliminating the less desirable outputs. In this process, the body continually interacts with the environment and has devised a highly ingenious was to deal with all information. The Five senses are in "contact" with outside world, collecting information and sending them to the brain through the nervous channels. The brain processes them and passes control instructions to the motor mechanisms of hand or foot or heart in what usually is a "timely" response. But the body is highly selective in what passes to the brain and what need not. If the sleeping person touches fire, his autonomous reflexes would prompt him to shift his burning limbs, — without the restful brain ever realising it or "remembering" it later. It is obvious that the human body deals with information hierarchically and only the most essential informations reaches the highest decision-making quarters, namely, the brain.

Do our organisations have a similar hierarchy of action? We can first describe an organisation's supervisors and clerks as the operational level; divisions, departments and profit-centres as the managerial level; and the top echelon of executives as the corporate or strategic level. Activity-wise, then, the operational level executes decisions and use resources in conformity with rules; the managerial level makes decisions, sets rules and allocates resources, besides measuring performance; and the strategic level sets objectives and determines resources for the organisation.

Hierarchy of Information Flow

Looking at the hierarchy of information now, clearly the information is immediate and real-time, limited to work-centres at the operational level. It is short-term and internal to the organisation at the managerial level. It is long-term and external to the organisation at the corporate level. Nature of information would be precise, readily available and tailor-made for the problems at the bottom; historical and fairly accurate and integrated at the middle; and prediction and imprecise at the top. Use of information would vary from just following directions, trough administrative persuasions, to being creatively analytical at the three levels.

It is important to notice that types of decisions that are made at bottom level are highly repetitive and structured, almost "programmed". At the middle, they are still respective but not programmed any more. At the top, they are one-time kind and totally unstructured, based largely on qualitative information, as distinct from the accuracy of quantitative information at the supervisory level. In fact, while it is possible to "optimise" one's decision at the lowest level with a judicious use of resources subject to the available constraints, this is possible distinctly less and less as one moves up the hierarchy, and it becomes only a question of compromise among a number competing and conflicting factors quite sub-optimally, best know as "satisficing."

Selectivity of Information

Having noticed these hierarchical variations, any judicious management of information has to recognise the cardinal principle that information has better be selective at the top in order not to deluge it or, in other words, what body does for the brain is just right to save the top from excessive information Such considerations have led to a fascinating hypothesis: information is really the knowledge of disorganisation, or, of what is not going right within the organisation, especially as one moves up from routine data full of certainty to a flexible unstructured decision-making in a highly uncertain environment

Does it add a new angle to handling of information and its selective use in decision-making? Single tasks or operations can cope with all the data available. But in the higher echelons, the whole organisation looms more and more in the view, and a ruthless, limitless process of "eliminating" garbage (does not the body do it?) is the only sane way for the top to confine its attention only to what is erring, i.e., departures from the set norms and targets, exceptions which bring out non-obedience of the rules and, generally, all deviations and aberrations to be rectified and to be put back to the right path.

Corollary Principles

A number of fairly significant principles follow from the above. First of all, since the top manager — with his understanding of the above — would no longer thump the table and ask for "all the information" (since he cannot handle it in the first place), there is a logical case for *delegation*. It lets decisions being taken where it is due based on information available in more details and, in the bargain, satisfy the subordinate's ego. Secondly, it helps to create far less file-bound "cases". More important, the spirit of delegation can go all the way down in terms of only aggregated, reduced or processed information being put up above which satisfy pre-defined yardsticks. For instance, certain "tolerance" limits can be easily specified (body does it again!) and what is controllable can be given attention to, without the wasting of time on what is uncontrollable.

The above enunciation militates against the age-old adage "information is power" and perhaps justly so. If the pathological craving to be "overinformed" is got rid of and the gear of "uninformed" decisions overcome, where is the need for clinging on to every opportunity for monopolising information?

Operational and Managerial Levels

It is precisely at the operational level that computers have helped the most by mechanising routine structured data, and that is how it should be. A lathe operator's acceptance or rejection of a turned-out part, is dependent upon the catalogue and part number, design-specifications, tolerance limits for different design-parameters, and a few other factors. These factors are specified according to prior directions, deterministic in nature and hence easily "programmable" onto a computer. The routine decisions can then be spelt out by the computer and acceptance or rejection takes place mechanically. A bank-clerk's honouring or refusing a cheque is another instance of operational level activity, where the verification of name and account number, amount at credit, signature, etc., can be smoothly entrusted to a computer, — with no qualitative factor involved. A foreman from stores department places a new purchase order for material, based on the re-order level and re-order quantity. The decision rules are so well-formalised that TISCO could use even its second-generation computers to trigger *automatically* new purchase-orders without any human intervention.

At the managerial level, the decisions may veer round a product mix. In an agricultural implements company, the capacity of different machines to produce these implements was determined, grades of skill and number of skilled personnel were assessed, and decision-rules were worked out according to a mathematical programming model for an optimal production plan every month according to upper and lower bounds of known current market-demand for each implement Quite often, these computer-based decisions were sufficient for managers to control production levels for the best profit-margins. Again, layout of a plant is a typical management-level decision needing many administrative considerations, but a general guideline to locate the physical facilities can be worked out with the help of computer. Recruitment of a group of staff-members can be considerably facilitated by a computerised data-bank on existing personnel (complete with skills, qualifications, experience and career-directions) and identifying the specific gaps to be filled by matching requirement with the availability of outside skills. Designing an advertisement campaign is a smaller management exercise based on the both historical and current data on product-profile and customer-profile on computer, and then using qualitative judgement for identifying the best campaign strategy. The point to be noted is that computer usage can be fairly selective in all the above situations, with many interfaces between the human decision and mechanised information.

Conclusion

At the strategic level, decision of an altogether new plant or introduction of a new production technology can all demand corporate attention. In the corporate planning group for TISCO, important decisions were arrived at on the replacement of old plant, establishment of new product-plant and adoption of a new steel-making technology all of which were essentially questions of compromises among a number of competing, conflicting and exceedingly complex factors. Again, in the execution of a collaboration or negotiation of an industry-level labour contract, the role of a computer can only be marginal (in the form of predicting forecasts on Implications of adopting different strategies), — with the onus of responsibility lying with the corporate brain alone, as the body will do in carrying out all its "intelligent" activities!

Utility of information in decision-making has always been realised by management. The increasing complexity in modern organisations, growing volume of data ascertained on a large number of parameters and the timeliness of critical decisions on many crucial problems are all phenomena of today, which often necessitate the use of computer. If management information system (MIS) can be defined as the essential capability of access, storage, processing and retrieval of all important information for control, monitoring and planning purposes, — such functions are admirably carried out for small organisations manually. It is only the volume of data, number of calculations and frequency of output reports which decide whether or not a computer need be used for MIS.

Responsibility Levels for Information

Managers at different levels of responsibility hirerachy information in characteristically different ways. The pre-occupation with day-today routine information at the operational level yield grounds to more semi-routine handling of information at managerial levels with less stringent rules for decision-making. At still higher corporate levels, the quality of information is only partly quantitative and the environment of decision-making is a highly flexible one. But at all levels, it is a cardinal management principle to concentrate upon only selective information on "as required" basis.

Let us look at an effective MIS from the above point of view. Most activities (at any level of responsibility mentioned above) can be assigned a pre-set norm or standard value (or budgeted figure) for the way the management expects it to be performed. In real practice, however, quite a few activities are not performed in an ideal manner due to the prevailing circumstances. It is only the deviations for those activities — of the way they have been actually performed from the way they should have been performed — that are of interest to management control for taking corrective action. It is therefore an essential function of MIS to monitor such differences and feed them back to decision-makers, as illustrated in the Fig. 1.

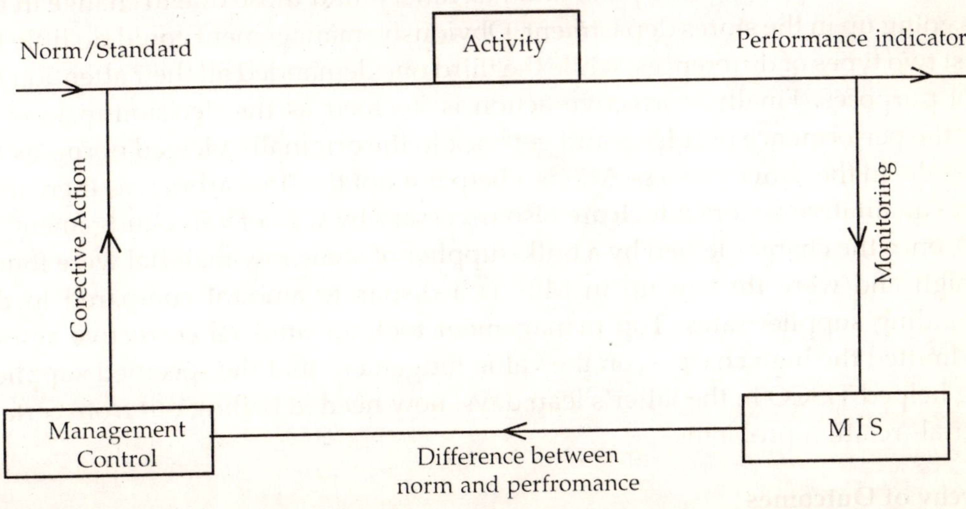

Fig 1: MIS for Control

Variety of Norms

A few points are to be noted here. First of all, norms and standards can be arrived at in many different ways. *Subjective* norms follow a decision-maker's own predilection perhaps followed by mature experience. *Historical* norms fall back upon past records while *analogical* norms draw from the experience of other organisations performing similar activities. *Engineering* norms are outcome of time-and-motion study and *mathematical* norms are derived by using calculations in performing specific activities. The commonly used norm is the *statistical* one which is assembling a large amount of performance data and then finding out the average (mean, median or mode) value, after eliminating the extreme readings. Secondly the differences between norms and actual performance indicators need not be fed back in their entirety. There can be differences which are small enough to be ignored and a prior management effort to define such tolerable differences can help considerably in reducing the volume of MIS reports. For instance, value-differences in inventory-items were watched every month, as compared to the beginning of financial year, in a large production organisation and were discussed in monthly production-meetings with departmental heads. Once the idea of tolerable differences was accepted with management concurrence, the inventory-value reports became small and very manageable ones. Thirdly, there are certain differences which are controllable, in contrast to certain others which are not so. It would be a futile management exercise to concentrate on the uncontrollable differences at the expense of the controllable ones. For instance again, the inventory-value reports mentioned above were divided into three parts, showing differences due to change in prices in the market, those due to introduction of pre-planned plant and machinery, and those due to change in the stocks going up in the stores department. Obviously, management could do little for the first two types of differences, while the third one demanded all their attention for control purposes. Finally, corrective action is deemed as the decision-making to rectify the performance problems and get back to the originally viewed norms as far as possible. In the above process, MIS is a help but not the final arbiter, as there may be some qualitative factors which are also necessary by way of value-judgement. In TISCO, once the charges levied by a bulk-supplier of some raw material were found very high and were thrown up in MIS as a disparate amount compared to the longstanding supplier-rates. Top management took an unusual corrective action, viz., admitted the high charges, on the value-judgement that the specified supplier, having helped TISCO in the latter's lean days, now needed bailing out from certain industrial- relation problems.

Hierarchy of Outcomes

MIS — with or without computer — should provide for a hierarchy of outcomes.

In routine data-handling situations where rules are unambiguous, it can generate almost automatically corrective actions (e.g., placing of purchase orders, etc.). In less routine cases, it can furnish regular exception-based report (e.g., production scheduling, machine-loading, etc.) At a still higher level of responsibility it can supply specific reports only on demand (e.g. resource analysis and cost allocation for a project management system, etc.). These outcomes apart, MIS can be geared to maintain an information-bank which can be delved into whenever necessary, like the using of a library resource. For computer-based MIS, the first three actions can simply be performed in a batch mode, while the updating of a data-bank and selective retrieval of information are best done on a lime-sharing mode.

Implementation of MIS must begin at the output end, by ascertaining what do the user decision-makers do need by way of selective information. Such a requirement analysis can shed new light on many angles of information-needs which are not — or inadequately — catered for in the current handling of information. After requirement analysis has been done, it should become clear as to what items of processed information would be required, by whom, at what level, at what frequency (periodic or ad-hoc, or one-time), on what formats and with what details. The last point about details is important as there has to be a balance between the desire for details and the expediency of data-collection.

Study of Information Flow

The next stage is to identify the input data which, when processed and reduced, could give rise to the needed outputs. At the input end, assessment of sources to generate data, agencies to collect data, frequency and format for collection, and level of details are all important considerations. Thereafter, design of permanent and current data-files have to be taken care of, manually or through computer, by adequately trained manpower and processing has to be tried out with sample data and dummy format first. Final implementation should be gone ahead only after successful conducting of trial runs.

If data-volume, calculation-complexity and output-frequency for MIS warrant computerisation, conceptualisation of computer-based system is needed at an early stage. This has to be done after a full scale study of the physical flow of information and in the flow-charts for computer-based MIS, enough provisions have to be built up for integration, modification and any other rationalisation of physical information-flow. The system design should specify through the flow-charts the necessary linkages and validation procedures, and envisage clearly the type and extent of codification needed. The programming action is then to follow in the shape of edit, update, sort, merge, calculate and point programmes, to name an important few.

The designed system needs careful desk-check (to see if all the desired logic has gone into it) and thereafter the trial-run should be obtained on computer with test-data. Final implementation may have to wait the above steps being repeatedly performed to achieve' complete confidence in the computer-based system.

A few important factors are to be noted for any MIS exercise. First, no MIS is better or worse than the data it is supposed to cater for. Therefore, data-validation procedures (both manual ana computer-based) are to be rigorously tested and implemented. Secondly, data-homogeneity has to be ensured to prevent unevenness in data to creep in from different data-sources. Thirdly, the authenticity of both source for data-generation and agency for data-collection is a crucial factor to build up trust in MIS. Fourthly, user education and training has a lot to do with the success of MIS. A "number-taker" of railway wagons in the marshalling yard or a "writer" of crime-records in the police-station or a "munshi" at the colliery-pithead to track the gang- performance below are the pillars of MIS and their familiarity as well as involvement are of paramount importance. Fifthly, data are to be regarded as a consumer non-durable commodity, — to be preserved only till required and to be weeded out thereafter to free their storage-space. Finally, the involvement of corporate management is very desirable right from the decision to implement MIS, to approve the system-design and to clear the test-runs up to the stage of monitoring what has been implemented. The *sine-qua-non* of MIS is its practical usage and any changed perception by the user management must get reflected in it with the least possible delay.

Useful information had often the dubious distinction of being confused with the raw, unprocessed data. The element of selectivity and aggregation in the data captured in greenfield condition is, although very desirable for higher-level decision-making, not always so obvious. New trends in Management Information System (MIS) have now happily coincided with the ethos behind the Shannon and MaCullogh's mathematical theory of information: the knowledge of disorganisation in an organisation can only be termed information; whatever activities are in a steady, pre-determined state do not give rise to any information.

Clerical Levels for Automated Control

The philosophy behind the above adage can be easily understood if one analyses the decision-making process itself. In any modern and complex organisation, hierarchies are clearly discernible: supervisory or clerical, middle management and top administration. Decisions made at supervisory or clerical levels (for topping "heat" in a steel-melting shop; distributing medicines in an outpatient department; or reconciling credits with debits in a bank) all deal with routine data under well-set rules, instructions and precedents. The data are essentially quantitative and quite short-term. The decision-making environment is pretty definitive and methods for optimisation (to achieve highest production or quickest dispensation of services to patients) can be applied well.

The above level of activities were computerised first in the last couple of decades and there has been no looking back ever since. In fact, the future trends are definitely towards *automated control* at this level, — where processes or services are designed to feed readings from instrument panels to computers which, in turn, draw upon the built-in logic and decision-rules and pass on (without any human intervention) the final instructions to control and regulate the process or the service.

There are examples galore of the automated control in the industry. In Indian steel industry, the nova and eclipse series of computers have been put to use at the steel meeting shops of Rourkela Steel Plant to monitor the end-point carbon and temperature of the incoming pig iron, and combine these readings with the polyvac laboratory analysis of the impurities to activate directly the blowing pressure and angle of the oxygen lance, — so that the right grade of steel can be made from out of the pig iron. Computer-aided manufacturing (CAM) is a recent trend in using automated programming to instruct the job-shop machines for carrying out milling and surfacing operations, apart from the simpler lathe-machine functions. Among the service organisations abroad, automated cash-dispensation is done by inserting cheques (with optically or magnetically sensitive characters) inside the public slot mechanisms connected remotely to the bank. In Indian service organisations, automated control has just started making its appearance, — notable among them being the Overseas Communication Service, where computer control is being used to press in service (or release) free (or occupied) trunk routes for transmitting calls to multiple destinations all over the world, and to indicate visibly the state of occupancy of every single route.

Middle-Management Decisions

Decision made at the middle management levels (for coordinating steel-making shop production in step with the blast-furnace Productivity and output frequency; allocating available hospital facilities according to the surgical clinical, radiological and Pathological needs; or deciding on the quantum of loans and advances to be disbursed in a bank's branches (with or without collateral are distinctive in their being semi-routine in character, — rules have to be combined with managerial discretions. The data can be partly quantitative and partly qualitative, involving a medium-term time-frame. The environment is fraught with risk and scope of clear-cut optimal solutions becomes increasingly unclear.

The above level of activities came for computerisation much later than the supervisory or clerical activities of a repetitive or accounting kind. The future trend points towards *operator guidance* at this level, — with computer being fed data by men and providing, in turn, a set of alternatives ready-reckoner tables which can be conveniently used by men to arrive at appropriate decisions.

There are many noteworthy examples of operator guidance in the Indian industry. Most on-line production planning and control, material management, and job scheduling systems on computer are of operator guidance kind, needing timely and effective human intervention both at the data-input end, and at the decision-making end. Among service organisations, Air India has now introduced on-line passenger-reservation system — with computer maintaining a data-bank for all flights and intending passengers, and linking them with current cancellations or changes as well as fresh intentions arising from passengers — so that operators can provide an up-to-date reservation service to all passengers. A similar operator guidance system is the Indian Railways plan for an on-line freight-control and wagon movement system, — to monitor movement, loading, unloading and idling of all railway wagons as to increase their effective utilisation by better planning through human intervention. An interesting application in a public utility like a dam is the monitoring of past meteorological data, current rainfall, tributary-flow, evaporation-loss and catchment-reserve data; linking them with the demand pattern for agricultural as well as hydroelectric water-needs; and providing computerised guidance to engineer-operators for adequate release of water through sluice-gates on a weekly or fortnightly basis. This approach was tried with the Nagariunasagar Dam operation with very successful results.

Top-Level Decisions

Decisions made at the top administration levels (for deciding on amalgamation or diversification in a firm's activities, planning new hospitals with extended facilities; or opening new branches for a bank) are fairly non-routine in character being almost entirely discretionary and seldom following any set decision-rules. Data used are largely and qualitative, involving long-term time-horizons. Decision-making environment is usually entirely uncertain, with an optimisation efforts being replaced by finding the acceptable satisfaction in the decisions to be made.

Although the top level of administration has come last in using computerisation, — this has been one of the most fruitful areas. Due to the very nature of non-repetitive data and unstructured decision-making, computer applications have to be highly selective. The trends are to provide *decision support* with an integrated MIS and other reports based on aggregation (for routine cases) and exception (for non-routine case). The earlier hypothesis about "information on disorganisation", as it were, comes more fully at play than at any other lower levels. Due to sheer pressure, the top executives cannot cope with "all the information at one's command" but necessarily a much reduced and filtered flow.

Indian examples of very selective MIS for decision support are many, including public administration, such as, Department of Steel and Mines, and Chemicals and Fertilisers which are mainly manual. The current trend in using computer for selective storage and retrieval of information, called from integrated files or data-bases, has started showing up in, for instance, Tata Steel in the private sector and BHEL and Hindustan Zinc in the public sector. A very significant decision support system is use of computer in aid of corporate planning. Formulation of possible corporate strategies, evaluating the various alternatives and arriving at the most preferred strategy can be immensely helped by computer-based simulation technique. The other usage of computer for corporate planning is to provide the return-on-investment (ROI) for various projects conceived, so that the best portfolio can be selected. ROI calculations can be based on simple project pay-back, discounted cash flow (for arriving at the present worth), the simple rate of return or the internal rate of return, — all on the computer, as done during the Tata Steel modernisation plan.

Conclusion

The interesting now development taking place abroad is to go in for *expert systems* which could use the entire knowledge-base and provide almost tailor made decisions. For such services as medical ones, diagnostic aids-combined with the past pathological history, can lead on to therapeutic prescriptions after searching through a vast array of medical facts and syndromes, and after matching with drug directories, among others. Such knowledge based systems would eventually combine the automated control at the execution level and operator guidance at the monitoring level,-and lead to far more efficient decision support systems using the "expert " status of the computer. Fifth- generation computer development plans in both Japan and the USA are poised for this kind of break-through.

APPENDIX A

CURRENT STATUS OF OPERATIONS RESEARCH

Introduction

Operations Research (OR) has been understood over the years to mean the application of the methods of science, particularly those of mathematics and statistics, to solve the problems of management and to help in decision-making. Having originated in the time of World War II, its practice has spread from the UK and USA to other countries including India, with an increasing use of computers.

In one of the recent annual conventions of the OR Society of India, there were 55 OR papers presented. Assuming the annual convention as the foremost gathering of the OR professionals of all shades, the papers could be taken to represent a fair sample of the current interest-areas. Looking into the cross-section of the papers, only 14 papers could broadly satisfy the criterion of practice papers, 3 were survey papers, and the remaining 38 could be termed academic and scientific papers whose concern was somewhat remote from the fields.

If 25 per cent papers above related to the grass-root applications of various types, it would only mean that the interest of the OR community at large in a developing country is still predominantly centred around methodology. This is not surprising, considering the excellence in formal sciences (such as. mathematics and statics) that this country is known to produce, and the encouragement given by our academic institutions to pure research. If, however, one accepts the premise that the *raison d'etre* of good OR lies in its real-life problem-solving capability, the situation is worth analysing further.

OR Methodology

Two factors are central to our observation. First, the status of OR methodology has progressed far from being purely *classical* (applying analytical and statistical methods to decision-making) and *technical* (applying highly developed techniques of optimisation, networking and simulation) to being largely *contextual* (applying knowledge of theory and practice of the context in which OR is sought to be used). In other words, OR methods have grown sufficiently diverse so as to keep up with the distribution of the functions of data gathering, information processing and control of a modern complex organisation. Secondly, the computational power of today's computers has grown even faster so as to provide a tremendous boost to the OR calculations in any mode: centralised or decentralised; at any level of hierarchy; and with any combination or networking of the two.

Technical literature for OR abounds in recording methodological development The evolution of macro-models has been particularly evident in the work carried out in the scientific and academic institutions. A striking feature is what Ackoff described as "systemic" modelling, where there is a systematic amalgamation of divergent models, such as, goal programming with statistical forcasting, or, input-output analysis with linear and mixed integer programming. While such an approach has widened the horizon of the capability of OR models, it has also helped the genre of micro-models for probing problems in depth. In particular, a lot of attention has been paid to diversity coverage, sensitivity tests, parametric ranging, variational analysis and consistency checks.

Macro and Micro Models

The main disadvantage perceived in the evolution of both macro-and micro-models within their academic constraints has been that basically any such model reflects a *snapshot* of reality at a given instance. It lacks the flexibility of an *open loop* system, under which the model-builder can handle a continuously changing environmental and can still remain in control all the time by suggesting optimal solutions to satisfy constantly shifting requirements. Also such a model lacks the capacity of a "see-saw" adjustment, where any one variable can be changed at a time introducing oscillations in the model until a balance is finally reached and optimal controls can be fully imposed.

Operational Research in practice, on the other hand, has followed a phenomenological approach which has been intimately connected with decision-making. At the operational control level, specific tasks are carried out effectively and efficiently. OR has been an invaluable aid at this level, making use of optimal decision parameters based on Linear Programming (LP), queuing and inventory control techniques. At the management control level, the managers have to ensure that resources are obtained and used judiciously in the accomplishment of the organisation's objectives. This is the design phase of functional relationships (e.g., rates of output, cost coefficients, market demands, etc.), objective functions (to maximise profit minimise cost, etc.) and prediction of outcomes for the best policy. OR methods help to define and determine the optimal policy. At the higher management level, all choices and values (with regard to objectives or goals) may not be very clear. While mathematical optimisation loses ground (unless based on unrealistic assumptions), the decision-maker may "simulate" the behaviour of the system under alternative courses of action and determine responses to "what if?" questions, in place of having a dear "What is best?" choice. At the corporate level of strategic planning, there is the process of deciding on objectives of the organisation, changes in these objectives, resources used to attain these objectives, and the policies that are to govern the acquisition, use and disposition of these resources. OR, in a technical sense, has been of little use here, although some trends exist in simple contextual modelling, such as, setting parameters, finding objectives, checking consistency, separating guess work from forecasts, and structuring combinatorial sets of scenarios.

Information System Links

Since decision-making is firmly linked with handling of information, it is necessary to understand the role of this linkage. At the operational control level, the physical source of information, the observational data, the inferential logic and the choice-parameters are all palpably obvious and action taken is virtually automatic. At the management control level, choices (and even inferences) are not so clear and hence the need of evaluating the best course of action and getting responses to "what if?" questions. At the corporate level, the decision-maker reserves the inferences, choices and actions, and uses only the physical source and the observational data. The need, therefore, of a good data-bank and a timely updating of its data is supreme for the corporate decision-maker.

It is evident from the above that a decision-taking information system, to help initiating automatically a purchase order when the inventory has dropped below the reorder point, will be fairly simple in nature at the operational control level. On the other hand, a data-bank information system to support corporate planning by top management will be highly complex. Furthermore, if OR methods have to make a transition from the trivial operational level to the top corporate level, two factors can be of immense help : a timely capture of data from the source and an understanding of the deep structure of the decision problem.

An interesting examples of the above transition is the computer-based decision-support system, developed at the TELCO, which uses forecasting techniques (adaptive filtering, double exponential smoothing and moving averages) as an aid to decision-making. In a fairly dynamic industrial environment, the system captures data from the source of application, viz., manufacturing of automobiles, analyses the data on consumption of small tools; makes suitable inventory modelling; and generates the desired decision parameters, viz., determination of order level, buffer level, order quantity, etc. What is more important, the recommendations and the computed decision parameters are, along with other relevant information, fed back to the source of application for the entire materials planning.

Diverse OR Modelling

State-of-the-art OR modelling is, in practice, largely evident today at the managerial control levels. This can be illustrated along with the diverse nature of modelling in the following cases:

(a) *Economic modelling :* A computation facility, needed for econometric model-building, was built up for the national planning exercise and given the endearing name VIDHATA. Developed in the form of a software package, VIDHATA used a number of sub-programmes and was linked with a data-base which contained all the information needed exogenously. The data-base could be updated and a new one created through a series of matrix manipulations (including addition, substraction, multiplication, division, inversion, transposition and creation of identity matrix). VIDHATA worked as an admirable interface between the complexity of the data base and the easy-to-use language of the user;

(b) *Environmental modelling :* Mathematical models applicable in hydrological problems have expanded creditably over the last two decades. These models are either deterministic with a definite linking between rainfall and river flood, or, stochastic when the chances of occurrence of the variables are taken into consideration. The SACRAMENTO model successfully applied he watershed concept to the upper Yamuna catchment and Tungabhadra river for the run-off simulation. He model, used a IBM 360/44 computer, calculated recursively the six-hourly values of water transfer (interception, evaporation and percolation) for the different phases of water cycle and the flow the area outlet (direct run-off, surface run-off, interflow and baseflow);

(c) *Exploratory modelling : Math*ematical models for various oilfields of ONGC was applied for the study and development of reservoir simulation, particularly for the three-dimensional three-phase black oil, radial coming and multi-component analysis. The models used IBM 370/145 studied the general behaviour of a complete reservoir or part of it. The radial coming model studied specific wells which may develop water or gas coning. The multicomponent model studied gas condensate, highly volatile fluids and retrograde phenomenon;

(d) *Industrial modelling :* This area, after defence, has the highest incidence of OR models of impressive quality, in order to illustrate a grassroot application (which can often be a very high dividend-earner, as is the case here) the LP model used repetitively in AGRICO product on planning can be considered. Several agricultural implements like spades, pick-axes and shovels were produced there tailored to demands which fluctuated widely based on seasonal factors. The production capacity varied according to the capacity available (against break-downs) of forges, presses and other mechanics. The labour, too, had a diversity of skills which had to be taken into account. The LP model was run every month and quarter within the upper and lower bounds of predicted market demands, on computer. The fine tuning of the production plan concentrated upon contribution to profits, and provided a highly effective and dependable document to management and

(e) *Health modelling : A* significant use of OR model in health application has been for the disease forecasting and control in the malaria eradication scheme. Taking an Andhra taluk of malaria-prone villages, both epidemiological factors (incidence of disease, rainfall, soil condition, drainage, etc.) and entomological factors (breeding of malaria germ) were studied to build a statistical model based or Markov process, where the probability of the spread of the disease to nearby villages could be forecast. This was an eminently useful model, helping the Andhra health authorities rush their medical and paramedical personnel to those villages, and spread them in advance with DDT.

Conclusion

The above, in a nutshell, recapitulates the current status of OR applications in India. While industrial and business applications are certainly gaining around, the same cannot be said for economic and social science applications where much more acceptance has still to find its place for OR modelling.

APPENDIX B

ROLE OF COMPUTER-AIDED OPTIMISATION

Introduction

The solution procedures in the Operational Research (OR) modelling efforts have also evolved from the pioneering days of static solutions arrived at without the use of computers. All OR applications based on earlier generation computers, working in a batch mode, were able to yield dynamic solutions. An example is the optimization model for slit combination of jumbo coils in Geep Industrial Syndicate, which ran on an early Reyad computer. The number and type of torches, to mention just one product, varied over a broad range. Each torch was made of a large number of components each of which, in turn, could be derived by cutting jumbo coils of varying dimensions. The OR model aimed at minimising the number of coils to be cut per slit. Dynamic batch solutions were derived by running the model every month to give production schedules to the factory, with a highly reduced wastage of coils.

Real-time Solutions

Real-time solutions are a further step ahead and are obtained on-line. There are two types of real time solutions: dedicated and time-sharing. Dedicated usage is based on a microprocessor chip which has the solution procedure as part of the built-in memory. For instance, the medium and light structural mill of any Indian steel unit has the need of cutting billets and yet reducing wastage. The OR model can be built into the microprocessor memory and thyristor control exercised to sense the dimensions of the incoming billets and to shear them according to pre-set calculations. Dedicated solutions are even faster when the micro-processor has the solution procedure built in as part of the hardware such 'firmware' has already become prevalent in India.

Time-sharing solutions, on the other hand, are obtained from terminals linked to mini or mainframe systems. Examples abound in industry where such terminals are made to operate on a real-time basis. For instance, the maintenance of thermal and chemical stability of a blast furnace can be achieved by letting the computer calculate the balanced burden-mix in order to satisfy all the requirements and assisting the operator to change the burden optimally. The inputs the system are the chemical analysis of material desired level of wind-rate, hot blast temperature, blast moisture and fuel injection to be used,— apart from the feed-back information about the previous cast, the actual raw material, and the actual hot metal and slag analysis. The printed output a provided at the terminal on the furnace, giving the quantities of each type of material to be charged into the furnace and the excepted analysis of the slag and hot metal, all on a real-tune basis.

Computing Power

In order to match the needs of the increasing higher level of management functions and allow the task to be amenable to OR methods, the state-of-the-art computing power can be examined from both centralised and decentralized points of view. A mainframe computer can handle many diverse tasks in running a complex modern organization. Alongside, a comprehensive data bank can be built up in different application areas and facilities provided for instant data updating. With such a centralised facility, every processing loop can have access to the data related to every other loop, and the task of supervision and maintenance becomes easy. On the other hand, such a facility is likely to have initial high cost independent of the size of applications, poor field expandability, unsuitability for certain fast processing loops and perhaps poor security and reliability problems (in the absence of a duplicate or stand-by centralized computer which may be economically unjustified).

An alternative to the above is the use of two or more low-powered central processing units (CPUs) in parallel to perform the trial task. The CPUs may be structured to operate *either* with shared memory and input/output (I/O) devices in a 'tightly coupled' manner *or* with own memory and I/O devices, but interconnected to other CPUs through communication interfaces in a 'loosely coupled' manner. The total task can then be split into clearly defined and related sub-tasks : each handled by multiple loosely coupled CPUs chosen for efficient handling of the specified task. This approach is based on the concept of decentralized control, distributed data acquisition and distributed information processing.

Hierarchical Functions of Control

In keeping with the hierarchical functions of operational control, management control and corporate control, a serial distribution of computing power can be attempted. At the operation control level, dynamic optimisation can be done by functional computers — with a very high degree of reliability and with the task of monitoring performance with mutual back-up support in the event of failures. In the TISCO set-up, more than 100 interactive terminals are already operational which serve this Junction by being hooked up to 4 minicomputers of Unisys 1955 kind located at the Stores, Rolling Mill-2 General Superintendent's Office and the main computer centre. Such intelligent terminals are able to read or alter any data in the host Unisys 6806 computer to achieve *overall* optimisation, if needed It is possible to build in control functions which would allow for local optimisation, on-line diagnostics and provision for switch-over to other terminals in emergencies. The mini-computers can be linked with each other through data communication links, for a local area network.

At the management control level, the mini-computers should have the capability to detect and react to any changes in the control variables, and then to optimise the performance of the unit under the constraints imposed by the host computers. The 'managerial' computer should handle a simple conversational language, have on-line programmable features and possess a powerful display capability. According to some authorities, the 'managerial' computer should react to individual operational exigencies and optimise over-all operations at any instance. In process industry, it should manage the tasks of energy management, maintenance schedules of plant and machinery, process yield, quality control information, raw material input, inventory control, sales management and so on, most of which functions are susceptible to OR approach. Since the expectations made and jobs entrusted are so widely varied, the CPUs should be modular and should have features to maximise throughout by choosing appropriate configurations of CPUs, memory and I/O devices.

At the corporate control level, a strong management information system (MIS) capability can come through a host mainframe computer. There should be from software viewpoint, a multi-user-environment with a high degree of data security. Facility for multiple storage of information coming from field, along with storage in the host computer, is useful in any distribution processing with an assured quality of inter-CPU communication.

Computer-Aided Optimisation

The above kind of computing power available today, can be made use of, along with the robust and contextual OR techniques, in real-life environment to achieve computer-aided optimisation (CAO) at all levels. We have seen how sources of physical activities and recording of data have to be linked with inference logic and rules for choice in order to facilitate decision-making. The more the logic and the rules made integral to the same computing device which also handles captured data, the better are the chances that unstructured decision will become structured by the appropriate MIS.

To the above extent, the state of the technology available simply demand use of CAO at all decision-making hierarchy. If we combine the types of usage with their tasks to be performed (under single or multiple criteria, as the case may be), there would emerge four classes of combination, viz., single-user single-task; multiple-user single-task; single-user multiple-task; and multiple-user multiple-task.

(a) *Single-user single-task applications* are among the most commonly occurred ones. In a refinery, industry, for instance, such operational level applications can comprise optimisation of shutdown scheduling of various HDS units and platformer unit; optimisation of crude-heat exchange train; blending of fuel oil and motor spirit; simulation of process, unit and equipment; and crude planning and tanker scheduling.

(b) *Multiple-user single-task applications* have the objective of optimal cost redaction at managerial level that can be achieved through minimisation of demurrage in computer-aided material handling and rail-traffic control system for watching over availability, movement and handling of rail-wagons through communication terminals for any major wagon-using organisation. The same objective can be viewed as optimal resource allocation, in which case the Indian Railways computerisation plan for an on-line freight control and wagon movement system, discussed earlier, may be cited for different zones.

(c) *Single-user multiple-task applications* can be commonly seen again in a process industry where various kinds of OR models for optimal resource allocation are tried out. For optimal allocation of energy (steam, power and fuel), the data communication facilities can be utilised to operate a real-time energy allocation model. Product-mix studies are found quite useful to achieve optimal use of resources in keeping with the market demand of steel product Simulation studies, too, are a common practice to achieve the highest utilisation of resources and carryout in a steel industry, the optimum scheduling of open hearth furnaces; the optimum scheduling of soaking pits; the improved utilisation of loco-power and captive rolling-stock; and determination of optimum number of iron-ladles, slag pots and ingot cars.

(d) *Multiple-user multiple-task applications* can be exemplified in two cases. The first case was that of the quantitative model for the Sixth Plan (1980-85) which could simultaneously treat both supply and demand, and their interaction between sectors and time. Its core-model had seven inter-dependent blocks, e.g., input-output, investment, private consumption, financial resources, import, employment and perspective planning. Its major sub-models were agriculture exports, demography, autonomous investment and public consumption. The model comprised a set of supply and demand equations, a set of inequality relations with given *upper* bounds (to ensure that demand did not exceed the market supply of commodities, services, capital, labour, foreign exchange and non-renewable resources) as well as *lower* bounds (to ensure that the community attained minimum welfare target). The model, although of a non-linear programming kind, had to cater for a multi-stage decision process and hence it was solved by iteration with the input of alternative values, for achieving a maximum growth rate.

The other case pertained to the copper mining industry in Zambia of Africa. Nchanga open pit there covered a vast expanse and had 14 shivols at different depths upto 1000 feet where the debris was transported by 75 gigantic trucks of 150 to 200 tonnes each. Given constraints were those resources, the travel-time form ore dumps and overburdens to shovels and back, the breakdown pattern of shovels the production priorities and the pit-manpower. The computer-based OPTIMA model used a dynamic allocation pattern for trucks to shovels, where parameters could be added and deleted on-line. Service call-ups were also generated for maintenance manpower to carry out an efficient maintenance management. Communication was not through terminals but shovel-radio, truck-radio, dump-location radio and route-monitoring radio. The output was flashed on signboards at strategic points.

Conclusion

The above is necessarily a birds-eye view of current status of OR methodology, its linkages with information system, and its interaction with latest available computing power. There is an unmistakable emergence of computer-aided optimisation (CAO) not feasible at any time earlier. The cases of single/multiple user, combined with single/multiple tasks, are further strengthened by the emergence of all India computer networks, such as, INDONET for 5 computer centres under CMC, NICNET for the Central Government and the State Government computer centres; ERNET for NCST, and IITS and other academic centres of excellence; and the proposed TRANSPORTNET for the Railways, the Air India and the Indian Airlines. The availability of the first and second generation INSAT satellites will, if anything, raise expectations for more public (and even private) networks. The sharing of OR models, as already done in tie ARPANET of the USA, for their pan-Indian usage is certainly not a distant dream anymore.

COMPUTER BIBLIOGRAPHY

SELECT BIBLIOGRAPHY OF INDIAN BOOKS

General/Introductory

Bitter, *Basic for Beginners,* Tata Mc-Graw Hill.

Chasen/Cohen, *Basic-Computing-Book D,* BPB Publications, New Delhi.

Chasen/Cohen, *Basic-Computing-Book E,* BPB Publications, New Delhi

Chasen/Cohen, *Basic-Computing-Book F,* BPB Publications, New Delhi.

Craddock, *An Introduction to Computer-Studies,* Tata Mc-Graw Hill.

ECC, *Computer Tutor - An Introduction,* BPB Publications, New Delhi.

Hanavan, P., *Basic-Computing-Book A,* BPB Publications, New Delhi.

Hanavan, P., *Basic-Computing-Book B,* BPB Publications, New Delhi.

Hanavan/Chasen, *Basic-Computing-Book C,* BPB Publications, New Delhi

Jain, S., *Introduction to Computer-Science (CBSE-XI),* BPB Publica-tions, New Delhi.

Margolis, A., *Trouble Shooting and Repairing PC's,* BPB Publications, New Delhi

Margotis, A., *Troubleshooting and Repairing PC's,* BPB Publications, New Delhi

Mehta, S., *Introducing Computers Part I,* BPB Publications, New Delhi

Mehta, S., *Introducing Computers* Part II, BPB Publications, New Delhi

Mehta, S., *Introducing Computers Part III,* BPB Publications, New Delhi

Mehta, S., *Let us learn Computers,* BPB Publications, New Delhi.

Pale & Orshalick, *Introduction to Pascal and Structured Design,* Tata Mc-Graw Hill.

Sharma, M., *Computer Ek Purana Parichay,* BPB Publications, New Delhi.

Sinha, P., *Computers Fundamentals,* BPB Publications, New Delhi. Verma R., *A Guide to Successful Computerisation,* BPB Publications, New Delhi.

Verma, R., *A Guide to Successful Computerisation,* BPB Publications, New Delhi.

Walker, R., *Understanding Computer Science Applications,* BPB Publications, New Delhi.

Walker, R., *Understanding Computer Science Applications,* BPB Publications, New Delhi.

Will is/Miller, *Computers for Everybody,* BPB Publications, New Delhi.

Programming

A.S.S., *dBase III Plus (Students & Instructor WKBK),* BPB Publications, New Delhi.

Ashton Tate, *dBase Programmes Utilities,* BPB Publications, New Delhi.

Ashton Tate, *dBase Programming Utilities,* BPB Publications, New Delhi.

Ashton Tate, *Introduction to dBase III Plus Programming,* BPB Publications, New Delhi.

Ashton Tate, *Using dBase III Plus,* BPB Publications, New Delhi.

Awate, *8085A Assembly Language and Applications,* Tata Mc-Graw Hill.

Awate, *8085A Assembly languages, Programming and Applications,* Tata Mc-Graw Hill.

Balagurusamy, E. and Sushila, *Computer Systems and Application:*

Recent Trends Tata Mc-Graw Hill.

Balagurusamy, E., *Fortran For Beginners: Including Fortran 77,* Tata Mc-Graw Hill.

Balagurusamy, E., *Programming in "C", Tata* Mc-Graw Hill.

Batis/Fortmo, *dBase III Plus Local Area Networks,* BPB Publications? New Delhi.

Beam, J., *Illustrated C Programming,* BPB Publications, New Delhi.

Bharucha, D., *dBase II A Comprehensive Users Manual,* BPB Publications, New Delhi.

Bharucha, K., *dBase III Plus: A Comprehensive Users Manual,* BPB Publications, New Delhi.

Bitter, *Basic for Beginners,* Tata Mc-Graw Hill.

Breem, G., *Clipper dBase Computer Applications,* BPB Publications, New Delhi.

Brown, *C for Basic Programmes,* Tata Mc-Graw Hill.

Brown, *C for Basic Programmers,* Tata Mc-Graw Hill.

Carlton, T., *dBase III Plus Applications Library*, BPB Publications,

New Delhi. Castro/Hanson, *Advanced Programmes Guide for dBase III*, BPB Publications, New Delhi.

Cowart, R., *ABC's of dBase III Plus*, BPB Publications, New Delhi.

Dale and Lilly, *Pascal Plus Data Structures, Algorithms and advanced Programming*, Tata Mc-Graw Hill.

Desai, *Fortran Programming and Numerical Methods*, Tata Mc-Graw Hill.

Freedman, A., *dBase II for the first time User*, BPB Publications, New Delhi

Gramillo R., *Illustrated Foxpro*, BPB Publications, New Delhi.

Kapoor, *Computer Assisted Decision Models in Fortran*, Tata Mc- Graw Hill.

Krishnamoorthy, *Finite Element Analysis: Theory and Programming*, Tata Mc-Graw Hill.

Krishnamoorthy, *Programme for Analysis of Structural Systems by finite Element Method*, Tata Mc-Graw Hill.

Marton, J., Basic: *Step by Step Programming*, BPB Publications, New Delhi.

Mathur, *Introduction to Pascal*, Tata Mc-Graw Hill.

Mueller J., *Illustrated Clipper 5.0*, BPB Publications, New Delhi.

Pugh, K, *C language for Programmes*, BPB Publications, New Delhi.

Ramkumar, *Programming with Fortran 77*, Tata Mc-Graw Hill.

Rao, *Computer Programming: Including MS-COBOL and COBOL-85*, Tata Mc-Graw Hill.

Roy and Distidar, *Cobol Programming: Problems and Solutions*, Tata Mc-Graw Hill.

Rugg, *More than 32 Basic Programmes — IBM PC*, BPB Publications, New Delhi.

Seigal, C, *Mastering Foxpro*, BPB Publications, New Delhi.

Sence, R., *Clipper-5 Programming Guide (2nd edition)*, BPB Publications, New Delhi.

Simpson, A., *Advanced Techniques in dBase III Plus*, BPB Publications, New Delhi.

Simpson, A., *dBase III Plus Programmes Reference Guide*, BPB Publications, New Delhi.

Simpson, A., *Understanding dBase II*, BPB Publications, New Delhi.

Stevens, A., *C-Data Base Development*, BPB Publications, New Delhi.

Thro, E., *The Database Dictionary*, BPB Publications, New Delhi.

Townsend, C, *Mastering dBase IV Programming*, BPB Publications, New Delhi.

Zaks, R., *Your First Basic Programme*, BPB Publications, New Delhi.

Application Software

Ahson, *Microprocessors with Applications in Process Control*, Tata Mc-Graw Hill.

Balagurusamy, E., *Office Automation and World Processing*, Tata Mc-Graw Hill.

Balagurusamy, E., *Selecting and Managing a Small Computer*, Tata Mc-Graw Hill.

Jain, *Basic Programming with Applications, Tata* Mc-Graw Hill.

Juneja et. al, *CAD/CAM Robotics and Factories of the Future*, Vol. I, Tata Mc-Graw Hill.

Juneja et. al, *CAD/CAM Robotics and Factories of the Future*, Vol. II, Tata Mc-Graw Hill.

Juneja et. al, *CAD/CAM Robotics and Factories of the Future*, Vol. III, Tata Mc-Graw Hill.

Operating Systems

Ashely, *Teach Yourself- Unix*, BPB Publications, New Delhi.

Cuthbertson, T., *The ABC's of SCO Unix*, BPB Publications, New Delhi.

3

MANAGEMENT CONSIDERATIONS OF THE INFORMATION SYSTEM

The purpose of this text is to analyze and discuss the many aspects of information system design. We have addressed the role of the information system as the primary interface between the management subsystem and the operations subsystem within the organisation. However, the information system is itself a large, complex resource that requires managing. We conclude Part III by providing several suggestions concerning management activities related to the effective use of the information system resource. Discussed specifically in this chapter are guidelines for the development of more maintainable systems, methods used to audit systems, types and pitfalls of project management systems, and managing change from a human perspective.

MANAGING MAINTENANCE

Organisations and their information systems are dynamic resources. All resources are subject to deterioration, malfunction, and the need for periodic upgrading. *Maintainability* is a systems requirement which is receiving more and more attention from both information systems designers and management. More maintainable systems require less attention, fewer modifications and changes, and are easier to change when maintenance is needed. In this section an analysis is provided on the causes of maintenance work, the problems it presents, and some ideas how to deal with maintenance.

Causes of Maintenance Work

What follows are some of the causes why programmes, data files, documentation, and general procedures must be changed in existing systems.

Emergency Maintenance. Emergency maintenance is directed toward resolving a malfunction or "bug" in the system. This maintenance is urgent and usually calls for immediate attention. Normally a system malfunctions because it has not been tested completely. In fact, it may be a system that has run perfectly for months or even years. Although this type of activity is associated with programming, frequently the information system user is the one who identifies the malfunction. Then a team of analysts and programmers must determine if the malfunction is in a computer programme or caused by a system input. The ability to diagnose rapidly and remedy the malfunction is of considerable value to the organisation.

Routine Maintenance. Routine maintenance activities are required to keep systems performance relevant as it reflects the organisational environment. This activity may take the form of rewriting manual procedures, conducting training sessions, altering information report formats and contents, and defining new processing logic for computer programmes. For example, a new tax law may require a change in the calculation of net pay, the production of a new report from the system, or the adoption of a new accounting depreciation method.

Special Reporting Requests. Special reporting requests are periodic requests for tactical and strategic management information not scheduled for routine production from a system. The analyst must define what is being requested, what is required to produce the information, and, finally, the most efficient way to produce the information based on available resources. While many of these special requests can be satisfied directly by a user via a data base management system, often the analyst assists in preparing the necessary parameters for the request. Even in an online environment users may be unfamiliar with all aspects of the data base available to them. Examples of special requests might include an analysis of pay rates during labor management bargaining sessions, a special report on selected products during a sales promotion, or a special analysis of a particular vendor's delivery performance.

Systems Improvements. After a new system is implemented, users may suggest additional improvements to the system. In short, many users' information requirements are subject to a rapid rate of change. To accommodate these changing requirements, an analyst must define what is needed, if it can be met with the existing data base, and develop the necessary manual and computer procedures to satisfy these requirements. The approach used by the analyst in this activity differs only in duration when compared to the development of a system.

Problems of Maintenance

Given the above causes for change, it is little wonder that existing systems are subject to almost continuous modification. Unfortunately, this can result in a number of problems.[1]

Cost. Changing existing application systems can be very expensive, requiring in some instances up to half of an organisation's allocated funds for systems. Many organisations have adopted the , principle of setting a budget for maintenance and then performing only the highest priority maintenance work.

Personnel Morale. Personnel working in the information system, especially programmers, often object to the amount of maintenance work they are asked to do. They do not want to spend most of their time maintaining or trying to patch up systems designed and implemented years ago. In some organisations, programmers are rotated from one project group to another on a one to three-year cycle. This policy of rotation has a number of advantages. First, it means new assignments for the programmer, even if much of the work is maintenance. Second, such a policy provides backup, since the experience base of the personnel is broadened. Third, rotation brings fresh outlooks, increasing the chance of better ideas being proposed. And, fourth, evaluation of personnel becomes more objective because a comparison can be made of the performance of two or more persons on the same job, and the performance of a person under several project leaders.

Failures. Maintenance programming has a history of causing more catastrophic failures than the original development programming. If the maintenance programmer is not familiar with the programme or if the documentation is poor, then it is possible that some changes made will result in serious failures. To remedy the first shortcoming, management should assign complex maintenance problems to the most knowledgeable people. For the second, it is the responsibility of management to ensure that all programmes are properly documented.

Extra-Training Costs. To maintain older applications that use outdated programming languages and run under primitive operating systems, means extra training for persons who will be working on such applications.

Unmanageable Conditions. Management may find itself faced with a complex and unwieldy problem; a problem that was not fully appreciated as it developed. This situation is characterised by inadequate documentation, rambling designs, a variety of incompatible hardware/software configurations, and outdated equipment and procedures. In such a situation information system management can rarely keep user departments satisfied. Few, if any, personnel hours are available. Practically no budget amounts are available for allocation to remedy the situation. In such a case, the severe problems of maintenance (and dissatisfied users) will continue indefinitely.

Procedures to Achieve More Maintainable Systems

The rate of change most organisations and their information systems experience is increasing rather than decreasing. Providing more maintainable systems and more efficient maintenance efforts are also likely to gain more emphasis. To achieve these goals within a dynamic environment requires action from both systems designers and managers.[2]

Designing for Change. This aspect encompasses a variety of procedures, some of which are:

1. *Standard data definitions.* The trend toward data base management systems underpins the push for standard data definitions. Many organisations now have redundant and inconsistent data definitions. These inconsistent data definitions are found in procedure manuals, source programme documentation, data files, and so forth, and only add to the problem of maintenance. A glossary or data dictionary of terms for data elements and other items in the system should be provided. For example, all data elements should have a name, description, size, source, location, and maintenance responsibility designation. It is also important to use the name, precisely as stated. ACC-REC-1 is not the same as ACCT-REC-1.
2. *Standard programme languages.* The use of a standard language, such as COBOL, makes the maintenance task easier.
3. *Standard set of configuration resources.* Standards should be developed, and the use of stipulated resources (such as core memory and peripherals) by a programme should be enforced.
4. *Modular design of programmes.* As with the maintenance of home appliances, where a repairman can determine which module is causing trouble and quickly replace it, the maintenance programmer can change modules of a programme much easier than trying to deal with the total programme.
5. *Use of decision tables.* Decision tables support modular programme design. They make programme logic clear to the maintenance programmer. Also, decision table preprocessors[3] provide a means for automatically converting decision tables into source code, thus reducing the chance for error.
6. *Documentation standards.* System, programme, and operation documentation is needed so that all the information required to operate and maintain a particular application is available. Since documentation is so essential, it is imperative that procedures be established and enforced for producing the documentation and keeping it current.

Design Changes. Even when programmes are designed to facilitate change, maintenance programmers need other tools to aid them in making and testing the changes. One tool that is needed is cross-reference listings of commonly used subroutines, files, records, and so forth. For example, when a change is to be made to a subroutine, the maintenance programmer wants to know all of the programmes that use that subroutine.

Configuration Design. The total configuration of an installation is subject to almost continual change. Maintenance requirements will be eased if the information system adheres to the policy of interchangeability (plug-compatibility), when making these configuration changes,. If a noninter-changeable alteration is made in the configuration, then some or all of the programmes will not run. A great deal of maintenance work is, therefore, necessary to make these programmes run on new, noncompatible equipment.

Organising for Maintenance. The issue here is whether maintenance should be performed by the development group, or whether it should be performed by a separate maintenance group. Some thoughts on this issue are as follows:

1. *Arguments for combined development and maintenance.* If both development and maintenance are performed in the same group, then the user departments will have one point of contact with the information system personnel who can effect change. User departments often do not know if a request for work will be classified as development or maintenance, since large revisions or system improvements are often treated as development. Furthermore, the analysts and programmers who originally developed the application systems have the best knowledge of those systems, and can best assess the full impact of changes. Some systems are so critical and complex that maintenance must be handled by only the most capable people and, in many instances, the most capable people are the ones who developed the system in the first place.
2. *Arguments for separate maintenance.* Separate maintenance tends to force better documentation, formal transfer procedures, and formal change procedures. Senior maintenance programmers may be promoted to development project leaders, since they have a good knowledge of documentation requirements, standards, operations, and so forth. And, for junior programmers, it is a good training ground.

AUDITING CONSIDERATIONS

Auditing is not only a legitimate form of systems work, but it affects directly the way systems work is performed. Consequently, the systems analyst should be aware of the different types of audits that the information system is subjected to, and the general approach taken by auditors, particularly when a computer is the heart of the system.

It is, however, the ultimate responsibility of management to see to it that the information system maintains a high degree of integrity. Therefore, all information systems should be audited both periodically and randomly. The general purpose of the audit is to detect inadequacies in the system and pinpoint defective operating procedures.

Types of Audits

A number of types of audits can be performed in the information system, each with its own particular objectives. All, however, are performed to ensure the integrity and operational efficiency of the system.

Post Implementation Audit. The basic purpose of this audit is to identify what actually occurred, versus what was projected during the development phase. In a large information system, a systems analyst may perform the post implementation audit. The audit, however, should not be performed by any analyst who was involved with the analysis, design, development, and implementation of the system. In many organisations a management consulting group is commissioned to perform the post implementation audit to ensure that a high degree of objectivity prevails.

From the perspective of the systems operations, this audit should determine that manual procedures are documented formally, that all computer programmes are documented properly, all operating personnel are trained, and that the level of accuracy and reliability of information outputs is acceptable to users. With regard to developmental projections, actual costs of each phase should be compared to projected costs. Likewise, actual developmental schedules should be compared to previously projected schedules.

Depending on the size and magnitude of the system implemented, the post implementation audit should not be conducted until the system has been operating for six months or more. This delay factor is intended to eliminate or minimise any learning curve effects on the system, which might distort unduly the auditor's findings.

Routine Operational Audit. In a large information system the routine operational audit is performed by a specially designated control group within the system itself. In a smaller information system, the routine operational audit may be performed by analysts or maintenance programmers. In either case the primary purpose of this audit is to determine how well operations are adhering to established control procedures and to provide assurance that the system is operating as designed. This audit involves such tasks as comparing output totals to input totals; reviewing console logs and error registers; verifying that input, processing, and output schedules are being met; and comparing actual procedures against standard procedures.

Financial Audit. The financial audit is a unique function of independent accountants. The primary purpose of this audit is to examine the organisation's financial statements and express an opinion as to their fairness, their conformity with generally accepted accounting principles, and the consistency with which the accounting principles have been applied from year to year. Since one of the major outputs of the information system are the financial statements, this type of audit serves as an excellent control over general operations of the system.

> ... If the CPA firm that performs the annual audit does not detect the inadequacies, and if serious losses result, the CPA firm can be sued by stockholders. If the CPA firm does detect the inadequacies, it will probably feel compelled to qualify the company's financial statements by noting such inadequacies in the statements. If such qualifications are made, and if there is not sufficient time to correct the control system and insure the integrity of the records, the company will be faced with the embarrassment of the notes in the annual statement.[4]

Systems Audit. Another service to top management is in the area of the systems audit. A systems audit generally involves review and evaluation of the following: (1) overall systems logic and design; (2) programming logic, operating system, and compilers; (3) computer configuration design and selection methods; (4) computer operation and utilisation; (5) systems backup and contingency plans; (6) security and procedure controls; and (7) documentation.

In summary, the post implementation audit simply answers the question posed by management: "Does the system do what the development people said it would do within projected schedule and cost?" The routine operational audit aids supervisors in ensuring that day-to-day operations meet standard operating procedures. Although CPA (certified public accountant) auditors are primarily concerned with satisfying themselves to the extent necessary to express an opinion on the financial statements, they may also be commissioned to perform many functions relative to a systems audit. During the course of the financial audit, the auditor may develop helpful comments and suggestions on improving the effectiveness and the efficiency of policies, procedures, and controls which pertain to the information system. Recently, the most significant advance in the role played by the external auditor is this extension from the traditional financial audit. Often, the auditor is charged with a broader responsibility encompassing many aspects of the systems audit.

Computer Auditing Approaches

In a computer-based information system, the auditor must determine how to validate that the processing done on the computer is correct. Auditing around the computer and auditing through the computer are two approaches to testing the processing logic of the computer.

Auditing Around the Computer. Previously, the typical auditor, being unfamiliar with computer technology, programming, and other techniques used in electronic data processing, developed audit procedures to review input documents and output reports only.

For example, the auditor selected source documents to be tested (e.g., employees' time cards), traced them through computer printouts (e.g., payroll accounts), and then reversed the order by tracing from summary accounts through computer printouts to source documents. The rationale behind this approach was that if source documents were properly reflected in the master files, and in turn the master files were properly supported by source documents, then the processing functions of the computer (e.g., the black box) must be performing correctly. Therefore, a review or

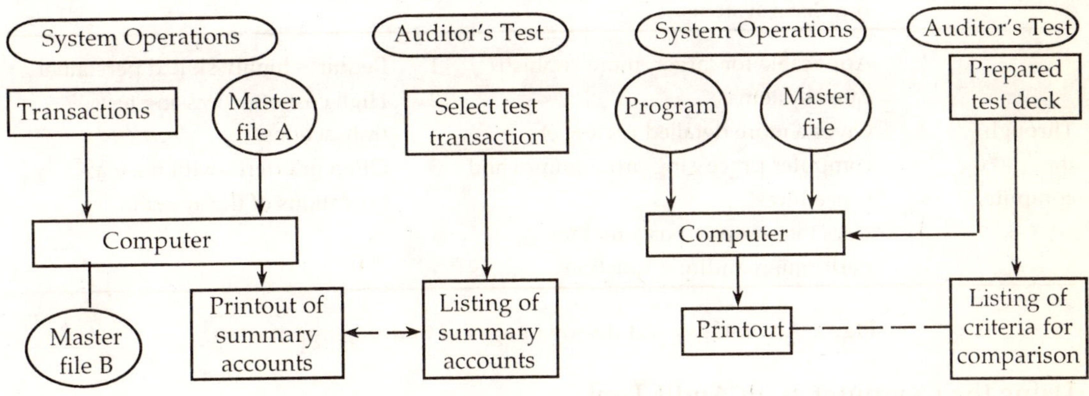

Fig. 1: Test of transactions around the computer.

Fig. 2: Test of transactions through the computer.

test computer programs or computer operations was unnecessary. These steps were bypassed completely as if the computer printouts were prepared manually, hence the term auditing around the computer. This approach is illustrated in Figure 1.

Auditing Through the Computer. As limitations of the above approach became more significant, as audit trails began to disappear with more sophisticated applications (e.g., the monitoring method), and as auditors became more knowledgeable in computer operations, auditing procedures also changed. Transactions began to be tested through the computer. With this approach, illustrated in Figure 2, the auditor verifies the effectiveness of control procedures over computer operations and computer programmes, and the correctness of internal processing.

Summary Comparison of Both Computer Auditing Approaches

Figure 3 is a matrix which gives the advantages and disadvantages of both approaches. It should be pointed out, however, that many auditors use a combination of both approaches for effective procedures.

Approaches	*Advantages*	*Disadvantages*
Around the computer	1. Logic is plausible. 2. Simple to use and is familiar to auditors. 3. Lessens need for specialised training. 4. Does not interfere with the normal operations of the system. 5. Applicable for audits of fairly small, simplistic systems.	1. Input data goes through many changes, limiting true comparisons. 2. A wide variety of transactions makes this approach tedious and time consuming. 3. Auditors fail to exploit the computer as a tool to help in auditing chores.
Through the computer.	1. Applicable for larger, more sophisticated systems. 2. Gives a more detailed review of computer processing programmes and procedures. 3. Uses the computer as a tool for performing auditing functions.	1. Requires highly skilled personnel. 2. High cost of processing test transactions. 3. Often interferes with normal operations of the system.

Fig. 3: Advantages and disadvantages of auditing approaches.

Using the Computer as an Audit Tool

To perform meaningful and comprehensive audits, the auditor should use an array of audit techniques rather than one technique alone. Most of these techniques require the computer to support their application. For example, to make compliance tests of programme controls, test transactions (traditionally called *test decks)* are prepared and run through the computer. Further tests (e.g., substantive tests), however, must be performed to test the accuracy and existence of records in the data base, and to retrieve from it various audit information. The following is a list of computer-assisted audit techniques.

Test Deck. Real data are simulated by dummy transactions (test data) that ideally include every possible type of condition, including those that the system, because of lack of proper controls, is incapable of handling. That is, the list of simulated transactions should test for both valid and invalid conditions.

Generalised Audit Programmes. Nearly all large accounting firms have at least one generalised audit programme to help them in their audit work. Normally, these programmes are written in a compiler-level language. Functions that audit programmes perform, along with practical examples of audit results, are as follows:

1. *Search and retrieve.* The auditor can have the programme scan large files and retrieve specified data segments that have audit significance. For example, it can search depositors' accounts for unusual charges, or identify dormant accounts.
2. *Selection of samples.* The programme can select a sample of records from a file population. Stratified sampling can be specified based upon upper and/or lower limits. Systematic sampling can be performed in which every *nth* record is selected for further review or confirmation. Or simple random sampling can be specified for record selection. Some programmes select a sample to meet desired statistical confidence levels. Furthermore, programmes calculate the arithmetic mean and variance of the population. Inferences can be made from these sample statistics, such as an estimate of the total book value of inventory.
3. *Perform basic calculations.* The audit programme performs the arithmetic operations of addition, subtraction, multiplication, and division. It also performs the logical operations of less than, greater than, or equal to.
4. *Prepare subtotals.* Totaling functions enable the auditor to print subtotals and item counts. For example, in payroll, auditing the programme can give levels of subtotals, by department, by plant, by state, by region, and so forth. It can also give end-of-file totals, such as numbers of records in the file and total debits and credits.
5. *Compare, sort, and merge.* Data, either alphabetic or numeric, can be sorted or merged in ascending or descending order. The auditor can match files on a given sequence, and compare the data in one file with that of another file. For example, a confirmation reply file may be compared with the confirmation log file, and a second mailing printed of those accounts not

responding. In another instance, the auditor can compare payroll files for different periods to see if there has been any significant change in pay rates, salaries, etc.

6. *Copy data.* This function simply copies records or fields from one file to another. It can produce a tape file of all accounts to receive positive confirmation. The auditor may have the programme create a work file of items that are of special interest, such as selling prices, item costs, pay rates, and commission rates.
7. *Summarise.* Large volume computer files can be summarised quickly to lessen the burden of making detailed reviews. This function creates desired totals and subtotals for a group of related records in a file.
8. *Print.* This function allows the auditor to specify the audit results in almost any format desired with descriptive major and minor column headings. Moreover, a great deal of flexibility is provided to the auditor for spacing, paging, and ordering of the output. This function enhances the organisation and readability of the audit information.

Tagging and Tracing. With application of tagging and tracing routines in the programming logic, any transactions and related data can be traced through the system. As each processing step is performed, the interaction of the selected transaction with other data and related tests is displayed. Control and selection of tagged transactions can be specified by the auditor through a terminal in his or her office.

The tagging and tracing audit technique flags, by some special notation or code, selected transactions. These transactions are processed as normal transactions by the programming logic. Displays of the status of these transactions are made to the auditor as they flow through the system. This technique, if installed into the programming logic while the programmes are being developed, requires relatively little extra time and cost, and provides a powerful technique to obtain a comprehensive transaction trail.

Three aspects to the tagging and tracing technique are: (1) some identifier must be used to tag the selected transactions, (2) programme instructions must be embedded in the application programmes to recognise the tagged transactions, and (3) routines must be prepared to print the results of the tagged transactions and related data at key points in the system.

General display points are: (1) where the transaction enters the system, (2) where the transaction enters each programme module, (3) where the transaction exits each programme module, (4) interface points between each transaction and a secondary record in the system, and (5) before and after displays of the master records changed by the transaction.

Integrated Test Facility (ITF). The ITF involves the establishment of a fictitious entity (e.g., customer, department, division, employee) in the data base, against which test transactions, unknown to the systems personnel, can be processed as if they are regular, live transactions. This approach integrates permanent test data into the system and permits the auditor to monitor continuously the performance of the system. The ITF requires the auditor to supply a system for recording and processing the test transactions so that predetermined results can be checked against the actual results produced by the computer system. Furthermore, the ITF gives the auditor a strong computer audit technique for auditing online systems, in that it tests the system as it is operating versus after the fact.

Monitors. Software companies and computer vendors (e.g., IBM's System Management Facilities—SMF) provide packages that can be put to good use by auditors to provide computer usage, control, and equipment performance information. This information is collected as a by-product of the normal operations, without requiring extensive programming or special work by the auditor. Six general categories of information furnished by monitors such as IBM's SMF package are as follows:

1. *Accounting records.* This category consists of records that show who used the system and for how long. The information contained in these records includes: (a) identification of job or job step, user, and hardware features; (b) job priority; (c) date and time of job initiation; (d) date and time of job termination; (e) type of job termination (for abnormal terminations, the reason for the ABEND is indicated); and (f) amount of main storage, in bytes, used to execute the job. These records provide an audit trail of the system resources used and the jobs or personnel responsible for the use of these resources. Information contained in these records is used by the accounting department as the basis for developing EDP cost allocation and charging users accordingly.
2. *Data set activity records.* These records provide information about which portion of the data base were used to perform a computer job or job step, and who requested the use of the data sets. The records furnish an audit trail of data usages. This trail is one of the principal benefits the auditor will derive if SMF is used. These records also supply considered information about the characteristics of the data base.
3. *Volume utilisation records.* These records indicate the amount of available space on direct access storage device and give basic error statistics for tape

files. They also record the number of records contained in each file. These records are used by the data processing department in its efforts to obtain better utilisation of space within direct access storage devices. In the case of tape files, the error statistics are helpful in assessing the quality of a particular reel of tape. For example, when the number of errors on a tape reaches a certain level, the tape should be either cleaned or discarded. The information in the volume utilisation records has little meaning for auditors. They might want to review this data in an attempt to determine whether or not the data processing department is making effective use of this information. Usually the auditor has no reason to look at these records, unless there are symptoms of a problem at the installation which such a review might clarify.

4. *System usage records.* This category contains records that show the portion of the hardware configuration being used by each job and job step. These records can be used to develop some appreciation of how effectively the resources of the system are being applied. Much of the information is technical in nature; for example, the amount of time the processor is idle. The auditor might want to be certain that this information is being used by the data processing department to achieve maximum system efficiency. Information that would be of particular interest to the auditor includes date and time of all file dumps, terminal initiation times, and times when a system halt command was initialised.
5. *Subsystem records.* Whenever a job requires a subsystem (subroutine, programme, or module) for some processing operation, that fact can be recorded by SMF. This information is of value to the auditor for two reasons. First, it provides an audit trail of which subsystems are being utilised by what jobs. Second, it gives the auditor an opportunity to determine what activity is being entered and from where it is being entered.

   One particular type of record will be of interest to most auditors. This record is written whenever a sign-on attempt fails because of an invalid password. A limited number of invalid passwords are normally allowed because of keying errors at the terminal. An abnormal number of such errors could indicate that someone is trying to penetrate the system. This error data are a potential signal for audit investigation.
6. *User written records.* When needed information cannot be obtained from one of the categories described above, SMF provides the user with the option of incorporating his or her own analysis routines into the system. The extensive capabilities for performing further analysis should provide

the auditor with unlimited possibilities for evaluating data processing. Auditors can build routines to review every transaction for conformity with organisation policies and procedures, to detect violations of systems standards, or to perform special analysis in support of audit objectives. In spite of performance degradation of the system, the use of analysis routines is an important technique because it potentially allows the auditor to analyze the operation of a system during execution time, without the specific knowledge of any other person or group. This could improve audit integrity, security, and independence in a computer environment.[5]

PROJECT MANAGEMENT SYSTEMS

The activities required to analyze, design, and develop an information system or subsystem are generally termed a project. The project concept is an effective technique for managing change. A project management system (PMS) is a system that supports the tasks of planning, scheduling, controlling, and accounting for projects. The essential feature of a PMS is a mechanism for delineating a project into measurable work units. What follows is a discussion of the types of PMS and an analysis of the problems they can create.[6]

Types of Project Management Systems

Project management systems can be classified into four general categories: (1) manual structured systems, (2) project tracking systems, (3) project networking systems, and (4) full project management systems. Many commercial packages are available for organisations to use.

Manual Structured Systems. These systems normally impose a standard structure of eight to twelve phases on all projects. Each phase is identified with work products and documentation. Project progress is reviewed at specific checkpoints where, relying on revised estimates of remaining costs and estimated benefits, management must make the decision on whether to proceed.

Project Tracking Systems. Project tracking systems produce reports showing actual schedule realisation and cost accumulation, based on a list of project activities and their corresponding time estimates and budgeted expenditures. Project tracking systems do not include a facility for project planning.

Project Networking Systems. Project networking systems use the well-known techniques of PERT and CPM (see Appendix A). Since time is the focus of these techniques, project networking systems are best suited for planning and controlling schedules; they are not particularly suited to controlling costs.

Full Project Management Systems. Full PMSs perform (or have the potential to perform) most of the functions (e.g., planning, work definition, tracking, and reporting) that were listed for the other categories of PMSs. Aspects of the planning function include (1) a work breakdown structure; (2) network capability, considering all projects; (3) resource scheduling; and (4) "What if?" analysis capability. This last aspect of the planning function is especially intriguing. When a project gets in trouble or a management redirection alters a plan, the "What if?" capability should help management analyze alternative courses of action and the concomitant impacts on the project.

A second feature of a full PMS is its work definition function. This includes aspects of (1) structuring projects based on phases, activities, and checkpoints; (2) preparing a precedence relationship among the activities (i.e., a network); (3) setting performance time standards for activities; (4) creating procedures describing how to perform the activities; and (5) defining documentation standards for the activities.

The tracking function of a full PMS entails collecting and validating data concerning work progress, schedule revisions, and resource allocation changes. Finally, the reporting function encompasses preparation of project reports to management, project leaders, project employees, and accounting. These reports detail actual versus plan for the last period, as well as planned activities for the next period. Furthermore, reports may be prepared on a departmental basis, showing the time distribution for all staff members over all activities.

Pitfalls in Implementation PMS

If suppliers of full PMSs were polled and they were candid in their comments, it is likely that they would report that over half of their full PMS installations have been failures. Moreover, an additional number of installations are making only limited use of a full PMS. This underscores that a full PMS is no panacea. It is not a solution to inadequate systems design procedures or poor programming practices. A full PMS is only of value in helping a smooth-running operation run even more smoothly.

Installing a project management system is like installing any other management procedure. If an organisation does not have any sort of PMS at present, then it would be unwise to install a full PMS at the outset. Regardless of the type of PMS implemented, it needs to be accompanied by large doses of management commitment, encouragement, and endorsement. Management sets the tone by either using, or not using, the reports that the system generates.

Impediments to Installing a Successful Full PMS

When installing a full PMS, three major problem areas to avoid are:

1. *Insufficient support.* Who will benefit from the successful installation of a full PMS? Not the analysts and programmers; while the chance of their being overloaded is reduced, the system can be a source of embarrassment, since their deficiencies will be highlighted. Not the project leaders; while the impact of schedule slippages will be pointed up, the mechanics of supporting the system can easily take up to 10 per cent of their time. So the only people in the organisation with a real incentive to make the system work is management. With an investment of little personal effort, the system can provide them with who is doing what and where each project stands.
2. *Costs out of proportion.* As a rule of thumb, no more than 5 per cent of the annual salaries of analysts and programmers should be spent on the purchase of a full PMS package. The purchase price of a full PMS system, however, is only the tip of the iceberg. Attention must be given to installation costs, and then to the annual costs of operating the system. For example, in a unit of 25 programmers and analysts, installation costs may be twice the purchase cost; operating costs may be four times the purchase cost.
3. *Lack of a realistic understanding.* The most common misunderstanding seems to be that the full PMS reports will provide a complete picture of the status of a project. This is clearly just not the case. Two important types of information missing from PMS reports are *quality of work completed* and *expected problems.* Quality of work done can only be assessed by conducting technical reviews. For example, at a checkpoint the programmes that have been completed might be reviewed from the standpoint of ease of conversion, ease of maintenance, effective utilisation of computer resources, and so forth. Information on expected problems might be obtained by instituting a hierarchy of periodic, manual reports. These reports could indicate the activities worked on during this period, what is planned to be worked on next period, and what are some of the anticipated problems where assistance may be needed.

MANAGING CHANGE

Many systems analysts, as well as managements, make the mistake of assuming that information systems development is controlled only by technical, economic, legal, and schedule constraints. A fifth constraint, *operation,* deals mainly with the people element in the organisation. In the long run operational feasibility often has a greater impact on systems development than the other four constraints combined. Much of the current literature related to the field of information systems reflects a concern that a preoccupation with technology and techniques has replaced the systems analyst's ability to deal effectively with people. While the dramatic and rapid developments in technology require an inordinate amount of attention from the analyst, these developments have also resulted in a greater need to pay attention to the human element of systems work.

All too often technical specialists have blind spots in dealing with people. Much of their work requires changes in the work of other persons, but they often do not recognise the social problems they cause. They are convinced that the technical part of their change is correct, and therefore any opposition to it must come from bullheaded or ignorant people. When they talk to workers, they sometimes use jargon and theories that do not "make sense" to the practical people of the shop. Further, they do not discuss; they tell—convinced that change is logical, they ignore the psychological![7]

The major result of the systems analyst's work is change, and many of the users or personnel in an organisation cannot deal effectively with the changes which they are being asked to accept. This problem is more acute in the areas of the organisation that traditionally performed many of the operations now done automatically by the information system. Moreover, these problems are found at each level of the organisation.

People and their social systems often resist change in organisations. In fact, the fear of change can be as disrupting to the organisation as the change itself. The reasons for this latter type of resistance are summarised as follows.

1. *Economic.* An individual fears becoming technically unemployed, demoted, or asked to work fewer hours at a reduced wage rate.
2. *Personal.* Change, by definition, imputes criticism that the present system is inadequate. The individual fears that, because of greater systematisation, his or her skill will be diminished or lost, and the personal pride derived from it will be lost or reduced. Moreover, most people dislike being required to relearn.
3. *Social.* Change frequently affects human relations and brings about new social situations. Old social ties must be severed and new ones must be made. The employee feels that the change, while perhaps benefiting the organisation, does little to benefit the individual or fellow employees.[8]

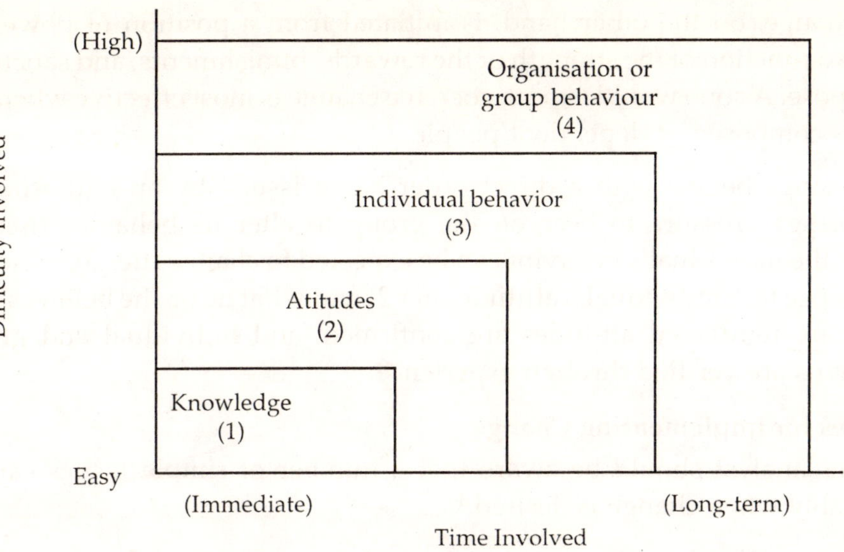

Fig. 4: Time duration and degree of difficulty in effecting change at each tier.

Participative Versus Coercive Change Strategy

Hersey and Blanchard[9] outline a four-tiered diagram of change: (1) knowledge changes, (2) attitudinal changes, (3) individual behaviour changes, and (4) group or organisational performance changes. The time duration and the degree of difficulty in effecting change at each tier is illustrated in Figure 4.

The systems analyst, when acting as a change agent, may attempt to move individuals from one tier to the next by employing a participative change strategy, a coercive change strategy, or a combination of both. If a participative change strategy is to be successful, then the analyst must possess a certain amount of influence over the individuals who will experience the impact of the change. Additionally, the group targeted for the change must be self-motivated and relatively independent.

Participative change begins when the systems analyst educates the individuals affected by the new system. It is hoped that this introduction of new knowledge (tier 1) will cultivate the development of the appropriate attitude toward the new system (tier 2). This attitude will, in turn, shape individual behavior via participation in such activities as goal-setting exercises (tier 3). Finally, individual behavior patterns will lead to formalised group participation (tier 4). While participative change may be slow and evolutionary, if effective, it is enduring.

Coercive change, on the other hand, is initiated from a position of power its permanency is a function of the strength of the rewards, punishments, and sanctions it is able to impose. As one would expect, coercive change is most effective when the target group is composed of dependent people.

Coercive change begins with a direct order being issued by an authoritative figure. This brings pressure to bear on the group to alter its behavior (tier 4). Consequently, the individual's behavior can be expected to change (tier 3), which in turn, can influence that individual's attitude (tier 2) and what he or she believes (tier 1). As beliefs are reinforced attitudes are confirmed, and individual and group behavior patterns are verified through experience.

Tactical Guides for Implementing Change

The systems analyst should be aware that a number of simple tactics can be applied profitably when change is desired.[10]

1. *Spaced practice.* Improvement in performance of a new task occurs more quickly, is mastered in greater depth, and is more permanent, if learning is introduced in relatively short periods with ample provision for rest. This can be contrasted to situations in which continuous or massed practice learning sessions are employed.
2. *Rehearsal.* Performance improves constantly with continued practice, until a plateau is reached. Practice beyond this point can lead eventually to overlearning, a condition in which the change routine or procedure becomes virtually automatic.
3. *Knowledge.* Considerable evidence indicates learning of a prior skill can have a negative transfer effect on the acquisition of a new skill. If the analyst moves directly to the new approach without first addressing established practices, negative transfer is likely to take place. In short, when introducing change, move from the known to the unknown.
4. *Goal setting.* Targets should be realistic, neither too easy nor impossible, but such that when attained they provide a feeling of achievement.[11] Moreover, they should be expressed, if possible, in numerical terms, described specifically, and be time-phased. "Net retail sales of Product X are expected to increase in the next calendar year by one million dollars," is one example of such an expression.
5. *Feedback.* Successful introduction of change requires that appropriate feedback information be presented to permit necessary adjustments to be made by those undertaking the change process. The systems analyst must provide for review and reporting sessions, not merely to boost morale, but as a control and correction requisite.

SUMMARY

To achieve effective information systems, management must be concerned with the activities of maintenance, auditing, project control, and introducing change.

It is inevitable that in working to get the information system developed, certain errors will be made and a variety of expedients employed. Moreover, users of the information system may suggest certain improvements. What is needed then is a plan of action that increases the maintainability of the information system.

Auditing activities are performed to ensure that management objectives are being met and that the integrity of the system is maximised. Many auditors, especially the independent certified public accountant (CPA), are extending the bounds of their traditional financial audit to include additional operational aspects of the system.

Project management systems are integral to the tasks of planning, scheduling, and controlling projects. Although project management systems may vary in their degree of sophistication, their successful introduction into an organisation will be a function of the commitment, encouragement, and endorsement given them by management.

In performing effective systems work and ensuring that changes in the system are accepted by the personnel in the organisation, both the systems analyst and the management of the information system must be acutely aware of human needs. If the technical potential of the information system is to be realised, then the various factors that relate to people and their social systems must be satisfied first.

REVIEW QUESTIONS

1. Why are more maintainable systems a major objective of management? Discuss fully.
2. List and discuss the four main causes of programme, data files, documentation, and procedure changes. Prepare your own example for each of these causes.
3. Why do you think most people dislike maintenance work?
4. List and fully discuss the procedures for achieving more maintainable systems.
5. Define modular design of programmes.

6. Should maintenance be performed in the development groups, or in separate maintenance groups?
7. List and discuss the types of audits.
8. Why should the post implementation audit be delayed until several months after implementation of a system?
9. List and discuss computer auditing approaches. Give advantages and disadvantages of each approach.
10. Prepare a list of computer-assisted audit techniques.
11. List and give examples of the functions that comprise a generalised audit programme.
12. In what way does the integrated test facility differ from the test deck and tagging and tracing audit techniques?
13. Describe how auditors can use different types of records produced by system monitors.
14. Describe four general classifications of project management systems.
15. Who will benefit most from a successful PMS, and why?
16. List the reasons individuals resist change.
17. Discuss some tactics that systems analysts might find useful when change is desired.

QUESTIONS FOR DISCUSSION

1. How can one differentiate between maintenance work, such as systems improvements, and new development work?
2. "We wrote all our programmes in LOGELNUM, the language promoted by the vendor we acquired our computer from. Now, we are planning on changing to another vendor but we are in a real bind because LOGELNUM is not compatible with the proposed new equipment." Comment on several ramifications applicable to this statement.
3. Compare and contrast systems work performed by a systems analyst, and the auditing function performed by an auditor. Discuss fully.
4. "During the course of the financial audit, the auditor may develop helpful comments and suggestions on improving effectiveness and efficiency of policies, procedures, and controls which pertain to information systems. In recent times, the most significant advance in the role played by the auditor is in this extension from the traditional financial audit." Discuss.
5. "Many systems analysts, as well as managements, make the mistake of assuming that information systems development is controlled by technical,

economic, legal, and schedule constraints. There is a fifth constraint which might be more severe." What is this fifth constraint? Discuss fully.

6. Is technological development a boon or a curse to mankind?
7. "Our programmers operate the computer themselves during testing periods." Discuss.
8. "The manager of systems development is a tough negotiator. When he disagrees with the users, he does it his way or not at all." Discuss fully.
9. "All your planning and control problems would be solved if only you were to install a full project management system." Comment on this generalisation.
10. "The marketing system I have implemented is the most sophisticated one of its kind. Now if only the sales force were bright enough to recognise this fact. . . ." Comment on this approach to introducing change into the organisation.
11. "Because of its many advantages, we rely solely on the ITF auditing technique." Indicate the conditions under which this might be an unwise course of action.
12. Comment on the statement, "When introducing change use the carrot first, and if that fails, use the stick!"
13. "Our goal is to increase the size of our membership by 5 per cent." How could this target statement be improved?

EXERCISES

1. What follows is a network with corresponding activity times estimated:

Activity	*Optimistic*	*Most Likely*	*Pessimistic*
A	5	8	16
B	3	4	9
C	2	5	7
D	6	8	10

Required

1. Calculate expected times for each activity.
2. Determine the critical path.
3. Calculate the cumulative variance along the critical path.
4. For each event, indicate the earliest, latest, and slack time.

2. Classify the following maintenance situations as emergency, routine, special reporting requests, or system improvements. You may feel that some of the situations cannot be appropriately classified under a single category; in this case use as many classification categories as necessary.

1. An order entry system has been operational for 18 months. During this period, the company's product line has been expanded, two new warehouses have been added, and three sales offices have been opened in Canada. Additionally, users have indicated that the report showing back orders would be of greater value if it were to reach their desk before noon, rather than by 4:00 PM.
2. You, as the maintenance analyst for the payroll system, have just received a memorandum from the Vice-President of Public Affairs. She has requested information on the year-to-date number of minority hires. It is indicated further in the memorandum that henceforth this information will be required on a quarterly basis.
3. As you leave the tennis courts, there is an urgent message requesting you to call operations immediately. It seems the sales analysis programme, which had been running smoothly for the last six months, has just abnormally terminated.
4. Due to the sharp decline in the cost of color CRTs, you are requested to modify the traffic control system, presently using black and white CRTs, to accommodate color.

3. Past experience has shown that a particular type of programme has an expected time of completion equal to 200 hours. David Wilson is assigned to prepare this programme. The plan provides the following tasks and related times for each task:

Design programme logic	50 hours
Code programme	40 hours
Test programme	70 hours
Document programme	40 hours

After reviewing the programme and developing a programme macro flowchart, Wilson begins to code. At the end of several days, Wilson reports the following:

	Planned	Actual	Remaining
Design programme logic	50	20	0
Code programme	40	4	27
Test programme	70	0	15
Document programme	40	0	12

You are the chief programmer. What is your reaction to Wilson's revised plan?

4. Conduct a post implementation audit of some system in your school or a local business. Prepare a report of your findings, highlighting the discrepancies between any projections and actual results.

PROBLEMS

1. Donna Henry, a systems analyst, in developing a production control system for Apex Products, needed to conduct some routine studies of machine utilisation and downtime in the manufacturing plant. Without explaining her purpose she set up records to be kept by each operator of a lubricant capper machine. These operators were paid on a piece-rate basis. The machine operators were told to report the length, time of day, and cause of all capper machine downtime. The supervisor was directed to require the operators to maintain these records for 30 days.

   Both the supervisor and the operators stalled and complained, and finally, kept such inadequate records that they turned out to be unusable. Donna Henry concluded that the department was full of obstructionists who did not have the best interests of the organisation at heart.

   Required: Identify the human aspects that Donna Henry has failed to recognise in dealing with the supervisor and the operators.

2. Heath Corporation is a manufacturer of quality sound components. It has a number of plants located in California and Oregon. Recently, a new labor recording system was installed in three plants in Oregon. A brief description of the labor recording system follows.

   Automatic time recording devices are located throughout the shop areas. For 2000 employees covered by this system, these devices completely replace human timekeepers and manually prepared time cards. Data from the system flows through to the company's payroll and job-order cost accounting and control records. Basic timekeeping tools are plastic employee badges, prepunched with charge number and other information about a particular job.

   The badge is assigned permanently to each employee. The job cards follow the parts or assemblies to be worked on. Exceptions are indirect labor and other special cards, which are located in racks adjacent to the input devices. Clock-in on reporting for work requires only insertion of the badge and one or more job cards, and depression of other keys.

   All input devices are linked electrically to a central control box, a master clock, and an online keypunch that creates a punched card for each entry.

The cards are converted to magnetic tape for passing through computer processes. The first of these, a match against an employee identification master tape, begins after the beginning of each shift.

Within an hour after shift start, an exception report has been prepared for distribution to shop foremen. This report indicates absences, tardy clock-in, preshift overtime, and failure to check in on a job. Each exception must be approved by the shop foreman. Transactions accepted in this first processing routine plus transactions accepted for the remainder of the shift are "posted" to a direct access file arranged by employee Transactions rejected must be analyzed and corrected for reentry into the processing cycle.

To evaluate the labor recording system, the internal auditors decided to use simulated transactions designed to lest not only routine processing, but also various exception conditions. Since the auditors wanted to perform the tests under normal operating conditions, using actual shop locations and job cards, a special set of employee badges and corresponding master records were created.

Required: For the labor recording system, prepare a set of transactions to test routine processing and exception conditions.

3. Listed below are the activities necessary to complete a project. For each activity lettered A through M, an optimistic, most likely, and pessimistic time estimate is included (O, M, and P, respectively). Additionally, predecessor and successor activities are indicated.

				Activities	
Activity	*O*	*M*	*P*	*Predecessor*	*Successor*
A	5	8	19	—	B, C, E
B	5	8	10	A	F, D
C	3	5	7	A	G
D	0	0	0	B	G
E	6	9	12	A	M
F	4	8	18	B	H, K
G	5	7	12	D, C	I, J
H	0	0	0	F	L
I	0	0	0	G	L
J	0	0	0	G	M
K	4	7	10	F	—
L	7	10	25	H, I	—
M	4	6	8	E, J	—

Required:

1. Construct a network for the project.
2. Compute the expected completion time for each activity.
3. Determine the critical path and the slack present in the network.
4. What is the probability of completing the project within 40 days from the day it started?
5. A $1000 late penalty fee is assessed if the project is completed after day 42. Is it cost/effective to purchase a new tool for $275 that will change the optimistic, most likely, and pessimistic time estimates of activity L to 6, 9, and 15, respectively? Assume that the tool, after being used in activity L, can be sold for $175.

4. Patty Randall, one of your more experienced and better maintenance programmers, has requested a meeting with you (her supervisor) to discuss the possibility of transferring to the systems development area.

   "I'd like to move to the development area because I'm tired of cleaning up someone else's mess. And I would like to get over to development because there is a greater chance for exposure to top management and, consequently, I might be able to progress a bit faster," she began.

   "My progress here has been quite good and I have nothing against you or the people in this area. It just seems that I might be able to do something more important—something I could call my own—over in development. I mean, that's where the action is and that's where they're creating all the new systems that are really going to contribute to the company," Patty continued. "Besides, development works with new equipment and new languages. It is not very exciting to be stuck here in maintenance and have to work with second generation languages and outmoded equipment."

   Required: How would you respond to Patty to convince her of the value of the maintenance function to the company, and the important role she can play within that function?

5. In establishing performance requirements for a proposed magnetic ink character recognition (MICR) demand deposit system, management indicated that the following qualitative factors were important:

   1. "The system should result in the most economical operation possible."
   2. "Items should not be posted to the wrong account."
   3. "The system must be able to handle unexpected future changes with minor difficulty."

4. "System downtime should be infrequent and cause as little disruption as possible."
5. "Customers should feel comfortable with the new system."
6. "The system should operate in a timely fashion."

Required: For each of the qualitative factors listed above, provide a corresponding quantitative measure that might be used to evaluate the new system when implemented.

NOTES

1. Summarised from "That Maintenance 'Iceberg'," *EDP Analyzer*, October 1972, pp. 4-8. Used with permission.
2. *Ibid.*, pp. 8-14.
3. See, for example, R.N. Dean, "A Comparison of Decision Tables Against Conventional COBOL as a Programming Tool for Commercial Applications," *Software World*, Spring 1971, pp. 26-30. Also see, "COBOL Aid Packages," *EDP Analyzer*. May 1972.
4. Computer Security: Backup and Recovery Methods," EDP Analyser, January 1972, p. 11. Used with permission.
5. This presentation on SMF summarised from William E. Perry and Donald L. Adams, "SMF—An Untapped Audit Resource," *EDPACS*, September 1974, pp. 1-8, and William E. Perry, "Using SMF as an Audit Tool-Accounting Information," *EDPACS*. February 1975, pp. 1-17.
6. "Adapted from "Project Management Systems," *EDP Analyzer*, September 1976.
7. Keith Davis, *Human Behavior at Work*, New York: McGraw-Hill Book Co., 1972, p. 517.
8. *Ibid.* For a more detailed list of human factors that contribute to resistance to change, see Ephraim R. McLean. "The Human Side of Systems: The User's Perspective," paper presented to the 1976 Western Systems Conference, Los Angeles.
9. P. Hersey and K.H. Blanchard, *Management of Organisation Behavior*, Englewood Cliffs, N.J.: Prentice-Hall, Inc., 1972, p. 160.
10. Condensed from M. Kubr (ed.). *Management Consulting*, Geneva, Switzerland: International Labour Office, 1976, pp. 36-41.
11. D.C. McClelland and D.G. Winter, *Motivating Economic Achievement*, Now York: The Free Press, 1969.

REFERENCES

"Approach Trains User to Read 'Alien' Code," *Computerworld*, September 12, 1977.

Auditing Standards and Procedures, Committee on Auditing Procedure Statement No. 33, New York: American Institute of Certified Public Accountants, 1963.

Canning, "COBOL Aid Packages," *EDP Analyzer*, January 1972.

Canning, "Computer Security: Backup and Recovery Methods," *EDP Analyzer*, January 1972.

Canning, "Project Management Systems," *EDP Analyzer*, September 1976.

Canning, "That Maintenance 'Iceberg'," *EDP Analyzer*, October 1972.

Davis, *Human Behavior at Work*, New York: McGraw-Hill Book Co., 1972.

Dean, "A Comparison of Decision Tables Against Conventional COBOL as a Programming Tool for Commercial Applications," *Software World*, Spring 1971.

"DP Auditing Viewed as Art Form Instead of Science," *Computerworld*, July 11, 1977.

Hersey and Blanchard, *Management of Organisation Behavior*, Englewood Cliffs, NJ.: Prentice-Hall, Inc., 1972.

Kubr (ed.), *Management Consulting*, Geneva, Switzerland: International Labour Office, 1976.

" 'Ideal' DP Auditor Needs Range of Experience," *Computerworld*, September 5, 1977.

McClelland and Winter, *Motivating Economic Achievement*, New York: The Free Press, 1969.

McLean, "The Human Side of Systems: The User's Perspective," paper presented to the *1976 Western Systems Conference*, Los Angeles.

Perry, "Using SMF as an Audit Tool-Accounting Information," *EDPACS*, February 1975.

Perry and Adams, "SMF—An Untapped Audit Resource," *EDPACS*, September 1974.

Perry and Fitzgerald, "Designing for Auditability," *Datamation*, August 1977.

Porter and Perry, *EDP Controls and Auditing*, Third Edition, Belmont, Calif: Wadsworth Publishing Company, Inc., 1980.

Study Group on Computer Control and Audit Guidelines, Toronto, Canada: The Canadian Institute of Chartered Accountants, 1971.

Thierauf, *Data Processing for Business and Management*, New York: John Wiley & Sons, Inc., 1973.

Toffler, *Future Shock*, New York: Random House, Inc., 1970.

Wadsworth, *The Human Side of Data Processing Management*, Englewood Cliffs, NJ.: Prentice-Hall, Inc., 1973.

Wilkinson, "An Application Audit," *Datamation*, August 1977.

4

TELECOM STORY

Information is data (for example, raw facts or observations) that have been put into a meaningful and useful context. This gives information value for specific persons and meets their particular information needs. Thus, information is a basic resource which is very essential for individuals and organisations to survive and succeed in society. In developing countries of the so-called third world, people live in an agro-industrial society composed primarily of farmers and industrial workers. In India, 80 per cent of its 850 million people live in villages. They earn their living mainly through agriculture. Only a small percentage of total workforce in the country is engaged in industrial activities.

In the developed and advanced countries of the West and the Far East, people no longer live in an agriculture society or an industrial society. Instead, they are living in an information society where a majority of workforce consists of *knowledge workers* engaged in service occupations. They spend most of their work time creating, using, processing and distributing information. The category of knowledge workers includes executives, managers, professionals, such as, engineers, scientists, accountants and teachers; and office staff, such as, secretaries and clerks. All those people earn their living using information technology to create, manage and distribute information resources which are then used to help them manage the human, material financial and other resources involved in their work responsibilities. Information thus is the most valuable commodity for knowledge workers, Their organisation and for the society. Their social, cultural and economic progress is heavily dependent on efficient management of information resources.

Information as a Resource

The organisations are faced with continual changes in environment and scope of their operations. Information is an important and valuable organisational resource that must be properly and efficiently managed for an organisation to survive and succeed. The organisation rely on information technology and information system to provide appropriate information for their efficient operations and effective management. This information must not only be reasonably accurate, it must also be timely. If accurate and timely information is not provided to the end-users, the organisation will suffer strategic disadvantage against its competitors. An information system and the adopted information technology which do not properly support an organisation to achieve its strategic objectives, corporate goals and do not lead to its overall progress may seriously damage that organisation's prospects for survival and success in a competitive business environment Thus information technology plays a vital role in our everyday life and in our society, dependent as we are on the effective use and efficient management of information resources.

The field of information technology is constantly changing and expanding, as dramatic technological development and research findings in human behaviour are opening new possibilities. Sociology, psychology and economics are the disciplines that contribute towards behavioural aspects while science, engineering, computers and telecommunications contribute towards technological aspect of the information system technology. The convergence of information processing technology (computers) and telecommunications has revolutionised the whole concept of information management. The direction of the computer technology today is toward increased connectivity where any computer in an organisation can communicate with any other one. This connectivity is provided by telecommunication links. A major challenge for the information society is to manage its information resources to benefit all its members. This, for example, means using information technology for efficient management of limited material and energy resources.

Telecommunications

Telecommunication is the sending of information in any form (e.g., voice, data, text and images) from one place to another using electronic or optical media. Transmission of voice is achieved through telephone network. Data communications is the term that describes the transmission and receiving of data over telecommunication links between one or more computer systems and a variety of input/output terminals. All forms of modern telecommunications now rely heavily on computers and computerised devices. However, in most developing countries including India, the telecommunications even today overwhelmingly mean voice transmission, i.e., telephone. Data communications is relatively at a very low key.

The importance of telecommunications as an essential infrastructure for the social and economic development of the society was realised in this country only in mid-eighties when it was declared as an essential infrastructure and included in the core sector. Since then the scenario has been changing rather rapidly. Today, the telecommunications is playing more important role in support of rural development, maintenance of law and order, defending the frontiers and in economic development of the country. The corporate sector depends heavily on telecommunications for vital support in its operations, management and strategic objectives.

The telecommunications have become an integral part of all human activities may be social, cultural or economic. It is impossible to conceive of a modern society without efficient and reliable telecommunication services. Today, the level of development of a society is measured by the status of telecommunications services. Worldwide, there are about 560 million telephones for the total population of 5.6 billion. The advanced countries of the West and the far East with less than 15 per cent of total world population have more than 80 per cent of the total number of telephones in the world.

While in the USA the telephone density is over 500 telephones per one thousand population, in India there are less than 6 telephones per 1000 population. Within the country also, there is wide disparity in telephone density among various States and also, between urban and rural sectors. Metro cities of Delhi, Bombay Calcutta and Madras, and also other major cities like Ahmedabad, Bangalore and Hyderabad have telephone densities ranging from 40 to 50 telephones per 1000 population. The whole of rural India have less than one telephone per 1000 population. This is clearly reflected in economic disparities between advanced and developing countries and also between rural and urban areas of a developing country like India. Modern, reliable and efficient telecommunication facilities are essential for efficient operation and management of corporate activities. Also, to accelerate growth of rural economy and to improve standard of living of rural masses, it is essential to extend and expand telecommunications facilities in rural areas. The role, present status and the trend of telecommunications in the two primary application areas, i.e., corporate sector and rural development is discussed here.

Applications of Telecommunications

(A) Telecommunication in the Corporate Sector

To survive and succeed in a competitive environment, an organisation big or small depends heavily on information resources for its operations, management and strategic objectives. The telecommunications requirement of big organisations are no longer limited to office telephone system or long-distance calling arrangement over telephone such as trunk calls and STD/ISD calls. They also need more complex computer-based telecommunication facilities, such as, data communication, text and messaging communications, image transmission and information retrieval, etc.

A list of specific applications of telecommunications for organised sector, grouped into major categories such as voice communications, data communications etc., is indicated below:

(i)	Voice Communications	Standard telephone service, Audio conferencing systems, Voice mail systems, Office intercommunication systems.
(ii)	Data Communications	Online transaction processing, Inquiry/response systems, Hardware/software sharing, File and database transfer.
(iii)	Text and messaging Communications	Teletype systems (e.g. telex) Electronic mail.
(iv)	Image transmission	Facsimile, Image processing. Video conferencing.
(v)	Information retrieval	Bibliographic search services. Videotex

TABLE 1

Examples of Business Objectives of Telecommunications Applications

Objectives	*Examples*	*Benefits*
Obtaining basic information about business transactions from remote locations.	Customer orders from remote sales offices to corporate data centre for order process, billing and inventory control.	Reduces delay in filling orders and issue of bills, allows quick updation inventory.
Supply of requested information to remote locations.	Credit authorisation at the point of sale by inquiry/ response of corporate data base	Credit inquiries and response can be made on-line, thereby reducing delay in credit authorisation.
Reduction in cost of traditional means of communications.	Audio and/or video teleconferencing.	Reduces business trips.
Strategic support	Electronic data inter-change to and from suppliers and customers,	Fast and conve-nient service locks in customers and suppliers.

In India, services and systems other than voice communications, teletype (telex), data communications (very limited extent) and facsimile are yet to be developed and popularised.

Some of the important business objectives of telecommunications applications and the benefit derived therefrom are summarised in Table 1.

Telecommunications is not only a method of electronic communications, but it is a means of organisational connectivity, a competitive weapon and a vital investment in technology for effective management of information resources. Managers can use telecommunications as follows:

(a) To compress the time taken to accomplish business activities;
(b) To expand firm's business activities geographically; and
(c) To restructure traditional business relationship with customers, suppliers, creditors, competitors and other organisations.

Managers can use telecommunications to improve operational efficiency, functional effectiveness and innovations. However, these values will not happen without clear objective and careful planning. The top management should have clear vision as to what extent the organisation's business strategy and business goals depend on the use of telecommunications. A business that chooses to remain a small local enterprise has less need of information technology than an organisation that has countrywide or worldwide operations.

(B) Telecommunications for Rural Development

India lives in villages where 80 per cent people of the country's total population reside. We can call our country developed and modern in its true sense only when our villages are also developed. The rural India is characterised by very low economic activity. In the absence of any kind of industrial activity, there is total dependence on agriculture. This is an example of typical agriculture society composed primarily of agriculture workers. The per capita income and standard of living are low. Lack of communications facilities has been one of the main reasons for the present poor condition of rural India. The gravity can be understood from the fact that there are only about 5 telephones per 10,000 of rural populace and only some 30,000 gram panchayats out of a total of 230,000 have telephone facility in the form of a long distance public telephone (LDPT). Further, these LDPTs are the only means of voice communication to nearby towns or revenue headquarters which the rural folks need to communicate for their day-to-day need. They suffer from poor reliability and low operational efficiency as a majority of these LDPTs are provided on conventional overhead telephone lines. These telephone lines are of ten snapped by climatic conditions, moving vehicles and also quite frequently by vandalism. The repairs are expensive and time consuming. High investment, low rate of return and non-availability. of indigenous technology and modern equipment had been the reasons for very slow progress. However, lately the importance of reliable telephone facilities in rural development has been recognised and following mile-stones have been set:

— Modernise rural telecommunications through use of electronic RAXs and multi access radio relay systems progressively;
— Cover all the remaining 200,000 gram panchayats by LDPTs by the end of the Eighth Plan.

As each LDPT costs on an average Rs. 150,000 an investment of over Rs. 3,000 crores will be required for this purpose.

Impact of Information Technology on Telecommunications

Development of digital techniques and convergence of information processing and telecommunications technologies have revolutionised the field of information management world wide. Telecommunications processors, such as, modems, multiplexers, concentrators, front end-processors, EPABXs and other similar devices perform a variety of support functions between the terminals and computers in a telecommunications network. The electronic exchanges are all central processor controlled switches. Also computers have simplified many vital support and control functions of operations and management of telecommunications services. Some of the important support functions which have been computerised are as follows:

— Billing functions for both telephone and telex,
— Online registration of new demand and management of commercial waiting list,
— Directory information service including updation of data,
— Customer information,
— Personal information and pay bills,
— Inventory controls,
— Project management and control,
— Fault repairs and Cable records.

Many new services have become technically feasible due to introduction of computers in the field of telecommunications. Some such services are indicated below:

- — Voice mail,
- — Electronic mail,
- — Cellular radio mobile telephone system,
- — Videotex,
- — Interactive data communications systems, etc.

Department of Telecommunication under its scheme named Communications Information System for Department of Telecom." (CIS DOT) has adopted an integrated computerisation plan for efficient management of information and various support functions, such as, finance and accounts, fault repair service, commercial waiting list, cable records, directory information, customer information, personal information, project monitoring and inventory control, etc.

Areas of Weakness in Telecommunications Services

- — Long waiting time for new telephones;
- — Large percentage of old and obsolete equipment in the network;
- — Inadequate funding resulting slow development and modernisation;
- — Low call completion rate for local and NSD calls;
- — Heavy dependence on operator assisted services;
- — High fault rate due to vulnerable outdoor plant;
- — Frequent damage of U/G cable plants due to vandalism; and
- — High initial as well as operational cost of rural telephone service and negligible return on the investment rendering rural network financially non viable. The services are accordingly provided as social obligation and the programme suffers cuts whenever there are more pressing demands on resources.

Thrust Areas for Over-all Improvement in Performance

- — Accelerated development to improve availability, accessibility and connectivity,
- — Modernised network to improve reliability and operational efficiency;
- — Improved quality of service and enhanced customer satisfaction;
- — Improved productivity and reduced operational costs;
- — Value-added and hone, plus services, such as, voice mail, electronic mail, videotex and audio/video conferencing for better exploitation of the network;
- — New services, such as, radio pageing, cellular mobile radio telephones and RABN, etc.;

— Liberalised indigenous production of telecommunication equipment to meet growing demand; and
— Extended reliable and efficient telephone facility to all villages in the country using digital state's and radio relay system.

Perspective Plan for Telecommunication is Services during 1990s

(a) Improved Availability

	Present	*1995*	*2000 AD*
Switching Capacity (million lines)	5.9	11.2	23.2
Direct Exchange Lines (million lines)	5.1	9.8	20.0
Telephone Density (number of telephones per 1000 population)	6.0	10.9	20.5

(b) Improved Accessibility

— An LDPT in each of the remaining 200,000 gram panchayats by the year 1995 and cover all the 576,000 villages by the year 2000 AD;
— Increased urban PCOs to 8 lakhs by the year 2000 AD;
— Provision of telephone facility on highways (every 10 Kms) as public utility service.

(c) Improved Connectivity by the Year 2000 AD

— Increased TAX lines to 449800 by 1995 and to 929800 by 2000 AD. (Presently 186800);
— All telephones in the country to have access to NSD.

(d) Development of Business Network

— Integrated services digital network with facilities, such as, voice, telex, data, facsimile, interactive "computer communications, audio and video conferencing with national as well as international accessibility.

(e) Expansion of Telex Network

Present	51670
Year 1995	87270
Year 200 AD	142270

(f) Long Distance Transmission Media (Thousand Route KMs)

	Present	*1995*	*200 AD*
Microwave systems	36.0	50.3	53.3
UHF systems	16.5	49.0	87.5
Optical fibre systems	7.1	23.4	31.5
Coaxial systems	27.9	31.5	

(g) Messaging Facility

— Modernised telegraph services through use of large size store and forward message switching systems (SFMS)

(h) Improvement in Quality of Service

— Reduced telephone faults to a level of 5 faults per 100 stations per month.

— Improved call completion rate to 60 per cent in live traffic.

(i) Improved Productivity (Staff/Telephone Ratio)

Present	72 per 1000 telephones
1995	47 per 1000 telephones
2000 AD	25 per 1000 telephones

Efficient management of information resources is vital for economic development of the society. We can afford to neglect development of modern telecommunications services only if we choose to remain economically backward perpetually. The services are financially viable in the urban and most of the semi- urban areas. However rural areas are to be covered as an essential social obligation. These objectives will be achieved by increasing investment, developing in digenous technology, liberalisation of equipment production and effective management of services. Availability well be improved to wipe out current waiting list and to provide telephones on demand. Accessibility and connectivity will also be improved to make the network flexible and more efficient to meet customer needs. To make optimum use of the network new and value-added services, such as, voice mail, videotex, audio/video conferencing and cellular radio mobile telephone services, etc., will be introduced.

History has several examples of primitive signalling by the fire and smoke. The invention of the telescope added a new dimension to the practice. The first steps toward modern communication were fostered by the French Revolution (1789) itself. France then needed a fast means of communication. A French engineer, Claude

Chappe (1763-1805) developed a system of optical telegraphy' in 1791 with which he displayed coded messages on towers. Paris and Lille were connected by such a system in 1794. The practice soon spread to different parts of the country and to England and America. An English, bishop, George Murray, established in 1795 a semaphore consisting of six independent shutters for the Admiralty in London to Link it to Portsmouth (Fig. 1). Different combinations of signals could be sent by operating the shutters differently. A brother of Claude Chappe, Ignace Chappe, was the first to use the word 'telegraph' in April 1793. The word signified the 'ultimate' in speed. However, the full advantage of telegraphy could be realised, only with electricity.

Fig. 1: A shutter board used in Britain as part of an optical telegraphic system during the Napoleonic wars.

In 1809, Professor Alessandro Volta recorded the production of electricity by chemical means. In 1819 Professor Hans Christian Oersted (1777-1851), a Danish scientist, discovered by chance that a current created magnetic effects. Electromagnets soon emerged. Magnets, needles and electricity encouraged the pioneers of electrical telegraphy to try out new ideas. One of the first electric telegraph systems was constructed by Georges Lesage in Geneva in 1774. He used a single wire for each letter. A Russian. Baron Paul Schilling (1768-1837) experimented in 1832 with deflecting compass needles under current flow and developed an electromagnetic telegraph. A 10-word telegram in French dictated by the Czar. Nicholas I, was transmitted. Schilling's work was taken up by academician B.S. Yakobi (1801-1874), a German mathematician, and W. Weber (1804-1879) to construct several types of telegraphy in 1836. Around 1840, a device known as ABC *telegraphic instrument,* consisting of two dials for sending and receiving messages was invented. A rotating needle picked out in turn the wanted letters.

Catching a Murderer

The railroads encouraged the use of telegraphy to prevent accidents By 1837. Prof. Charles Wheatstone and Cooke developed a working telegraph which had five-needles to spell out 20 letters, known as *Wheatstone working.* The first telegraph line was constructed between Euston and Camden in England, spanning less than two kilometres. Later, a 21-km link was set up. The telegraph clicked into fame in 1845. when news about a murderer on a train was sent on the wire. His subsequent capture fired the imagination of the people. The countryside was soon crisscrossed by telegraph wires.

The famous Morse telegraphy was operated in 1845. Samuel Finley Breeze Morse (1791-1872) designed a code for alphabets on the basis of the deflection of a pen to mark a strip of paper under the influence of an electric current through an electromagnet. After abandoning an underground line laid in 1844 as impracticable. Morse started to construct an overhead line. On 1 January 1845, the first, words were transmitted over the lines between Washington and Baltimore. The message transmitted, viz. "What hath God wrought?" has become historic.

The dots and dashes of the Morse code could be operated only with a strong current. Converting the code into plain language was also a problem. The difficulty was solved to some extent with the invention of plain language telegraphy in 1855. David E. Hughes (1831-1900), a British, inventor, won a patent for it. Known as *Hughes-type printing telegraph,* it had a rotating wheel with the alphabet, which stopped when the wanted letter appeared on the paper. Hughes' machine could transmit 40 words a minute as against 25 in Morse telegraphy.

The Five-Unit Code

The next advance came in 1875, when an officer of the French Telegraph Service, Emile Baudot (1845-1903) introduced a five-unit code to represent each letter of the alphabet. Five impulses were sent over the lines to actuate a set of five magnets. He could send 60 words a minute. The Baudot telegraph was used in England from 1879 and in his honour, the speed of transmission is now called the *baud.*

In America, Thomas Alva Edison (1847-1931), who was himself a telegraph operator at the age of 15, developed a technique of sending more than one message on the same line. He took out patents for devices that would help send and receive telegrams at the same time and invented a method of sending two messages in each direction. Meanwhile in Vienna, a single telegraph wire was used in 1853 to transmit two messages, one in each direction.

The new medium caught the imagination of a newsman. Julius Reuter (1816-1899). He used telegraph lines to communicate news. Paris was linked with Berlin and other places. Newspapers, railways and governments were among the early users of telegraphy. Around 1850, telegraphy crossed the sea. John and Jacob Brett laid the first submarine cable in the open sea between France and England. The first transatlantic telegraph cable was laid in 1858, but it operated only for 20 days!

In India

In India, semaphore signalling was started in 1813 between Calcutta and Sagar Island. Even as Samuel Morse was laying the telegraph lines in the United States, the first experimental electric telegraph line in India was set up in 1839 over a distance of 33 km from Calcutta towards Diamond Harbour. In 1851, the circuit was established between Calcutta and Diamond Harbour for the East India Company. The telegraph service was opened to the public in 1855. An Indo-European telegraph line was built during 1867-1870 by a German firm, connecting London with Emden. Berlin, Torun, Warsaw, Odessa, Teheran, Bushehr, Karachi, Agra and Calcutta. In 1860, a telegraph cable linked London with the Indian subcontinent through the Suez Canal. A London-Bombay telegraph service over a submarine cable was inaugurated in 1870. Bombay and Calcutta were linked by a telegraph system that allowed simultaneous transmission in both directions. The Baudot system was used in printed telegraphy in 1906 between Calcutta and Bombay.

Telegraphy made its way to other countries also. A telegraphic code book in Chinese was published. Four-digit numbers were used to indicate over 6.000 commonly used characters. The numbers were telegraphed! In France, the first telegraph line was completed in 1845 and in Russia in 1853. In 1849, Austria and Russia signed the first treaty aimed at linking the telegraph systems of the two countries. Some years later. 20 States signed the first International Telegraphy Convention in 1865. This meeting set the pattern for cooperation among the countries in the world in telecommunications.

A common feature of telegraph communication is that messages are converted into the dot-dash Morse code, transmitted and decoded at the other end (Fig. 2).

Operators sent the messages in the early days by coding them and depressing a key at the other end and heard the 'clicks' on a Morse sounder and decoded them.

This process was slow and prone to error. It took several decades of effort to mechanise the process of encoding and decoding messages for electrical transmission. The *teleprinter,* as the machine was known, came into general use in the late 1920's. Earlier in 1894, an Austrian teleprinter was designed to transmit messages as they were typed. The 'start-stop' *telegraphic printing,* which was later adopted in teleprinters, was devised by a Soviet technician N.P. Trusevich in 1921. The first teleprinter was made in a Berlin laboratory in 1928. Each character consisting of five units was preceded by a start condition and succeeded by a stop condition. At a speed of 50 bauds per second. 6-2/3 characters per second can be transmitted. Assuming that a word has an average of five characters. 80 words per minute could be sent.

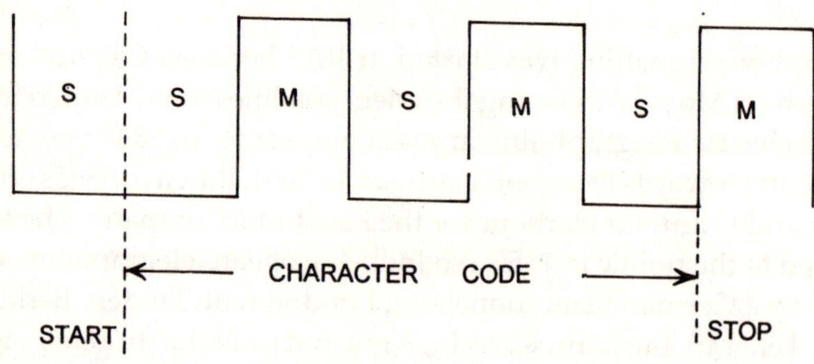

Fig. 2: Letter 'R' represented by a code of current pulses. The character code is SMSMS. Current 'on' condition corresponds to stop condition also called Mark (M). while current "off" corresponds to start condition, also called Space (S).

In India, an early teleprinter was reported to have linked two offices in the city of Calcutta in 1929. During the Second World War, a few high-speed teleprinters set up. But the majority of the telegraph lines continued to be on the Morse key and sounder system till the 1940's. It was only after 1960. when the Hindustan Teleprinters. Madras was set up, that teleprinters were made and used in the country on a wide scale.

"GOOD HEAVENS, IT TALKS!"

Sound has fascinated man from time immemorial. However, the nature of the sound waves came to be understood scientifically only since the eighteenth century. Indeed, the word 'telephone' (from the Greek words *tele,* meaning far and *phone,* for sound) meant acoustic methods of communication. It was only later that the word was used to indicate sound transmission aided by electricity. The telephone arrived some 45 years after telegraphy. In fact early experiments to improve the telegraph led to the invention of the telephone.

An Englishman. Robert Hooke (1635-1703). was among the first to suggest that speech might be transmitted over long distances. In 1831. Charles Page (1812-1868), an American inventor, discovered that rapid changes in magnetisation of iron caused a musical note. The properties of sound waves were better understood as a result of the work of a German scientist. H. Von Helmholtz (1821-1894) in 1863. This was followed by new ideas on the use of a magnet to increase the sensitivity of receivers and a diaphragm to operate contacts and interrupt the electric current. These ideas were put into practice in 1860 by Philip Reis of Germany (1834-1874) who transmitted musical notes electrically over a distance. He called his instrument, the *telephone.*

The first man who was clear about the principles of telephony and demonstrated the instrument for speech was Alexander Graham Bell (1847-1922). He was born in Edinburgh on 3 march 1847. His father, Melville Bell, was a phonetician. Young Bell helped his father in teaching deaf children how to speak. After studying in Edinburgh and London, he emigrated to Canada and later to the United States. In 1871. he became a teacher at the Boston School for the Deaf. He continued his interest in electricity and acoustics. Two years later, he become a professor of vocal physiology and elocution at Boston University. He was attracted by telegraphy.

The capacity of the human ear fascinated him. He wondered whether it could be emulated in some way for the transmission of speech signals over the wires. He said. "If I can make a current of electricity vary in intensity 'precisely as the air varies in density during the production of sound. I should be able to transmit speech telegraphically."

The idea of variations in a continuous current through a vibrating membrane came to Bell's mind while he was experimenting on combining separate telegraph signals for transmission on a single wire. One of the needles in his experimental instrument got stuck to its electromagnet. When he asked his assistant. Watson Thomas, to remove the sticking reed. Bell found that the corresponding reed in the next room vibrated, producing a sound of the same pitch. Sound was electrically transmitted, though speech was not intelligible. Bell concluded that speech could similarly be sent—that was on 2 June 1875.

"Mr. Watson, Come Here"

After several attempts, the first complete sentence was heard on the phone on 10 March 1876. Watson was in one room with the receiving instrument, pressing his ear closely against it. The transmitting instrument was in another room. The doors of the rooms were closed. Bell shouted into the horn of the instrument. "Mr. Watson, come here. I want you." Watson rushed out and confirmed. "Mr. Bell. I heard every word you said, distinctly.

The first telephone had an electromagnetic receiver and a variable-resistance transmitter having a horizontal diaphragm attached to a metal rod in a vessel of acidulated water. The transmitter and the receiver contained a thin circular metallic diaphragm and a horse-shoe magnet with a coil of wire. Sound waves striking the diaphragm caused it to vibrate and produced changes in the magnetic field which varied the electric current in the coil. A connecting wire conveyed the current to the receiver coil, which produced a changing magnetic field, resulting in the vibration of a diaphragm in an exactly similar way as in the transmitter.

The first public demonstration of the telephone invention was on 10 May 1876, at the American Academy of Arts and Sciences. At an exhibition in Philadelphia, marking the centennial of the US Independence, the telephone was a modest entry. The Emperor of Brazil. Dom Pedra who was one of the jury to adjudge the inventions tested the instrument and exclaimed. "Good Heavens it talks!" Congratulating Bell, the Emperor said the invention would change the way people would live all over the world. He was indeed prophetic.

Still the telephone had to get wide support of the Public. The telegraph companies saw in it a potential rival. Some people even said it was a gimmick fit only for "the laboratory. There was also competition. Elisha Gray (1835-1901) was working on the telephone. In February 1876 he applied for a notice of invention. He would have got it had not Bell preferred his claim a few hours earlier. The two knew each other's work even in 1874. Both were however primarily concerned with the development of the telegraph.

Bell and Watson worked hard, started a company and started installing telephones. It was, however, Bell's visit to England that expedited the growth of the telephone He demonstrated it before Queen Victoria, who asked for two of the instruments for her palace. The telephone became popular in England and later in Europe. This had a good effect at home. The telephone spread rapidly across the United States.

A Genius

Characteristic of a genius, Bell tried several innovations. He proposed eeho sounding for measuring the depth of water. He attempted speech transmission over a light beam, with the help of a detecting selenium cell. He improved Edison's phonograph. He invented the aileson and financed studies to determine the speed of light. He suggested the use of radium for the treatment of cancer. Above all, he remained a humanist and campaigned vioro-ously for the education of the deaf. It is interesting to note that Bell did not keep a telephone in his study, as he did not like any interruption! Important as it was. Bell's invention was only the first step. The early telephones were rather crude devices. Several developments were needed to make them convenient reliable and attractive.

The first home telephone which came in 1877 served both as a microphone and an earphone. A speaker had to make it clear that he had finished speaking and was putting the instrument to his ear. ready to hear the other person.

A year later, a second receiver-transmitter was added so that one could talk and listen easily. Telephones grew in popularity. The first telephone directory was issued on 21 February 1878, at New Haven, Connecticut, USA.

A Curate's Discovery

That year, a country curate in England, Bolton Percy, discovered that crushed coke was suitable for varying the contact in a microphone. An English clergyman. Henry Hunnings, developed a transmitter in which granular carbon was used. Thomas Alva Edison, too, invented (1877) a transmitter with carbon granules. Indeed, he and his colleagues tried some 2,000 materials before selecting carbon. Another inventor, Anthony C. White, made a device placing carbon granules between a fixed and a movable electrode. Several variations of the carbon-granule microphone appeared and after a decade, a practical model came up.

In 1880, Francis Blake designed a set which was able to transmit the voice with clarity. Edison developed a loud-speaking telephone in 1879.

France had handsets for subscribers by 1882. In Austria an automatic connection was made with another subscriber by manipulating four levers. Also in 1882, the Magneto Wall set appeared, with a crank to be turned for signalling. Four years later, a voice transmitter for long distance use was developed.

Efforts to make the telephone elegant continued. Desk sets were developed in 1892 and 1897. A common battery to provide power for the telephones from an exchange was introduced in 1900. Early in this century, wall models with a built-in generator and provision of interlinks within the home emerged, much to the delight of ladies.

Dials Appear

With the growing practice of calling subscribers by numbers instead of by names, the idea of dialling the numbers began to take shape. The rotary dial was developed in 1896. In 1919, a dial telephone was made in the United States. It called for new switching techniques. Early table telephones in Germany had a rotating finger plate of 25 holes !

Streamlined models of European phones in different colours soon became popular. A combined receiver and transmitter in the handset was developed in 1928, popularly known as the *French phone.* New desk models with dials appeared, in 1937, the bell and the related equipment were placed inside the base of the phone itself. A year later, six buttons were added with one 'hold' button, to help those who have separate phones for each line. Extension phones and buttons for handling numerous calls in more and more elegant designs and colours followed.

Outside the United States, several models were developed in various countries from Sweden to Japan. An early English receiver was designed by A.E. Dolbear, a physics professor, in 1876. Two Russians. A.A. Stolpovskyi and A. Kanger, developed a desk telephone in 1886. An early coin-operated telephone equipment was used in Austria in 1910. The Swedish Telegraph Administration made a phone in 1884. Bulgaria started the first public telephone system in Sofia in 1886. An automatic table telephone was used in Germany in 1908. A French-model appeared in 1924 with one of the first dialling systems.

Despite the sophisticated features, the basic elements of a telephone set remain the same. The carbon-granule microphone was invented in the 1890's. The bell dates from the last century, while the dial is almost the same as it was at the beginning of this century. The receiver continues to be basically the same ever since its invention.

Still innovations continue. Though the carbon-granule microphone gives good output, it is a little troublesome at times. Semiconductors, under direct pressure of sound waves, amplify speech better. The bell too has been improvised to give a pleasant sound with the help of circuit which converts the ringing current into a frequency.

In several places, the dial has been replaced by a key-pad with buttons. Normally signals originating from the dialling are stored in the instrument temporarily and then sent out as pulses from a dial telephone. Key-pads come with 12 or 16 buttons. The operation of these buttons will generate pre-set frequencies for signalling purposes. An advantage of having the push buttons of this type is that the telephone can be used to 'converse' with the computer directly.

A telephone has as many as 400 intricate components. The quality of every one of them determines its efficiency. Efforts continue to improve the components and redesign the telephone instrument to make it lighter, more elegant and more reliable.

The Indian Telephone Industries (ITI). Bangalore, has for example, taken up the work of improving the transmitter so as to get a more faithful reproduction of speech with lower extraneous noise and less distortion. A governor has been developed to retain the correct speed of the dial throughout its life. Several inner components are mounted on a printed circuit board, which eliminates wiring within the instrument.

Basic Principles

While the shapes and sizes of the telephones have changed the basic principles have remained almost the same. The main requirements of a telephone set are the transmitter. which converts the sound into electrical energy, a telephone line or microwave route to serve as a medium for carrying the signals and speech and a receiver which converts the electrical energy into sound. Then there are other components like the bell and a dial (Fig. 3).

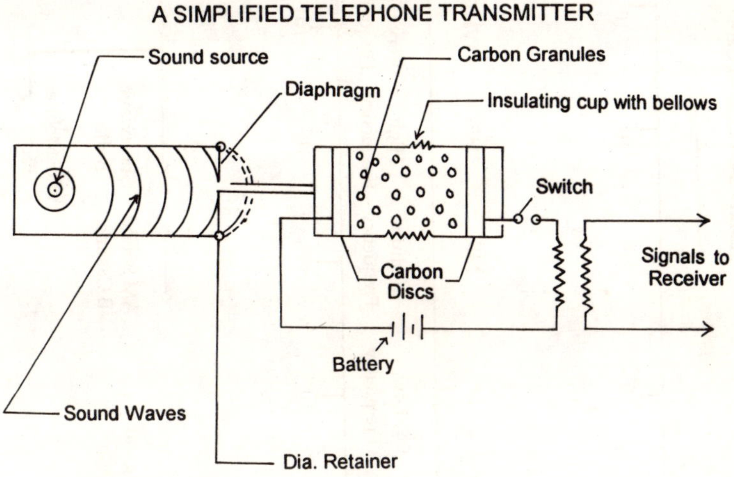

A SIMPLIFIED TELEPHONE TRANSMITTER

Fig. 3: A simplified telephone transmitter, which converts the sound waves into electrical waves.

The mouthpiece, the transmitter, consists essentially of a diaphragm and a capsule filled with carbon granules. The capsule is in between two electrodes connected to a battery at the exchange. The sound of the speaker causes the diaphragm to vibrate in sympathy. which compresses or releases the carbon particles. The carbon particles provide paths to the current, admitting more current when the particles are compressed and less when they are released. The sound waves are thus transformed into fluctuations of electricity.

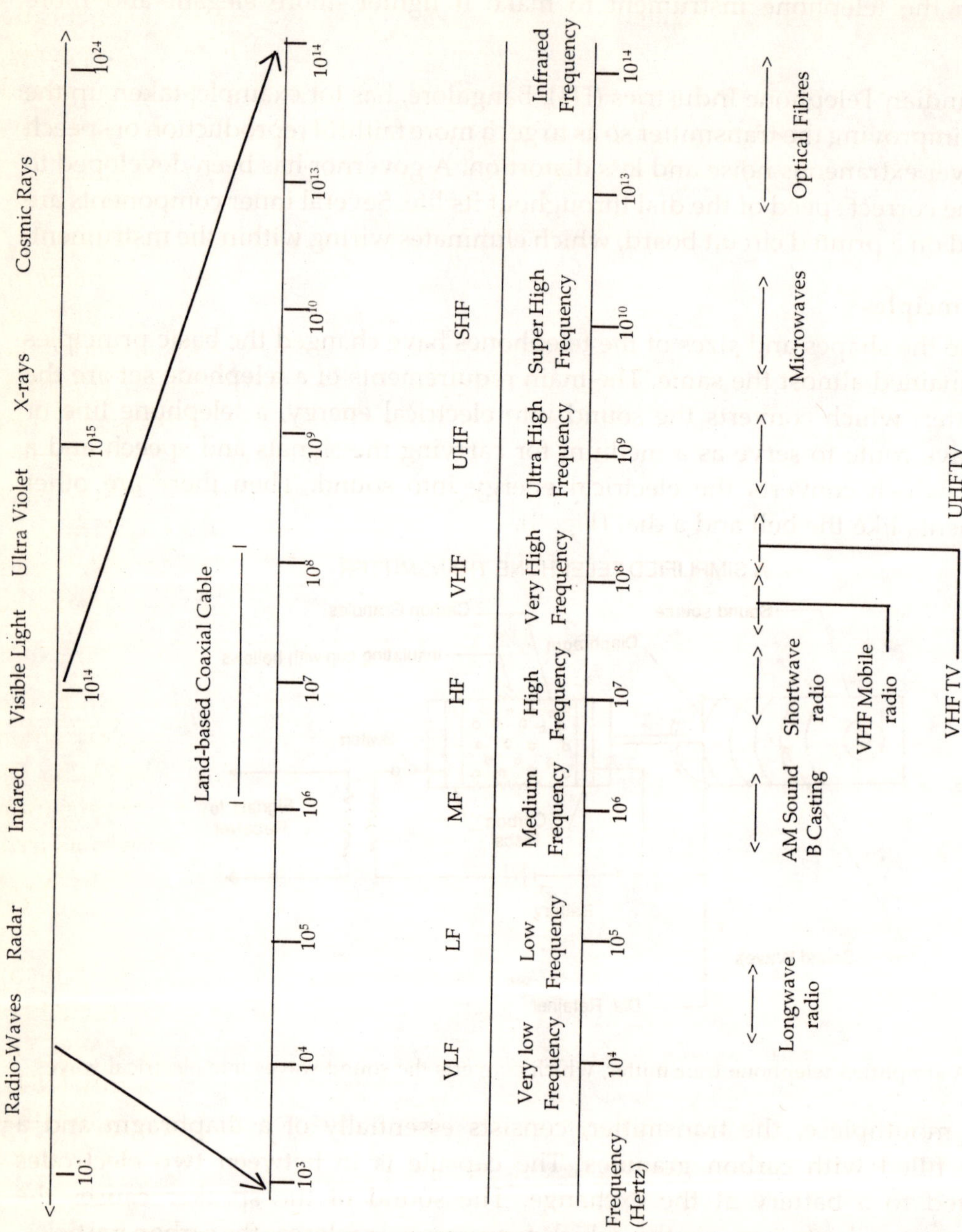

Fig. 4: The *electromagnetic spectrum:* Extends from radio waves to cosmic rays, in which visible light is a small window. The spectrum available for communication extends from 10^4 Hertz to over 10^{14} Hertz, a range of, wavelengths from 30,000 metres to one millionth of a metre. More signals need more frequencies (bandwidth). The microwave band is 2.000 times wider than the medium waves but quite small compared to the optical fibre's capacity

The receiver converts the electrical waves back into audible sound by magnetically vibrating a diaphragm in unison with the incoming current, through an electromagnet. A fluctuating magnetic field is created so that the diaphragm vibrates and the sound reaches the ear of the listener. The receiver is also capable of getting the dial tone, engaged or the ring-back tone, which are sent by the exchange.

A LIMITED SPECTRUM

Visible light is only one form of radiant energy described as electromagnetic in nature. There are other forms Different waves of energy varying in frequency per second and in their length constitute the electromagnetic spectrum. At one end of the spectrum are long radio waves followed by short waves, microwaves, infrared, visible light, ultraviolet. X-rays and gamma rays (Fig. 4). A Scottish professor, James Clerk Maxwell (1831-1879), published in 1864 equations on electromagnetic radiations. He showed that light has the same velocity regardless of the velocity of the object emitting it relative to the observer. He held that all electromagnetic waves travel at the speed of light. His calculations had practical implications. But Maxwell was ahead of his time. His mathematics did not enthuse people. Even Kelvin, a notable scientist, did not encourage his ideas.

Most of the laws that control radio waves were forecast by Maxwell, even before such waves were produced. People realised the importance of his finding only when a German, Heinrich Rudolf Hertz (1857-1894), produced radio waves in 1889 (Fig. 5). The experiment is so epoch-making that frequencies of radio and telecommunication waves have since been named after him. A unit of frequency is now known a *Hertz* (Hz). The term, frequency, refers to the number of cycles an electromagnetic wave makes in a second (Fig. 6).

A man who repeated the experiment of Hz was Oliver Joseph Lodge (1851-1940). He transmitted wireless signals across a hundred yards in Oxford in 1871. He kept a transmitter and a receiver with a tube called *coherer* to detect wireless waves. The discovery of the coherer is attributed to a French physicist. Edouard Branly (1844-1940). hailed in France as the inventor of the electric telegraph. He found that electromagnetic waves, produced 25 metres away, caused metal particles of iron or silver in his coherer to stick together and pass a current.

Meanwhile, the first radio receiver was developed. In 1896, a physics lecturer in St. Peters berg, A.S. Popoff (1859-1906), developed it and sent the words, "Heinrich Hertz" over a distance of five km. In Italy, a charming young man thought that the Hertzian waves might be used for communication. Twenty years after the telephone was invented. Guglielmo Marconi (1874-1937) sent a telegram by radio over three

Fig. 5: Hertz, who discovered radio waves.

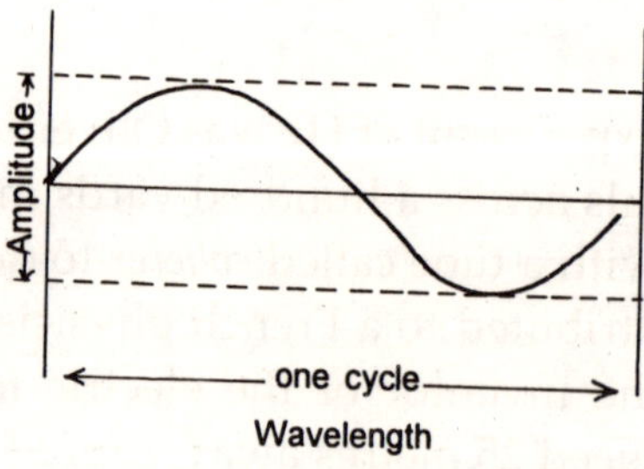

Fig. 6: *Wavelengths:* One cycle of a wavelength per second is called *Hertz,* named after Heinrich Hertz, the scientist who first produced electromagnetic waves in 1887. Radio waves travel at the speed of light which is constant. To Increase frequency; wavelengths are reduced so that more can travel in a given amount of time. A *Kilohertz* is one thousand cycles per second: a *Megahertz,* one million per second; and a *Gigahertz,* one billion per second.

km. He went to England to try his luck with the Post Office. He had by then transmitted radio waves over a distance of 32 km. Led by William Preece of the Post Office, the engineers were quite impressed with the young man but they could not get any funds and Marconi had to return to Italy in 1897.

By then he had found that the wireless signals could be sent farther, if the height of the aerials could be increased. He began to master kite-flying so that kites could support the aerials. In an effort to prove his ideas, he crossed the Atlantic and reached Newfoundland, where he flew an aerial and caught the radio waves transmitted from Cornwall, England. In 1901, he received the three dots in telegraphy representing the letter 'S' That was a big triumph for man.

Several development promoted the use of radio waves. A Danish radio physicist, V Poulsen. succeeded in 1902 in producing continuous electromagnetic waves by means of an are lamp. It was however the vacuum tube that solved the problems relating to the essential devices for radio-telephony, viz. an oscillator to generate continuous high-frequency waves, a means to modulate the waves with speech and a receiving amplifier to increase the power of the waves. A professor of electrical engineering in London University. J.A. Fleming (1849-1945), who had helped Marconi in transmitting waves across the Atlantic, developed in 1904 a thermionic valve, which emitted a strong current when struck by electromagnetic waves. An American inventor. Lee De Forest (1873-1961), working independently of Fleming, developed in 1906 an improved device called a *triode vacuum tube* which amplified weak signals. Initially, he had problems and he was even prosecuted for selling "gas bottles full of nothing!" Besides amplifying signals, the tube could generate a precise and controllable broadcasting frequency. In 1908. De Forest tried a broadcast from the Eiffel Tower in Paris, which was heard in Marseilles in southern France.

Another significant event happened in 1906. A Canadian. Reginald Fessendon (1866-1932). with his friend Alexanderson put speech and music in radio waves. Two speeches, one song and a violin solo on Christmas eve. heralded entertainment broadcasting. The two men used a high frequency alternator and sent the programme over a distance of 320 km.

It was however the arrest of a murderer on board a ship in 1910. with the help of a wireless message that caught the imagination of the public. Radio communication became popular. Newspapers hailed it as a great achievement. Shipowners hastened to use it. Weather reports and distress messages began to be sent to ships. And the wireless was used when King George V visited India in 1911.

The First World War (1914-1918) gave a further impetus to the use of radio. Crystal sets appeared in the market, followed by big receivers.

Efforts were continued to perfect the transmission of speech. In 1915, intelligible speech was transmitted by radio from Arlington to Hawaii and to Paris. A concert was broadcast from England in 1920 and it was heard in Europe. In 1923, a 60-KHz frequency was used to set up one channel of communication across the Atlantic. Three years later, a two-way radio telephone link was established between England and the USA. In 1927, the first commercial radio telephone link was set up between these two countries. Links between Berlin and Buenos Aires soon followed. In 1930, the UK and Australia were linked by radio.

In the early days of radio broadcasting, it was found that frequencies in the range of 3 to 30 KHz were useful for low-speed telegraphy. Later, higher frequencies (above 1.500 KHz) were used to reach more distant places. Scientists began to probe the medium which reflected the waves from the sky. Two scientists, O. Heaviside of the UK (1850-1925), and A.E. Kenelly (1861-1939) of the USA, suggested the presence of the ionosphere, the direct observations of which were made in 1924 by E.W. Apple-ton (1892-1965) of the UK and others. It was discovered that the ionised layers could send shortwave frequencies from 3 to 30 MHz more than half way round the earth. It was also found that these frequencies could take on more channels (Fig. 7).

Nature of Radio Waves

Perhaps the nature of radio waves can be likened to the movement of waves in the sea. The distance between successive crests is called the *wavelength* which is measured in metres. The number of crests that pass a fixed point in a given time, usually a second, is called the *frequency,* which is measured in Hz or cycles per second.

Radio waves travel at the speed of light. 300 million metres per second in vacuum. If the distance between two successive peaks, i.e. the wavelength is 30 metres, then the number of peaks passing a fixed point in one second will be 10 million, i.e. a frequency of 10 mega Hz.

The rule for converting from one to the other is to di vide 300 by what we know (metres or mega Hz). For example:

$$15.07 \text{ MHz} = \frac{300 \text{ metres}}{15.07} = 19.91 \text{ metres}$$

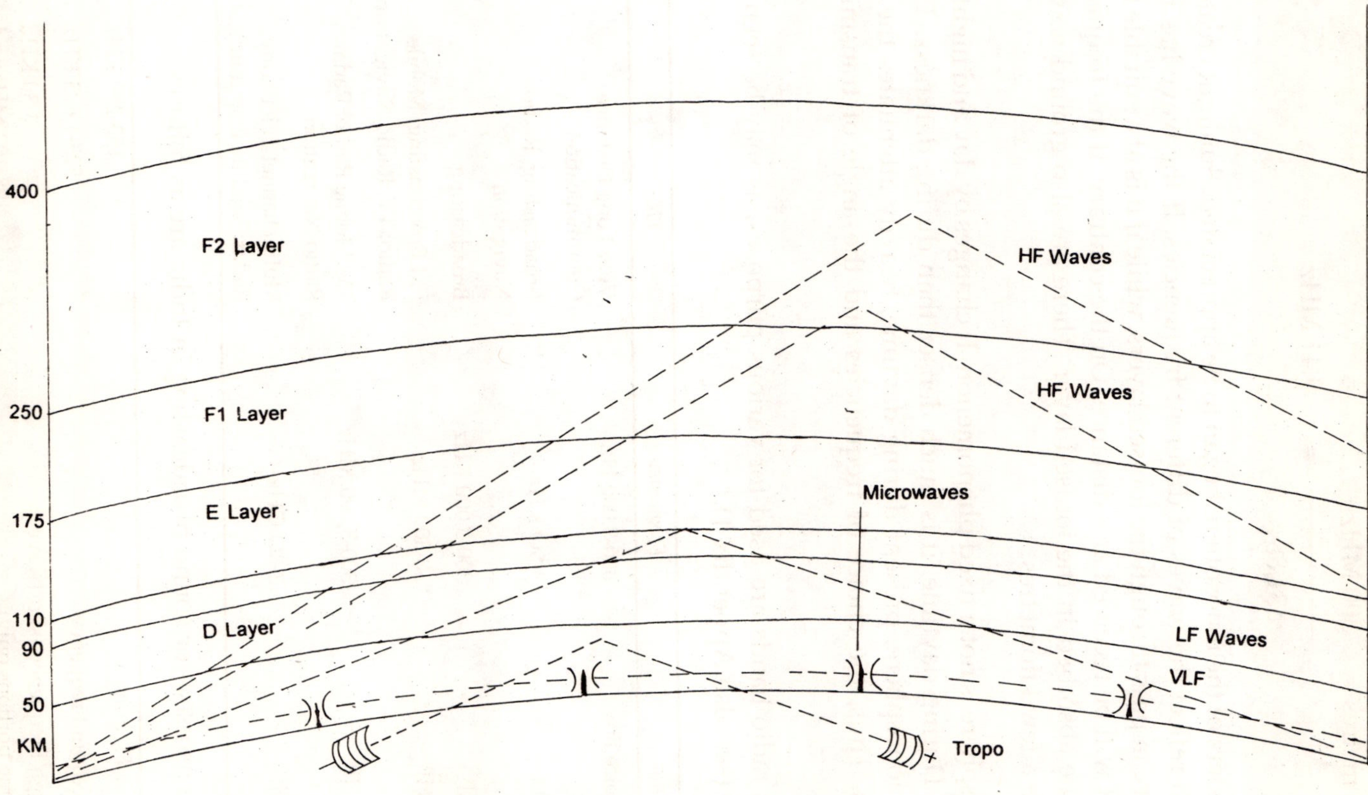

Fig. 7: The ionosphere which reflects radio waves of different frequencies. Long waves are reflected from the lower portion, while short waves are bounced back from the upper layers. Higher frequency waves follow line-of-sight paths and need to be reflected from lower to tower. The lowest part of the atmosphere, called troposphere, helps in setting up troposcatter linked on routes where repeaters are not feasible.

$$31.88 \text{ metres} = \frac{300 \text{ MHz}}{31.88} = 9.41 \text{ MHz}$$

The wonders of the ionosphere began to be appreciated. Sunlight creates ionised layers which reflect the waves of different frequencies. If the wave has too high a frequency, it can pass through the ionised layers, while if it is at a suitable frequency and angle, it will be received at a distance. On the contrary, if the frequency is too low, it will be absorbed in the ionised layer. There are also ground waves which extend up to a few kilometres.

The ionosphere is not a fixed phenomenon. It changes by day and night and over the months. During daytime, it is much denser than during darkness. The lowest layer of the ionosphere, present during daytime, heavily attenuates the medium-wave bands. Thus, the choice of frequencies and the angle of transmission are important.

Different radio bands are used for various purposes, as may be seen from the Table below (see also Appendix 1).

Band	*Frequency*	*Use*
Voice Fre.	300-3,000 Hz	Very Long Distance Communication
VLF	3-3O KHz	Broadcasting: Radio Navigation
MF	300-3,000 KHz	Broadcasting
VHF	30-300 MHz	FM Broadcasting; Mobile Radio; TV. Radio Navigation
UHF	300-3,000 MHz	TV: Mobile Radio: Radar: Radio Navigation.
SHF	3-3O GHz	Multi-channel Telephony: Radar; Satellite Communication

The portions used for sound broadcasting in India are as follows:

Low Frequency	150-280 KHz
Medium Frequency	525-1,605 KHz
High Frequency (shortwave, some portions only)	3-30 KHz 98-102 MHz and
Very High Frequency	106-108 KHz

The effectiveness of a broadcast depends on noise, mutual-intereference-between-transmitters and propagartion features of the radio waves. Thunderstorms and human interferences form electrical gadgets constitute noise. Signals at LF. MF and HF cut across national boundaries and should therefore be strong enough to overcome the interferences form other transmitters. The propagation features of radio waves depend on their frequencies. Low frequency waves travel along the ground for some distance, but there are only few channels for use in this band, even if its use is permitted by ITU. Medium waves cover hundreds of km in daytime and get reflected by the ionosphere during the night, thereby covering long distances. Short waves are transmitted by the ionosphere and by varying the antennas, the target areas could be separated and long distance coverage ensured. The vagaries of the ionosphere require the use of more than one frequency for a circuit to ensure reliability.

Careful planning is necessary to prevent mutual interference form transmitters, operating on the same frequency or on frequencies very close to each other. There will be interference even if the signal strength of the unwanted transmitted is much lower than that of the wanted transmitter. The magnitude of interference depends on several factors such as the relative power of the transmitters, the distance between them, frequency and the time of the day, season, sum spot number and related phenomena.

In general, interference during the day is negligible in medium frequency and lower HF bonds (lower than about 5 MHz) unless the transmitters are too close or one of them is of higher power. Interference is felt even during daytime on higher frequencies (e.g. 12 MHz) and above. During night, interference from distant transmitters will be found in MF bands, because of good sky wave propagation.

These examples show that radio spectrum is a limited natural resource. It is utilised for several types of telecommunications, including broadcasting. The International Telecommunication Union (ITU) lays down radio regulations as well as technical and operating standards. In 1959, the World Administrative Radio Conference (WARC-59) in Geneva evolved a detailed procedure for co-ordination of frequencies in the high frequency (HF) bands for broadcasting. This involved the preparation of tentative HF broadcast schedules four times a year followed by international coordination for improvements, even during the operation of each schedule. This has improved broadcasting in the HF band.

Another major conference, WARC-79, resolved certain issues to promote a more equitable use of the radio spectrum by all countries.

International Coordination

However, coordination of medium frequencies became rather complex with the increase in the number of high-power transmitters all over the world. Moreover, channel spacing was not uniform in different regions of the world. In Region 3, which includes India, the channel spacing was 10 KHz throughout the Medium Frequency band. In Region 1, consisting of Europe and Africa, the channel spacing was 8, 9 and 10 KHz, depending on the particular portion of the band. This resulted in excessive mutual interference in the operation of transmitters in the MF band.

During 1974-1975, a Regional Administrative Radio Conference for Low and Medium Frequencies for broadcasting in Regions 1 and 3 was held. For the first time, an agreed frequency plan was drawn up to be effective from 1978.

THE MYSTERY OF LIGHT

The idea of using light to transmit information has fasciated people. Bonfires and torchlights conveyed simple signals in war and peace. But a more sophisticated and improved way of using light for conveying information emerged only after more and more properties of light itself were discovered.

Some scientists thought that light was composed of particals. Newton's experiments with a prism showed how white light is indeed a mixture of seven spectral colours. The experiment supported the idea that tiny particles constituted light. Light does slow down while travelling in water. But some questions remained unanswered. Why does one colour refract more than another? The idea that light is composed of waves and that different colours have different wavelengths was suggested by a Dutch physicist. Christian Hugghens. Still, it was a mystery how waves of light could travel in the vacuum of space between the sun and the earth. A French physicist. A.J. Fresnel (1788-1827), lent credence to the wave theory by showing how in certain circumstances light waves do bend around objects. A German physicist. Max Planck (1850-1947), imagined light as discrete units of radiation, called quanta. This idea attracted Albert Einstein (1879-1955) who said light travels as photons which possess characteristics of both particles and waves. Mecwell had meanwhile clarified the idea of light as part of the electromagnetic spectrum.

Normally the term light refers to the portion in the electromagnetic spectrum varying in wavelength from 400 to 700 nanometres (billionth of a metre or nm). For purposes of transmission, a broader region in the spectrum is considered, including the infrared region. For example, 'some windows' can be chosen in the infrared region around 850 nm or 1,500 run or above. Over the years, the trend is in favour of changing from the shorter wavelength to the longer one.

The use of the infrared portion of the spectrum has to await the development of semiconductors. A device was necessary to turn a pulse of electricity into a pulse of infrared light and another to convert it again into electricity. The growth of transistor technology made these devices possible. Certain semiconductor diodes emit light when an electric current is passed through them. They are called Light-Emitting Diodes (LED) and some of them ran be switched on and off more than a hundred million times a second. A LED, made of gallium arsenide, emits Infrared light in response to current. The opposite of a light-emitting diode is a light detector—a silicon photodi-ode—that puts out electric current in accordance with the light falling on it. Electrical signals can be transmitted after being converted into pulses of light.

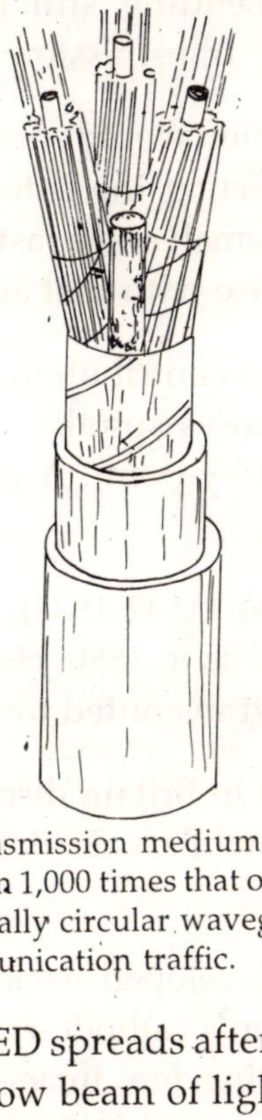

Fig. 8: *Optical Fibres:* The latest transmission medium that carries information as light waves. The frequency of light is more than 1,000 times that of the highest microwave band in use. The hair-thin fibres, which are essentially circular waveguides for guiding light, have thus enormous capacity to handle telecommunication traffic.

As the light produced by LED spreads after travelling for a while, another device was invented to ensure a narrow beam of light that would not spread at least over short distances. Such a device is called *laser* (for light amplification by stimulated emission of radiation). The first laser was constructed by an American physicist, Theodore Maiman (b. 1927) in 1960, based on the principle applied earlier by another US scientist. Charles Townes (b. 1915) in 1953. The light produced by a laser is so pure that it does not spread quickly. When focused on a point on the moon, the laser light spreads only 800 metres, after travelling 400,000 km. Moreover, laser light can be switched on and off much faster than is possible in a microwave system. But the laser beam can be blocked by rain, clouds or snow. Even temperature variations on its route can affect its propagation. Nor can a laser beam turn corners. If therefore, light from a laser or LED is to be used, a tube or a tiny waveguide is necessary, the answer was optical fibres, which are hair-thin strands of glass. They have started a quiet revolution in telecommunications (Fig. 8).

The Emergence of Television

The discovery that light waves of images could be transmitted as microwaves for subsequent recovery of what they represent, led to the development of television.

Even though the technique of sending still pictures was known, several developments were needed before TV transmission could become a reality.

It was found that the picture definition would come out well, if portions of it were scanned sequentially instead of projecting the entire light from it on to a photoelectric cell. For this, the cells must be small and a fast scanner is required. A scanner at the receiving end should synchronise with that at the transmitter.

A person who made a fundamental contribution was Paul Nipkow (1860-1940). His perforated scanning disc, with lenses spirally arranged, enabled engineers to transmit the image of a picture point-by-point. A photoelectric cell converted the light into electrical signals.

A Frenchman, Constantin Senlecq (1842-1934), made an invention, vising a rotating perforated disc of selenium cells in 1880. He became blind and was unable to see the first TV pictures that were transmitted towards the end of his life.

In 1897. J.J. Thompson (1856-1940) in Britain discovered the electron, an almost weightless unit of negative charge, while C.F. Braun in Germany invented the cathode ray (electron) tube.

In 1906. M. Dieckmann in Munich developed an electron camera, and an electronic projector, the *kinescope.* based on Braun's cathode-ray tube. In Russia, Boris Rosing demonstrated at device for transmitting few images. He died in a concentration camp but his pupil. V.K. Zworykin, escaped to the USA. In 1929, he demonstrated in New York the electronic scanning of pictures. He showed that the tiny photoelectric cells can store the charge between scans. Zworykin also drew inspiration from the ideas of A.A. Campbell Swinton of England, who wrote in *Nature* in 1908 about using cathode rays, with a mosaic of photoelectric cells for the transmitter.

By then, the first practical demonstration of TV had been done in London. On 27 January 1926. John Logle Baird, a Scottish engineer (1888-1946). was 'the first to achieve television.' He demonstrated to scientists transmission from one room to another of an image of a man talking. In 1928, he used radio waves to send his picture signals across the Atlantic. People in New York saw some persons in a London room. At about this time, the first commercial TV receiver was shown to the public. In 1929, the BBC granted Baird fecilities for using its transmitter. Sound was added a year later. At first 12-1/2 pictures a second were transmitted and each picture had 30 lines of scanning. It occurred to engineers that the pictures would improver if more lilies were scanned in a second

The use of Baird's Invention continued with the transmitting of a horse-race, some entertainment and even a newspaper Interview. The Nipkow disc was replaced by a mirror drum. Photoelectric cells were improved. In 1932. Baird demonstrated the use of short waves for transmitting TV signals. Unfortunately for Baird, the Post Office preferred another system of transmission as it could scan more lines. The electron beam moved very much faster than any mechanical device and over 400 lines could be scanned in a second, producing 25 pictures.

Basically, the television camera converts the variable Light intensity of a scene into a video signal. The scene is focused on to a surface, which is scanned, making one complete 'frame' or picture. A picture consists of two interlaced fields. Every other line is scanned first and then the missing lines interlaced. In this system, 50 fields or 25 pictures per second are transmitted.

The composite video signal has the picture component (the brightness and detail) and the synchronising signals to enable the receiver to reconstitute the picture. The picture signal voltage varies between two reference levels representing the maximum and zero tonal values.

At the receiver, another electron beam traces out the same pattern on a phosphor-sensitised picture tube. The incoming video signal modulates the intensities of the electron beam.

In colour TV, there are three cameras, one each for red. green and blue which are primary colours for television broadcasting. Colour information is added to the video signal. At the receive-end, there are three kinds of light-emitting phosphor, one for each colour, coated in the form of numerous dots. The received signal is decoded into its components and made to modulate three independent electron beams. Each beam strikes one set of colour dots. The colour component of the video signal will contain the basic colour information and the degree to which it is mixed with white.

The video signal is sent out as electromagnetic waves from the TV tower, which has dipole arrays for the purpose. The antenna gain at the receive-end is tenfold. If the signal is weak at the receive-end a complex structure of antennas is required. A 100-metre TV tower can 'cover' an area of 60 km radius. Microwaves are used to transmit the TV signals between distant places on a point-to-point basis. Satellites are used for nationwide, multipoint transmission.

The role of the telecommunication engineer is to transmit the programme given by the TV authorities. It can be transmitted on coaxial cable to a limited extent but sent over long distances, along with telephone and other messages, by microwave lines. However, a TV programme would occupy a large chunk in the communication highway, at the cost of several hundreds of telephone conversations, unless enough transmission capacity is provided for.

THE WONDER CHIP

Modern telecommunication relies on computers so much that people have started wondering whether the two are in fact separate systems at all. All information—voice, data or video—is turned into digits and transmitted as digits. The binary system wherein all numbers are represented by ones and zeros is suited to telecommunication and computer systems as the information can be recognised by the presence or absence of the corresponding electrical signals.

Mechanical aids to calculation of numbers have been in use for a long time. The abacus and the slide rule are well-known examples of such aids. The mechanical machine of Charles Babbage (1791-1871), an Englishman, did automatic calculations using electrical circuits and magnetic relays though the device was quite heavy.

In 1948, an invention changed the world in a unique manner. It was the *transistor*, developed by three scientists of Bell Laboratories—John Bardeen, William Shock-ley and Waltair Brattain. Basically, it is an electrical valve used to boost or amplify electrical signals. It soon replaced the Fleming tube in various applications including telecommunications.

Transistors are made of silicon, which is the most abundant element in the world next to oxygen, although it does not appear in pure form. Silicon is neither a. good conductor of electricity nor a good insulator (hence the name, semiconductor). It is very sensitive to the presence or absence of Impurities.

The Basic Technique

A material either passes electric current or does not. There are some materials which do not pass current but will do so, when property 'doped' with impurities. Such materials include germanium or silicon and they can be doped with small doses of arsenic, indium and other impurities. The impurities change the electrical properties of the material. This is the basis of semiconductors.

An element's capacity to allow a free flow of electrons depends on its atomic structure. Copper and gold, for example have loosely bound atoms in which electrons are free to move. They are good conductors. When the number of electrons in the outer ring of an atom is less than the maximum possible spaces for electrons, they are called 'free' (or valence) electrons. Silicon and germanium have four free electrons in their atoms. The electrons bind the silicon atoms together. When an atom of silicon is surrounded by another silicon atom, each nucleus appears to be surrounded by eight electrons and the resulting crystal structure is very stable and will not let the electrical current to flow unless the stable valence electrons are disturbed. If we want the electrical current to flow easily, we should dope the silicon crystal by phosphorus and boron. If phosphorus, which has five electrons, is added to a silicon atom (which has four electrons), there is an extra electron not required to bind the crystal and it is of negative charge. It is free to move about and carry current. Phosphorus is called *n-type impurity,* meaning it has a negative charge. In another method, when a boron atom which has only three electrons is inserted into a silicon atom, one electron is absent. A 'hole' is created since the fourth silicon electron has no impure electron to pair with. The hole or absence of an electron will mean that the positive charge of the nearby silicon nucleus is still there and so the hole has a positive charge. Boron is called a p-type impurity, as absence of an electron gives it a positive charge. By doping a silicon crystal, half with a *p-type impurity* and the other half with a n-type impurity, a p-n junction is formed and an electrical current can be made to flow across it. The p-n junction is the basic building block of transistors (Fig. 9).

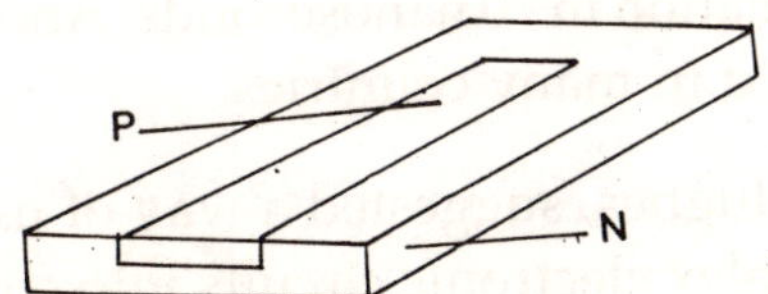

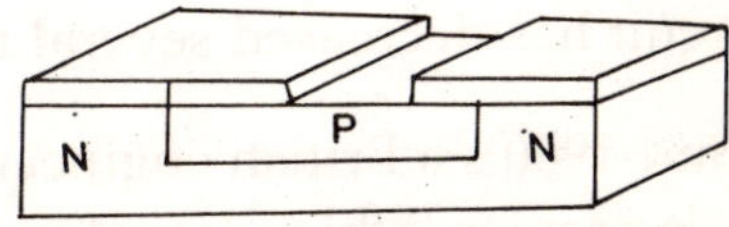

Fig. 9: A typical microelectronic process. On the surface of a silicon wafer, a 'window' is etched and Impurity is diffused. An N-type of region is created. Repeated etching and diffusion create NPN areas, which form a transistor. Electrical contacts to the N-region are made by depositing an aluminium conductor. On the left is a diode and on the right, a transistor.

Besides transistors, other components can be made. While a transistor amplifies signals, a resistor regulates the level of current; a capacitor stores it and a diode allows the current to flow in only one direction. (It can thus detect the presence or absence of pulses).

The Integrated Circuit

In the initial days of transistors, one had to wrestle with the problem of connecting thousands of components by hand. A circuit with several components needed a large number of soldered connections linking them. This problem of numbers was solved by an American electrical engineer. Jack St. Clair Kilby (though another. Robert Norton Noyce is also reported to have got the idea independently). Kilby suggested a novel method of interconnecting the different devices as part of the manufacturing process instead of connecting them later. For this purpose, the components will have to be miniaturised and placed in a single medium. The result was a monolithic integrated circuit (IC) or semiconductor chip. Developing from early transistors, modern ICs involved as many as 100 inventions. By 1960, mass production of chips started and soon their reliability and power became proverbial. In the early 1960's, each chip contained 12 transistors. In a decade the number went up to 1,000 and more, called *large-scale integration* (LSI). In the early 1980's, several hundreds of thousands of components (very large-scale integration) were put on a single chip.

Japan developed the world's first 256 k bit (256,000 bits) Random Access Memory (RAM) chip (with 600,000 circuit components) in an incredible area of 6 millimetre (mm) square that has an access time of 100 nanoseconds (one nanosecond is a billionth of a second) consuming very little power.

A one-million bit (megabit) chip has also been developed in Japan, which has four times the capacity of the earlier generation chip. Each chip can store the equivalent of four pages of a newspaper text! It is also claimed to have the world's fastest access time for such chips. It can read information in 70 nanoseconds. And the cost per circuit has decreased several thousandfold in many countries.

In the mid-1960's a British engineer, Charles Hughes, suggested a way of using the micro-electronics (which meant building complex electronic circuits into chips) for telecommunications. He called his device a *miniprocessor*, which was later known as the *microprocessor*. It is a small, stored-program computer using Metal Oxide Semiconductor (MOS) technology allowing large-scale integration. The device itself contains the computer program. The logic program is held in a read-only memory chip; it has an arithmetic unit and control. It could be designed to perform several operations in the exchanges such as registering dialled digits, signalling between exchanges and services such as checking coin payphones. Semiconductor companies worked out these ideas in the USA and developed microprocessors. From about 1960, production techniques have steadily been improved for obtaining transistors and then integrated circuits.

A New Art

A new art has come up, which includes skills in photography and physical and chemical processes.

The process is quite elaborate. Silicon is doped and cut into wafers,. which is called the *substrate* Again, it is doped to get another layer of silicon, which is coated with a photo-sensitive resin. In is then masked and exposed to ultraviolet light. The resin is removed from the unexposed areas. There is a 'window in the chip through which other parts of the chip may be exposed. The impurities will diffuse into the silicon in areas not protected by the silicon dioxide layer. The routine of coating, masking, exposing, etching and diffusing is repeated over and over again. With each process, another function is added. When the impurity is diffused into silicon, a new oxide layer forms over the entire surface. NPN areas now form a transistor.

The development of the silicon chip is not over. The progress of technology is so fast that it is cheaper to produce one chip than many separate ones for eventual combination. Chips of greater purity can be produced if they are smaller in size. The most advanced features printed on a silicon chip are approaching the width of a micrometre (millionth of a metre). If less width is required, electron beams, will be needed instead of light beams used now. That will mean a millionfold increase in the number of transistors on a chip.

MIXING SIGNALS

One may wonder how several telephone conversations are transmitted on the same path and recovered individually. It is a complex process that has evolved as a result of several inventions and discoveries.

The human voice generates sounds of many different frequencies all at once. A range of frequencies transmitted is called the *bandwidth.* It is a telecommunication highway; more bandwidth is required to send more information in a short period. For transmitting music, for example, more space is needed in the highway to create fidelity (30-12,000 Hz). A telephone channel has a band-width of 3 kHz which ranges from the lowest (300 Hz) to the highest (3,300 Hz) frequencies chosen. The band for telephone is restricted to this range; frequencies in a conversation higher than about 4,000 Hz are filtered out, as they are not necessary to comprehend normal speech.

The wires and cables that carry the signals can however transmit more conversations or information. Several phone calls take up different slots of 4 kHz each in the transmission medium. For purposes of transmission, each call is given a different frequency just as different stations can be tuned in a radio at various frequencies. The different frequencies are obtained by mixing the initial frequencies with a carrier. A carrier wave has a constant single frequency so that its highest and lowest amplitudes (a measure of the signal's strength) and the wavelength are constant. Different frequencies (say from telephones) modulate the carrier which then a band of frequencies. The advantage of this arrangement in the modulated frequencies can efficiently be transmitted.

The first carrier system was installed in 1918 between Baltimore and Pittsburg. with four two-way channels over a single open-wire line. Two years later, three I two-way channels were installed using different frequencies for each direction of transmission. Eventually a carrier system which can take 12 channels was developed and operated in 1938 on a transcontinental cable route. Carrier systems were further developed in the 1940's. With the coming of transistors, frequencies could be controlled precisely and hundreds of conversations could be sent on the same line.

Transmission lines were also improved. The first telephone circuits employed a single wire with a ground return. Later two closely paralleled wires were used to avoid electrical disturbances. One of the wires provided the return current path, instead of returning the current through the earth.

The weakening of the signal became a problem as the length of the wire increased. A professor of mathematics of Columbia University, Dr. Michael Idvorsky Pupin 1858-1935), found an answer. He developed a device called *inductance* or *loading coil* which reduced the fading of higher frequencies. Installed at every mile or so along open wires, the device made it possible to have a thin instead of thick wire and cut costs. The use of the coil in underground cables extended the distance covered. The first such cable was installed between New York and Philadelphia and put into service in 1906. However, Pupin's coil could only reduce the fading; it could not amplify the signals.

Vacuum Tubes

The need to detect and amplify electric current led to research in the field. Around 1900, only crystal detectors were used in a few wireless telegraph sets. By 1915, Lee De Forest's triode detectors were used. They made a big change in communications. The device amplified the telephone signals, though weakly. A telephone company soon bought his technology and developed it further with the work of Harold D. Arnold (1883-1933) and his team. By 1912, a very high vacuum tube was available. The vacuum tubes proliferated and by the mid-1950's, there were more than 1.800 different varieties of them. In order to improve the performance of repeaters in amplifying telephone signals, a negative feedback amplifier was invented in 1927 by Harold S. Black (b. 1898) of Bell Laboratories. The device fed back part of the amplified signal into the input thereby improving the stability of the signal and reducing its distortion. In the process, the gain obtained fay the amplifier was somewhat reduced.

With a view to minimising the loss in transmission over long distances, a four-wire system was developed, one pair for the receive frequencies and another for the send frequencies, mainly because the amplifiers, being unidirectional, cannot handle the signals going in both directions. The line from the subscriber to the telephone exchange, called the *two-wire connection,* would transmit and receive the signals in both directions. An interface became necessary between the two-wire system and the four wire link. Such a device, known as *hybrid,* was developed. It separates the incoming and outgoing signals and sends them on different lines. The hybrid converts the two-wire signal on the subscriber line into a four-wire signal (Fig. 10). A similar arrangement is made in the telephone handset which converts the two-wire signals from the exchange into separate channels requited for the earphone and the mouthpiece and also prevents the echo of your own voice from reaching your ears.

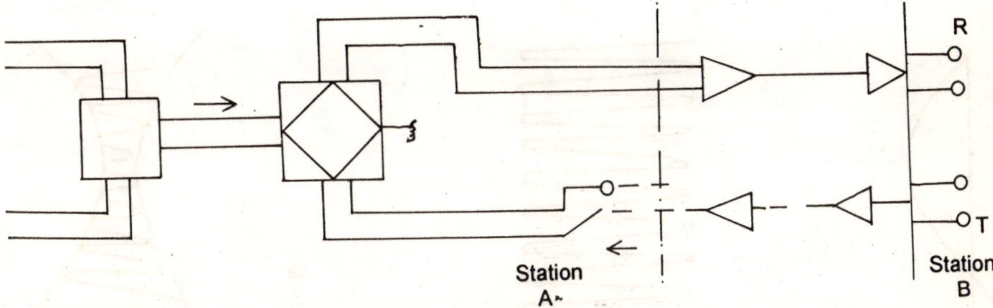

Fig. 10: Incoming and outgoing channels on trunk lines or microwave are on different paths, called a four-wire link. The line connecting the subscriber to the exchange, called two-wire line, takes traffic in both directions. An Interface, called hybrid, converts the two wire path into a four-wire path (and vice versa for incoming traffic).

Modulation

As demand for telephony Increased, the need to transmit more speech channels on the same wire became imperative. Moreover, the telecommunication path could accommodate more than one channel. Different frequencies are used to transmit different channels. The process of shifting the input signal to the assigned frequency

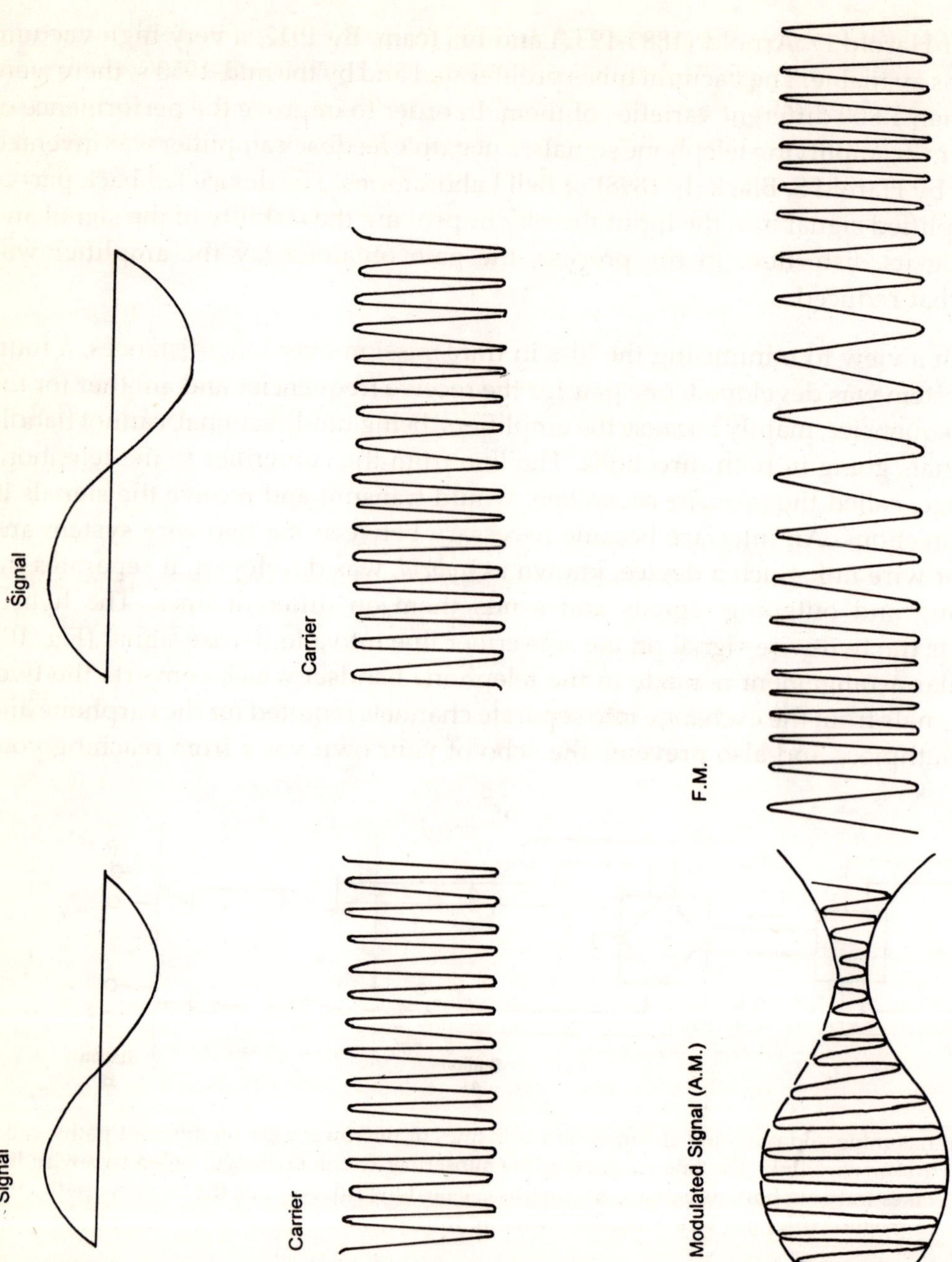

Fig. 11: In Amplitude Modulation (AM), the amplitude of the original wave directly modulates the amplitude of a carrier wave having a uniform frequency.

In Frequency Modulation (FM), The amplitude of the original wave form is used to alter the frequency of a carrier wave of constant.

slot is called *modulation* and the reverse process at the receive end is called *demodulation.* In modulation, the signal is superimposed on the undèrlying carrier in a form suited for distribution. Demodulation recovers the original signal from the altered carrier. For example, a carrier wave of constant amplitude and frequency of say, 1,000,000 Hz is modulated by a modulating signal of 1,000 Hz. The resulting amplitude envelope of the modulated carrier will contain the carrier frequency of 1,000,000 Hz and the sum as well as difference of the carrier and modulating frequency (viz. 1,001,000 Hz and 999,000 Hz. respectively). The signal in other words, modifies a carrier frequency both above and below the bandwidth of the modulated carrier. The frequencies above and below the carrier are called the *sidebands.* Each sideband carries full information on the amplitude and frequency of the modulating signal. Thus it is enough if either of the sidebands of a resultant signal is transmitted. The other can be suppressed conserving power and bandwidth. At the receiving end, the sideband is mixed with a carrier frequency which is identical to that used for modulation.

There are two types of modulation, viz. amplitude modulation and frequency modulation (Fig. 11). In Amplitude Modulation (AM), the sound wave directly alters or modulates the carrier wave's amplitude, i.e. its up and down oscillation. (The carrier wave has uniform frequency). A detector at the other end reproduces the original wave form. The other method. Frequency Modulation (FM), was pioneered in the early 1930's by Edwin Armstrong to improve the quality of radio transmission. In this method, the amplitude of the original wave form is translated so that it alters the frequency of a carrier wave of constant amplitude. At the receive-end, the original wave form is recovered. In practice, AM signals require a minimum of bandwidth, while FM signals need more of it. But FM is less prone to noise, as one can notice in the quality of FM broadcasts or in the audio channel of a TV set. The bandwidth in FM depends on how much the frequency is varied in accordance with the amplitude of the signal changes. The bandwidth can be increased without increasing the signal power or increasing the noise.

Transmission of a specified band of frequencies needed special filters. Theoretical investigations of electrical networks by G.A. Campbell (b. 1915) led to the invention of the electric wave filter in 1917. Today, it is usual to use advanced filters (called *low-pass filters* or *high-pass filters)* that allow only those frequencies which are below or above a specified frequency. A band-pass *filter* will transmit a specified band of frequencies, suppressing all others.

Stacking Conversations

Modulation is a step in the process called *multiplexing*— an important development of the late 1940's. In multiplexing, a number of messages of the same type are stacked for simultaneous transmission on a *single line* or radio carrier. The combined multiplexed signal is termed a line signal or, in the case of radio transmission, *baseband signal*. Different speech channels are 'translated' into different frequencies. By varying the amplitude or frequency of the carrier wave, the information in the modulating frequency is transferred to it. Multiplexing can be done on the basis of frequency division or time division.

The equipment which translates the frequencies is crucial to this formation and transmission. Such equipment is being made indigenously. It is necessary that the frequencies generated have to be stabler if all the careful combinations have to work. To ensure that, there are highly stable master oscillators which generate basic carrier frequencies for each of the translation stages. From them other desired frequencies are obtained.

Multiplexing is thus a means by which several circuits are combined for transmission over a common transmission path. Frequency Division Multiplex is the most widely used method for assembling voice signal over a single medium. In a 12-voice channel, each with a 4 KHz wide, the first channel will be from 60 to 64 KHz. while the last channel will be from 104 to 108 KHz. The composite signal of 48 KHz (12 x 4 KHz) is transmitted. At the receive-end, the signal is demodulated into its 12 components (Fig. 12).

Groups—Basic, Super and Hyper

In a 960-channel multiplexing, all the 960 are not modulated individually with a different carrier to get the combined signal. First, a block of 12 channels is obtained in the frequency of 60 to 108 KHz, called a *basic group*. Five such basic groups (12 x 5) will make a 60 channel chunk, known as a *super group*, with a bandwidth of 240 KHz in the frequency range of 312 KHz to 552 KHz (Fig. 13). Each one of the five basic groups modulates one of the group carrier frequencies and forms the 60-channel band. Fifteen super groups are combined to make one hyper group of 900 channels. Three such hyper groups can be combined to form a 2,700 channel (Fig. 14) band in the 312-12,336 KHz (or 12 Mega Hz) range. The first hyper group is taken direct without modulation. Hyper groups 2 and 3 (each between 312 and 4,092 KHz) are modulated with 8,432 KHz and 12,468 KHz, respectively. Twelve hyper groups combine to produce a 10,800-channel baseband for 60 Mega Hz systems.

Suitable guard space is provided between the groups so as to prevent overlapping. Advances in filter technologies have reduced the size of the multiplex systems.

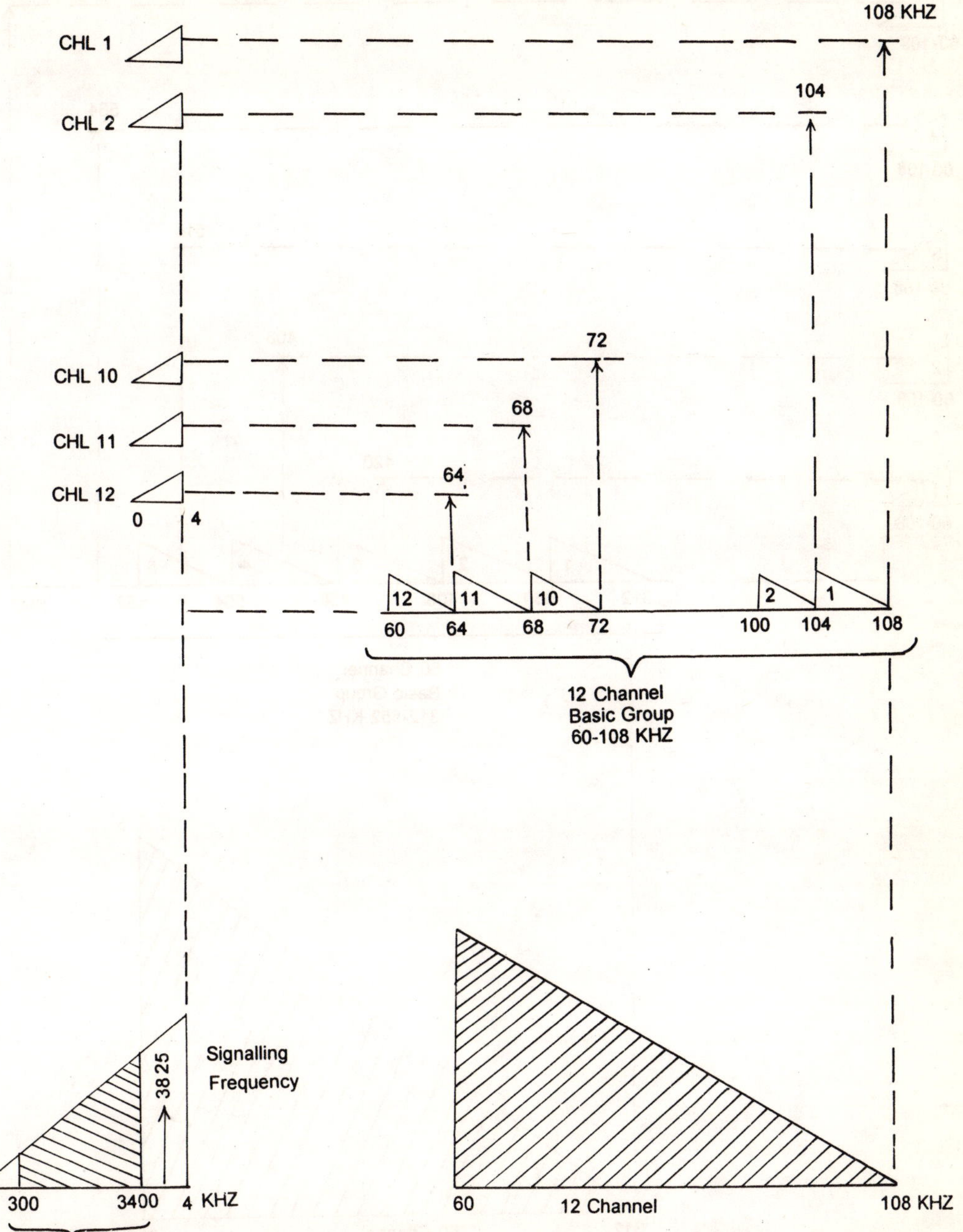

Fig. 12: *Fequency Division Multiplex:* Most widely used method for assembling several voice signals for transmission over a single medium. 12-voice channels, for example, each with a bandwidth of 4 KHz, are transposed upwards in frequency to occupy 12 adjacent bands, each 4 KHz wide, to form a basic group of 60-108 KHz. At the destination, the signal is demodulated into its 12 components.

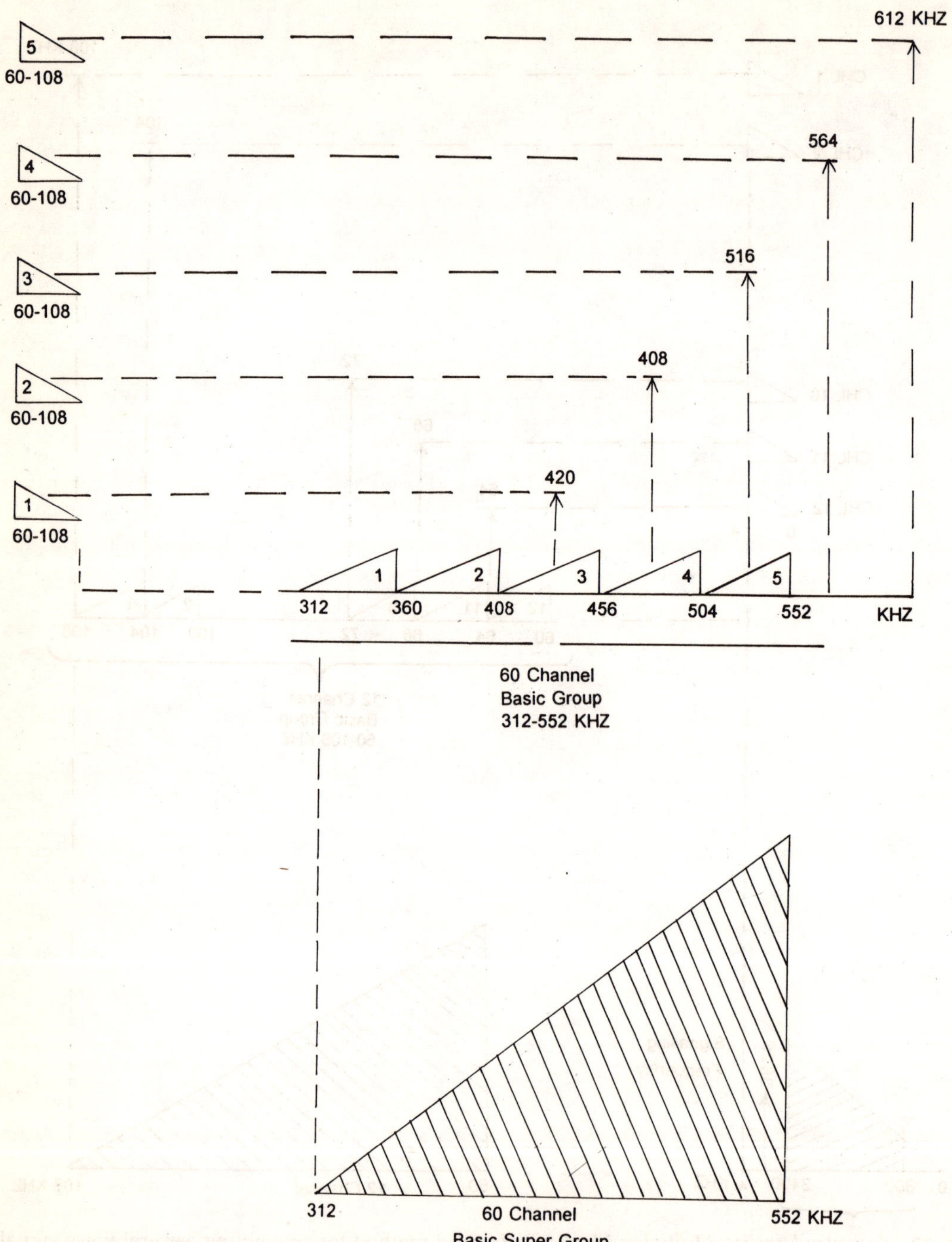

Fig. 13: A basic super group of 60 channels is formed of five basic groups of 60-108 KHz in the frequency range 312-552 KHz. The carrier frequencies which are modulated are given above the slots showing the basic groups.

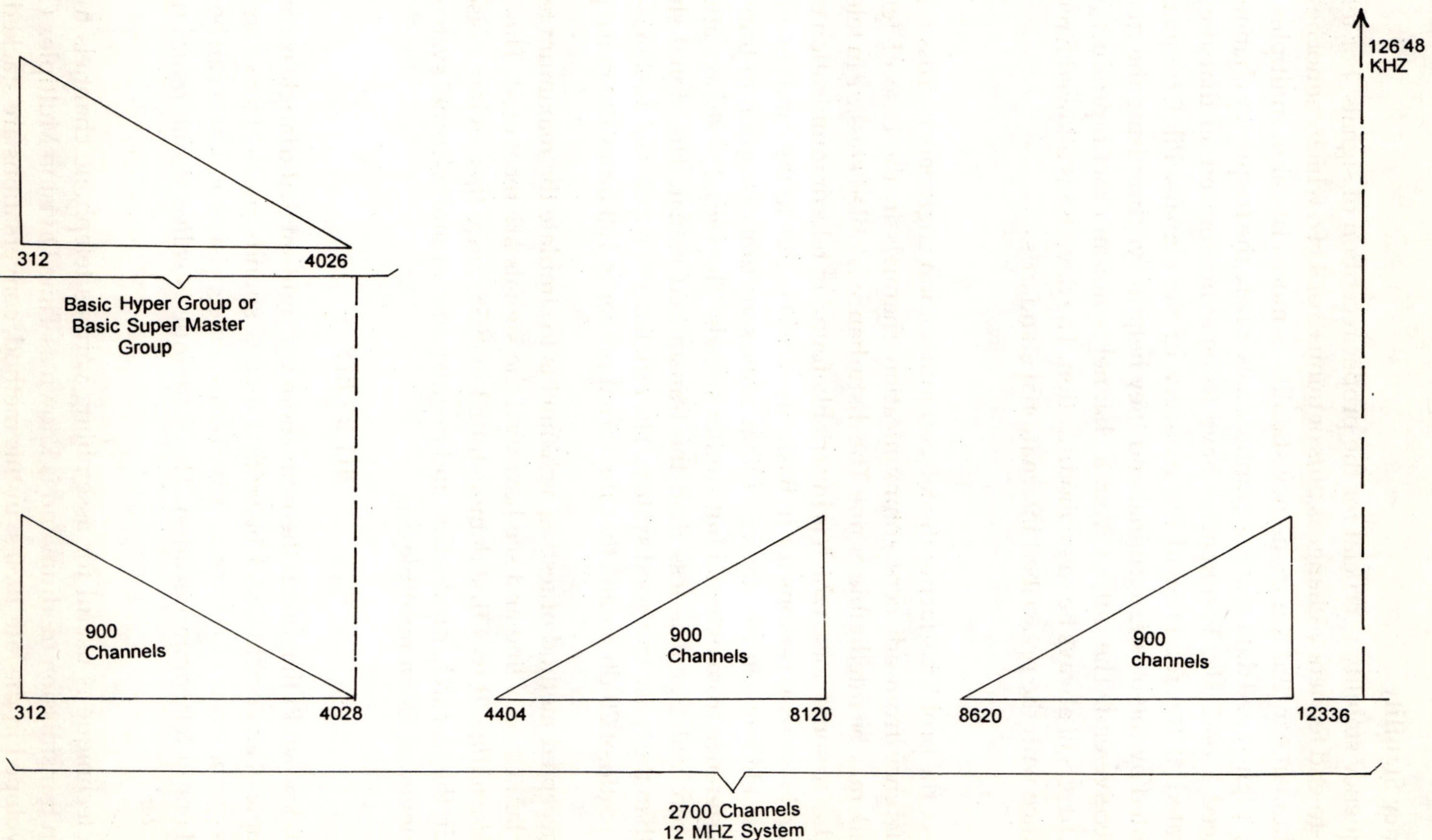

Fig. 14: A 2,700-channel system is formed by combining three hyper groups of 900 channels each. The first hyper group is taken without modulation while the others are modulated.

Frequency Stability

Frequency stability is crucial for the proper reception of signals. For telephony, the end-to-end fequency change is plus or minus 3 or 4 Hz. which cannot be detected by the human ear. But the frequency stability is more critical in multiplex systems carrying high-speed data and telegraph signals where the frequency changes should not exceed 1 or 2 Hz. Frequencies have to be synchronised so that they can be regenerated at the receive-end for recovery of the signals. Pilot frequencies are transmitted by the master terminal and they help in synchronising the frequencies at the receive-end. The output from a channel is not an exact reproduction of the input. There will always be some modification. The deviations allowed have to be in accordance with the prescribed international standards.

Noise

One of the problems facing the telecommunication engineers is cross talk which is interference from adjacent communication channels in the case of telephony. Cross talk may be intelligible or not. The disturbance is called *crossfire* in telegraphy. This is due to some noise which is invariably found in telecommunication channels. There can be several reasons for it. Basically, noise is due to the random motions of atoms and electrons in the devices. Other causes include distortion in transmission and interference from external but similar signals. The signal is always attenuated, i.e. the received signal is less than the transmitted signal. The signal should be louder than the noise in a good system. The efficiency is expressed as signal-to-noise ratio. A. ratio of 20 db means that the signal power is 100 times the noise power.

An accepted method of testing a channel is to simulate the maximum telephone traffic planned on a line and see how well the signals are recovered. This is called *white noise testing.* It was first demonstrated in 1955. Since then, white noise testing is done in the research, production and maintenance of multichannel systems based on frequency division multiplexing.

BIT BY BIT

The well-known Pythagorean theorem about the right-angled triangle is considered an example of an ancient Greek belief that shapes, sounds, musical tones and, in fact, all ideas can be expressed numerically. Today, voice, vision and data can be reduced to numbers in telecommunication. The technique is called *digital transformation of information.*

This technique is useful for assembling various telephone channels to share a common transmission medium and is known as Time Division Multiplex (TDM). It was developed in the late 1930's. In this method, conversations are stacked in time.

The different channels time-share a transmission path. In contrast, in the Frequency Division Multiplex (FDM), the channels occupy different frequency slots in the path. In TDM, each channel is assigned a short time slot and the channels occupy the slots in turn. Instead of sending the entire signal corresponding to a conversation, momentary samples of the signal's amplitude are taken and their numerical value is transmitted as coded pulses. The signals can be sent and received much faster by machines than by humans. TDM is used in a digital exchange which has a time-switch for allotting the signals.

The new technology is based on a rather simple approach. Information can be presented in two different way the analogue and the *digital.* The analogue technique is seen, for instance, in the movement of a compass needle or the hands of a clock. What is shown by them is an analogous signal which varies continuously. In contrast, Morse telegraphy is based on on-off electrical pulses. In the digital way, the phenomena measured are presented as binary digits (bits for short) symbolising 'yes' or 'no'. Binary numbers make up the language of the computer. Corresponding to ones and zeros on-off electrical signals are transmitted. (A bit is not to be confused with byte which is a combination of bits normally, though not always, forming an 8-bit word).

In the analogue way, variations in the originating sound or brightness of a picture correspond to the variations in electrical signals. In the digital method, the variations are expressed as ones and zeros.

Though the human ear responds only to an analogue signal, engineers have found that voice can be changed into a digital format for transmission. It was discovered that the analogue signal of the voice from a telephone or the entire band of electrical waves corresponding to the speech waves need not be transmitted. Though the ear can respond to a large bandwidth of 200-20,000 Hz, it is found that speech can be recognised and understood at a frequency range of 300-3,300 Hz. It would be enough if the electrical wave is sampled at a suitable rate for reconstruction at the other end.

Sending Samples

A sampling idea which can work efficiently was first suggested in 1938 by an American engineer, Harry Nyquist (1889-1976). The practical application of the idea has to await the advent of the transistor since the system demands devices that can switch on and off at a fantastic speed. It was found that if the sampling is at a low rate, the signal would not be reproduced correctly. Even if the sampling rate is extremely high, it would not improve the quality beyond a point. The ideal sampling rate was found to be at least twice the highest frequency of the signal. For voice, the desired sampling rate is 8,000 times a second, which is double the maximum voice frequency (4 kHz) in a telephone channel Similarly, a television signal of 6 MHz should be sampled at 12 MHz.

A unique way of conveying samples of the speech was suggested in 1938 by Alec H. Reeves of Britain. Each people conveys a numerical value corresponding to the amplitude of the signal at a point of time. The values sampled are quantised, i.e. measured according to a chosen scale. The train of sample pulses can be sent through a carrier wave. This process is called Pulse Amplitude Modulation (PAM).

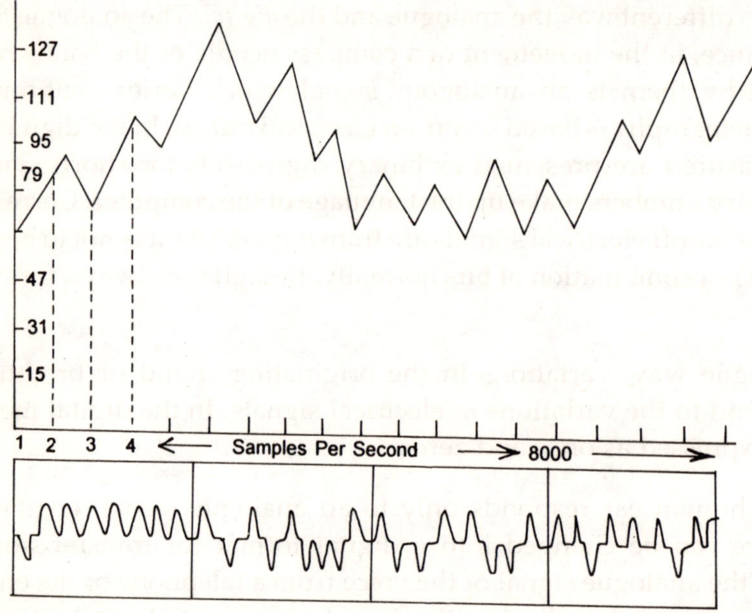

Fig. 15: In Pulse Code Modulation (PCM), the amplitude of the original voice signal is sampled 8.000 times a second and the sampled values are put as binary codes consisting of ones and zeros. Codes consisting of bits can convey 256 levels of amplitude of the original signal.

If the sampling rate is 8,000 times a second, each signal is sampled once every 125 microseconds. Each sample can be expressed in an 8-bit code. The code can represent 256 levels or values. The codes correspond to the nearest level in a scale of 128 positive and as many negative amplitude levels (Fig. 15). The values can be rounded off to the nearest number in the scale and this process is called *quantisation.* The greater the number of quantising levels, the more accurate will be the value represented. Digital conversion of an analogue signal thus involves three steps, viz. sampling, quantisation to the nearest value and encoding in an 8-bit combination. This method of modulating pulses is called Pulse Code Modulation (PCM).

A simple calculation would show how many bits are necessary to transmit a telephone call. If a 4 kHz telephone channel is sampled at 8 kHz (8,000 times a second) and each time eight bits are required to describe the amplitude encoded in the sample, 64,000 bits are needed per second (64 kbit/s).

The capacity of different transmission channels as well as the complexity of a message source can be measured in terms of bits per second. A mathematical theory of communication applicable to this field was given by Claude E. Shannon (b. 1916) in 1948. In effect, the theory held that if the information rate does not exceed the capacity of a channel (also expressed in terms of bits per second), messages can be sent with hardly any error. If properly sent, the information flow (as bits per second) can approach the channel capacity. The theory enables engineers to predict and evaluate the performance of a transmission system in terms of speed, characteristics of the signal and the interfering noise.

The information rate of human speech is perhaps less than 1,000 bits per second (bit/s). The telephone channel can transmit 60,000 bit/s. The channel capacity for radio is 80,000 bit/s; for FM radio, 250,000 bit/s and for colour television (525 lines.) 90 million bit/s. These calculations are based on Shannon's theory.

With 64,000 bits transmitted each second, excellent quality can be obtained in voice communication. A fairly good quality signal can be derived at a reduced speed of 32,000 bit/s.

Combining Bits

Bits from various sources are generally combined for— transmission. If a telephone speech is sampled (at 8,000 times a second with 8 bits per sample) we need 64,000 bit/s. If there are 24 telephone channels, there are as many time slots of eight digits with a total of 192 digits and a spare one for synchronisation. The time slots are repeated 8.000 times a second making a total of 1,544,000 bit/s. In fact, the United States and Japan have adopted a basic unit of 24-voice channels with a bit rate of 1.544 Mega bit/s (Mbit'/s).

The rest of the world has adopted the 30-voice channel grouping at 2.048 Mbit/s. The 30-channel system (with two additional channels for synchronisation and signalling) has 32 basic time slots, teach with 64 kilo bits per second capacity, making a total of 2,048 Kbit/s or 2 Mbit/s. The sample information from 32 different channels is continuously sent, one sample after another (Fig. 16). The 2 Mbit/s transmission forms the primary level of a digital hierarchy. Digital pulses from four of the 30-channel multiplexes can be interleaved on a single cable; which will then carry 120 conversations as eight million bits every second. Subsequently, four sets of eight million bit multiplexes can be interleaved on one cable to get a 480-channel link with a 34 million bit stream. Also, four of these streams can be sent together on a single telephone cable. All the series of pulses are 'reconstructed' again into speech at the receive-end.

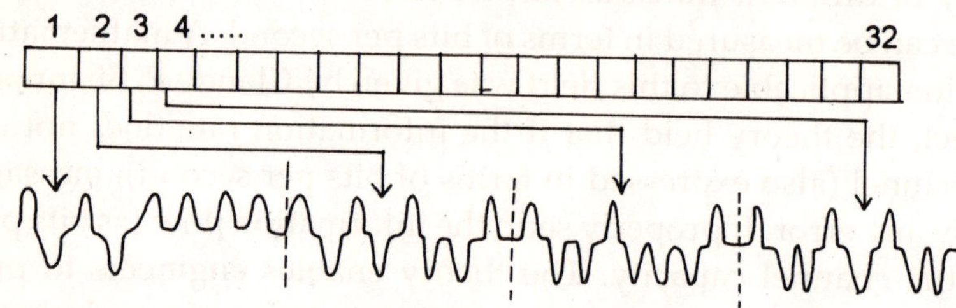

Fig. 16: Time Division Multiplex uses pulse code modulation. Here 32-voice channels are sampled in sequence. 8,000 times a second and the amplitude of each sample is represented in binary form as in PCM, which are Interleaved and transmitted as 1's and O's. 32 Timeslots of 8 digits (256) plus a spare (257) are repeated 8,000 times a second for a total of 2,056,000 digits per second.

Merits of Pulse Code Modulation

Pulse Code Modulation (PCM). sampling at 8,000 times a second, to reproduce any frequency up to 4,000 Hz can reduce costs per telephone channel on short routes and can enhance line utilisation within a city. The advantage offered by PCM are several: PCM is not affected by line noise or cross talk. Even a rough medium such as an old cable can do the job well. PCM is ideal to handle the higher data transmission rates from computers. The technique is used in satellite communication, as bit streams to be sent to a satellite may have to be time-division multiplexed. Control of the network and provision for privacy are some other advantages.

There are, however methods of encoding telephone signals into a smaller number of bits, thereby increasing the capacity of the digital trunks.

Already, lower sampling rates are in use where fine sampling of speech is not needed to get the message, as in some military or emergency communication systems. Known as *delta modulation*, coding in this method only ascertains whether the amplitude of the speech signal is more or less than the previous sample. If the sample is more, it is one; and if it is less, it is zero. This sampling is done at 32,000 times as against 8,000 times a second in PCM. Thus in delta modulation, there will be 32,000 bits as against 64,000 bits per second in PCM. The obvious advantages of the method are only half the bandwidth and power are necessary to transmit the same information, compared with PCM. Though the samples are not as accurate as in PCM, the delta method is less prone to error as the coding is simple, just one bit for each sample.

Sophisticated error detection techniques are used in digital communication. It involves adding one or more bits to a binary character code of fixed length. In a 6-bit code for instance, a seventh bit (also called *parity bit)* is added for verifying the accuracy of transmission.

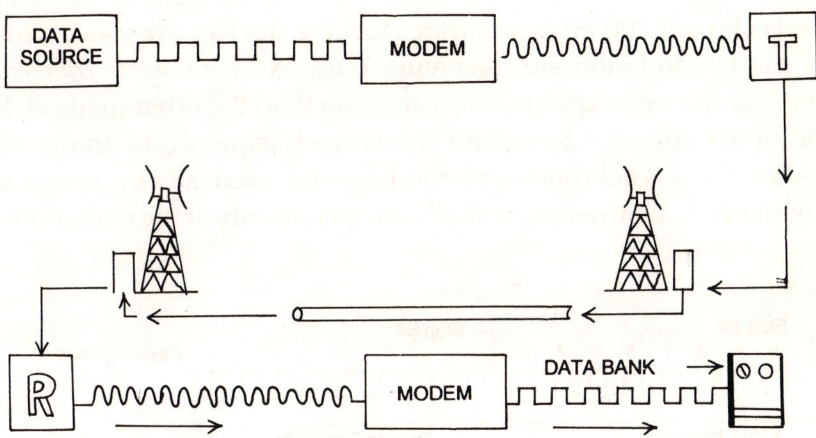

Fig. 17: Digital data transmission is facilitated by modems, which condition the signal to travel along the telephone cables or on microwaves.

Special Devices

Transmission of data needs some special devices. The transmission medium such as the telephone cable is meant for carrying-analogue signals. So long as the telephone network is used to transmit digital information, a device is necessary to condition the digital output to suit the transmission medium. Such a device is called *modem.* short for modulator and demodulator (Fig. 17). It is an interface that transforms a digital signal into an analogue-looking signal for transmission by cables or microwaves. For this purpose, a modern modulates a transmission frequency by a digital input. Either two amplitudes of the transmission frequency or two frequencies of the transmission path can convey the two states of the digital input. A modem at the receiving end demodulates the transmitted signal and helps recover the original digital output. Different bit rates can be sent. Up to 300 bit/s, they are called *subvoice speed,* while medium speed ranges from 600 to 9,600 bit/s. Rates at 64,000 bit/s are in the high-speed category. Bit rates up to 300 can be handled on a full duplex mode which means data can be sent and received at the same time between two points. Speeds above 300 bits are sent in a half-duplex mode i.e. they can be sent or received but not simultaneously. There can also be a simplex mode under which a station can only send data to another.

The sender and the receiver of data should have perfect coordination. If for instance, the receiver samples a signal every 10 microseconds, while the duration of one pulse is 100 microseconds, it may register only 10 pulses at the receiving end. For low speeds (below 1,200 bit/s) start-and-stop bits are added to each 8-bit character to distinguish the bits. This is called *asynchronous mode of transmission* (Fig. 18). For speeds above 1,200 bit/s, accurate clocking devices are used, which would synchronise the transmission and receiving rates. A *synchronous transmission* can send more bits for the same speed of transmission than the other method. However, it needs additional circuitry to ensure the correct sequence in transmission and reception. Also, the asynchronous method can be used at any speed up to the maximum, while the synchronous method can operate only at the maximum specified speed.

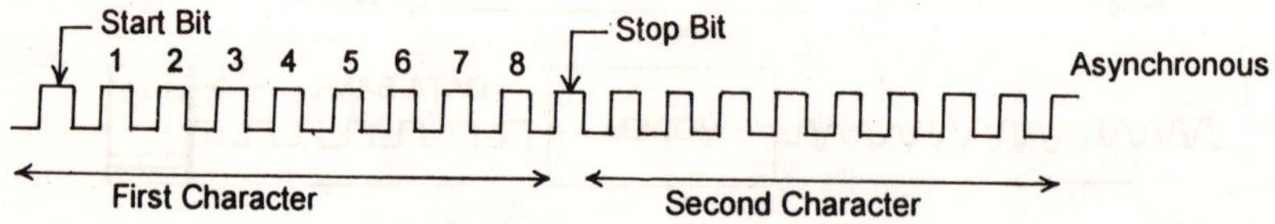

Fig. 18: Speeds of data below 1,200 bits per second can be sent in an asynchronous mode with start and stop bits with each character (with an 8-bit coding) to distinguish the bits. The synchronous method for speeds above 1,200 bits does not use the start and stop bits but requires accurate clocking devices.

Several Advantages

Digital technology offers several advantages. We have seen how in the analogue method repeaters not only amplify the signal but also the noise. In digital transmission, boosting is still needed but the repeaters will not amplify noise. It would only be necessary to recognise the presence or absence of the pulses to recreate them. The result will be greater clarity of speech or picture reproduction.

The superior transmission quality of the digital system commends its adoption particularly on routes with interior telephone cables. Junction cables that connect telephone exchanges in a city can use digital system which can increase the number of conversations (generally 30 channels) over the same pair of wires—an obvious advantage in crowded areas where laying of more cables may be difficult and costly. A 120-channel system is used on specially conditioned cables. A higher number of channels (480 for instance) can be carried on small coaxial tubes or microwave routes while 1,920 channels and more are used on big coaxial tubes.

Digital technology has started a change that goes far beyond junction cables. The digital technique is a great leveller, reducing all information—be it voice, music, picture or data—to the same format. The voice sent over telephone wires can now be transmitted as data bits that cannot be distinguished from data bits of computers. The same transmission path—cable, microwave or optical fibre—can handle data. However, the use of the telephone network for data transmission is limited to speeds up to 2,400 bit/s, Higher speeds need some devices called *equalisers* that counteract any distortion and condition the lines. Still higher speeds demand special networks. In fact the modern trend is to provide an Integrated Services Digital Network (ISDN), that would handle voice, high-speed data and pictures in one system based on a standardised digital telephone network. Digital technology is changing the nature of telecommunication.

VOICES UNDER LAND AND SEA

A single grounded wire connected two telephones in the early days, until the emergence of a switchboard in 1878. The first long-distance line for public use was opened between Boston and Providence in the USA, a distance of 64 km. on 12 January 1881. The circuit consisted of several sections of galvanised iron wire, with ground used as the return conductor. In 1884, the commercial service was inaugurated between Boston and New York. The idea of sending more than one speech on the same channel became a reality. The capacity of open-wire and multi-pair cables was increased. However, the bandwidth limitations allowed the provision of about 24 channels only.

After the Second World War, the search for methods to increase the transmission capacity of the cables was intensified. Cables with capacities of several hundreds of channels began to be used. A coaxial cable system was developed in 1929 at Bell Laboratory, USA. Early systems provided 300 channels. It was, however, only in 1941 that a system was set up between major cities in the eastern United States to transmit 640-message channels. Soon. big capacity cables were laid from coast to coast.

The system (known as Bell LI) had a limited bandwidth. Later, repeaters and multiplexing equipment were developed to combine speeches and boost signals. By 1953, the capacity of the message channels increased to over 1,000 or 600 message channels and a TV channel. Another system (Bell L5) had 9,000 channels per tube and 22 tubes in a cable sheath. Systems of 300, 600, 960, 1,380 and 2,700-channels were developed. In recent years, the capacity has been increased to 10,800 channels.

Coaxial Cables

The limitations of the open-wire system were overcome by the coaxial cable. Basically, it consists of a single wire in the centre of a cylindrical conductor, placed like a lead in a pencil. This wire is surrounded by an insulating layer of polyethylene foam. The insulation is surrounded by a tubular shield of copper wire or a seamless aluminium sheath. The axis of the inner and outer conductors is the same and hence its name. Usually, a number of tubes are combined inside one sheath. It is shielded from outside interference and the signals undergo very low attenuation, since the electromagnetic propagation is confined to the tube and cannot radiate off it. It has more conducting surface area than a two-wire transmission line. It can thus take on higher frequencies and that is the secret of its enormous capacity.

Service pairs and interstitial tubes are also provided inside the coaxial cable. These are used for transmitting control signals and for voice traffic for maintenance purposes. The coaxial cable can carry telephone, telegram and telex signals. Radio programmes are also sent through them.

A layer of heavy insulation and lead sheath protect the cable. Still, it is vulnerable and any digging of the road can cut the cable. The signals carried by the coaxial cables need boosting at regular intervals. The higher the frequency of the signals, the higher would be the attenuation and hence repeaters have to be placed closer. The power for the repeaters is carried by the same cable. Up to 280 km, power can be fed from one point. As power is at a lower frequency than the speech signals, the two do not interfere.

There are different sizes of the coaxial cables, known as big and small tubes. While the inner conductor is a straight copper wire, the outer conductor is made of a copper tape, formed into a circular tube. The inner diameter of the outer conductor can be 0.375" (9.5 mm) or 0.174" (4.4 mm), the former known as the *big tube* and the latter as the *small tube* (Fig. 19).

In a bid to reduce investment on copper efforts are under way to replace it by aluminium. Recent research on aluminium alloys has given it more suitable properties. A move to use aluminium in cables is under way in some countries.

Though the system permits transmission of very high frequencies up to several mega Hz (MHz) on a pair of conductors inside a tube, without interference, equalisers and repeaters are needed en route to drive a strong signal at the line. Repeaters are necessary at every 9 km for the big tube system of 960 channels and at every 4 km for the small tube carrying the same channels. If the cables have to carry a higher number of channels, viz. 2,700, the higher frequency involved will reduce repeater spacing to 4.5 km for the big tube and 2 km for the small tube.

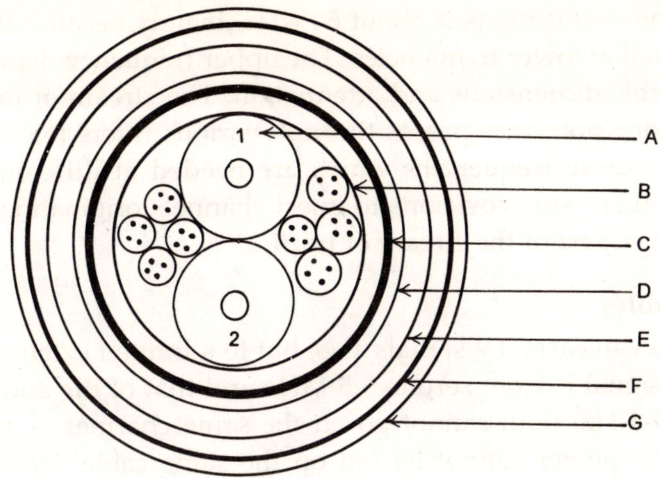

Fig. 19: A Two-Core Coaxial Cable (.375-Type):

A. Coaxial cores.
B. 8 Quads (0.9 mm), 16 pairs used for control circuits and short-haul carrier systems.
C. Lead sheath.
D. Two layers of impregnated paper tapes.
E. Two layers of hessian beddings.
F. Two layers of pre-compounded steel tapes.
G. Two layers of Impregnated hessian.

10,800 Channels

For the largest yet system of 10,800 telephone channels. repeaters at every 1.5 km are needed, as it operates at a high frequency of 60 MHz.

The cost of laying the cable varies with the size of the cable. The cost of coaxial cable system has come down, with the increased use of transistors in repeaters. These trends have made it feasible to increase the number of repeaters, thereby enabling the use of higher frequencies and wider bandwidth. The mean time between failures, as they call the lifetime of a part, is an unbelievable 1,000 years, even when the underground repeaters are buried at a depth of about 1.5 metres.

Being the life-lines of communications, coaxial cables are protected from lightning discharges. Copper conductors take care of it, but when lightning reaches the lead sheath, power trips and the line is down. In case of such an interruption, the point where the cable is affected has to be located, often in rain and darkness, and the cable dug out for repair.

Although a coaxial line will transmit signals down to zero frequency, the practical lower limit for communications is about 60 KHz, mainly because the coaxial tube does not shield well at lower frequencies. The upper frequency depends on several factors such as cable dimensions and attenuation. The stream of information that goes on the transmission lines passes through various filters (electronic devices), which allow only those frequencies which are needed at different points. On a coaxial highway, there are provisions to inject channels originating from wayside stations and recover part of the stream of traffic.

TV Signals on Cables

Coaxial cables can carry TV signals also, but to a limited extent. The frequency range of a video signal is from zero to 5.5 MHz and that of the audio programme, from 50 Hz to 10 KHz. Both cannot go on the same charmer as the signals will overlap. Moreover, power cannot be fed on the same cable. However, one-way transmission of TV signals from outside the studio is economical up to a distance of 10 km. This would be useful where high-rise buildings make microwave transmission of TV signals impossible or cumbersome with several antennas.

At the time of Independence in 1947, the trunk network in India consisted entirely of open-wire routes. Improved cable carrier systems were introduced in the 1950's. The first coaxial system was installed on the route from Delhi to Agra in 1959. Asansol. Varanasi, Allahabad, Kanpur, Jaipur, Udaipur, Ahmedabad and Bombay were soon connected. Later, the link from Bombay was extended to the south via Pune, Belgaum, Bangalore, Madras, Coimbatore, Ernakulam and Trivandrum. The Madras-Calcutta route was commissioned in 1974. The systems range from 300 to 10,800 channels. Another feature of the Indian network is the programme to augment the capacity of the existing cables. For example, a 4 MHz system can be upgraded to a 12 MHz system so that more channels can be sent on the same cable. Only at the repeater points, the cable has to be cut and rejoined to the new repeater equipment. Repeaters housed in huts on the ground are put underground, as more reliable components are available.

An area that is not so glamorous but very relevant in the urban context is the huge investment on copper that gets buried in a network. In some systems, copper accounts for almost one half of the total investment. Several efforts are under way to economise its use and find a substitute. The efforts include the use of plastic insulated and sheathed cables, cheaper joining techniques, aluminium conductors, use of air pressure in the cable to detect punctures which otherwise show up only during the monsoon and the introduction of Pulse Code Modulation, by which more speech signals can be sent on the same pair of wires.

Undersea Cables

Telephone calls across the Atlantic were first sent in 1927 as radio waves reflected off the ionosphere. It was only in 1956 that the first Trans-Atlantic Cable (TAT-1) was opened, providing for just 36 conversations between Oban (Scotland) and Claren Ville (Newfoundland). Soon afterwards TAT-2 was laid between the UK and France. The capacity of TAT-l was increased by an innovative method. The technique was called Time Assignment Interpolation (TASI), which doubled the number of speech channels. Essentially it did so by connecting the talker to a channel only when a signal is present. A new modulation system was also used, under which the 4 KHz voice channel was reduced to 3 KHz. The distance between channels was also shortened to 100 or 200 Hz. As a result, 72 channels—double and designed capacity—were obtained.

The spread of undersea cable truly began with the invention of the light-weight cable and long-life repeaters by the British Post Oflfice (as it was then called). The new cable was laid for the first time in 1961 in Cantat-1 between Scotland and Newfoundland. Later, the cable was used in other links. The turning point came with *repeaters,* the wonder electronic devices, that are put into the cable at regular intervals to amplify calls during their undersea journey. The gain of the signals varies with changes in sea temperature. Without repeaters, pre-War cable routes could hardly go beyond 130 km.

The man who pioneered the introduction of the world's first silicon transistor used in submarine cable repeaters is Dennis Baker (b. 1933). With the new device. repeaters were certified as reliable for 20 to 25 years, as long as the cable was in good condition. The performance of the transistors was checked under above-normal conditions. One test, for example, confirmed that it would take 26 years for a little gas to get out of it. The repeater needs little power, unlike valve amplifiers.

Semiconductor devices were first used in the links with Europe TAT-5 between the USA and Spain was laid in 1970 with a capacity of over 720 circuits. In 1974. Cantat-2 was opened between the UK and Canada, with 1,840 circuits, which was then the biggest single telephone cable across the Atlantic. It was soon followed by TAT-6 with 4,000 circuits between the USA and France. The next link. TAT-7, with another 4,200 circuits was started in 1983 with a video conference between London and New York. It could handle, besides phone calls, computer data and telex between the USA, Canada and Europe. The latest is TAT-8 between Europe and North America. It carries the first-ever optical fibre link and can transmit the equivalent of 40,000 simultaneous phone calls. It transmits voice, computer and video calls as pulses of laser-generated light over hair-thin glass circuits laid across

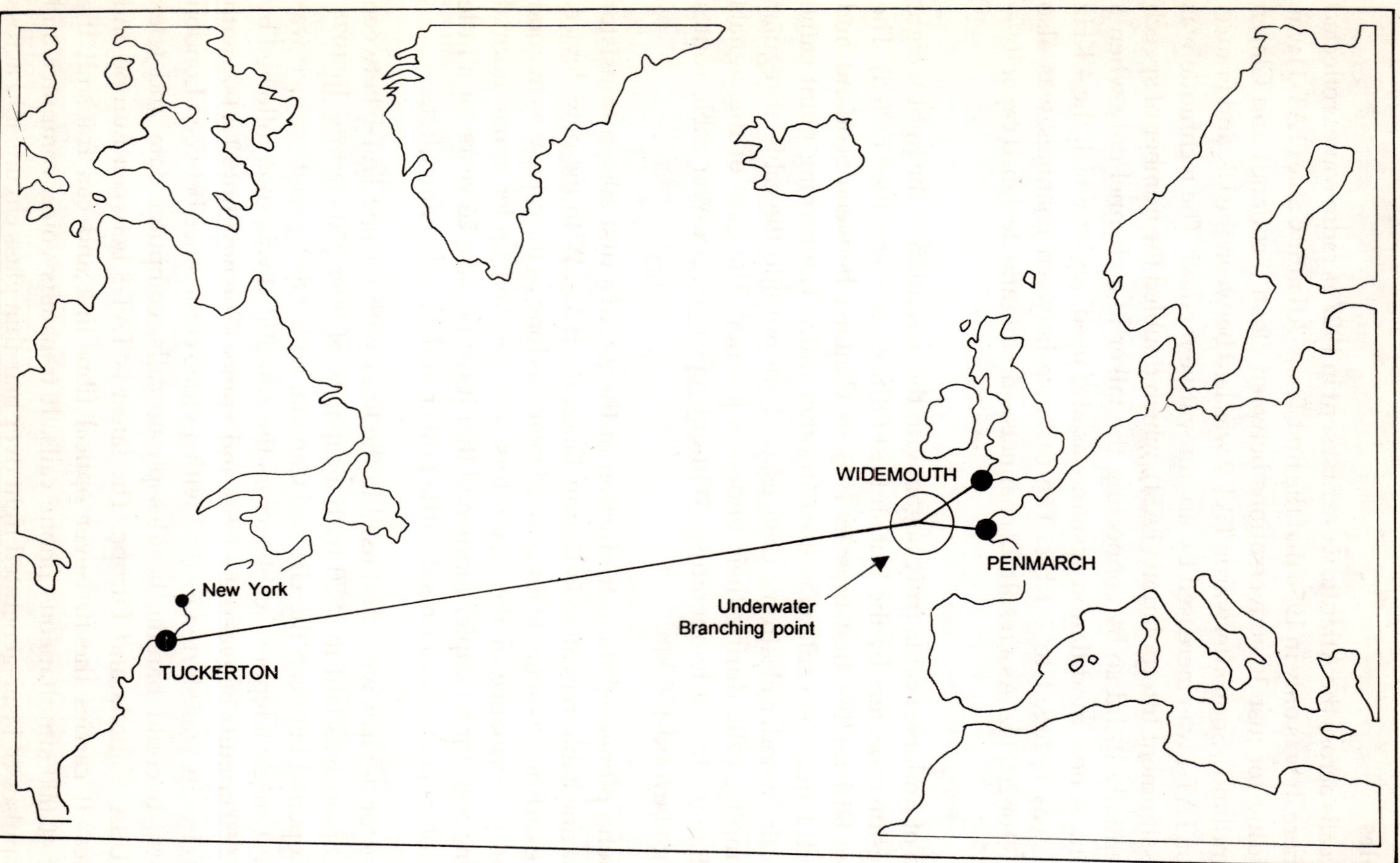

Fig. 20: *Transatlantic Optical Fibre Link* (TAT-8): The first seven cables under the Atlantic are conventional links, though with long-lasting repeaters.

the floor of the Atlantic. It has another first, viz. a sea-floor junction box, thus enabling it to land in three countries (Fig. 20). TAT-8 is joined by the first fibre optic cable under the Pacific. A second transatlantic link, TAT-9. will be ready in 1991-1992, with a capacity of 80,000 calls at a time.

The cable system is watched for defects with the aid of a computer. Checks are automatically made every few minutes. Faults are detected and alarms sounded at terminals. In the early period cables were laid along existing shipping routes. Today it is possible to avoid-deep trenches, stay clear of earthquake centres and rough mountain ranges under the sea. Oceanographers supply a lot of data on all these features. Cables can be cut and washed away by earthquakes, landslides, ship anchors and trawlers. Most of the damage occurs in shallow waters. TAT-6. for example, is the first telephone cable to be laid to a depth of 2,000 metres to avoid interference from fishing fleets. Specially equipped cable ships keep the cables in good repair.

A Good Complementary

The increase in undersea cable capacity has made the system a good complementary to satellites. Links to distant countries go through satellites as well as cables. For examples a call from Bombay to New York goes via satellite up to the UK and from there, through the undersea cable. The use of two satellites—a 'double hop—is avoided in view of technical problems.

Cables that can handle phone calls and other services are called *wideband links.* While such links are increasing in the Atlantic and in the Pacific, there are only few of them in the Indian Ocean areas. One of the world's longest undersea telecommunications cable called ANZCAN runs more than 15,000 km (8,100 nautical miles) between Australia, New Zealand, Fiji, Hawaii and Canada. Inaugurated in 1984, it can carry 1,380 simultaneous phone circuits on the major route between Canada and Australia. It meets the growing demands for data transmission, telex and facsimile. An undersea optical fibre cable has also been laid between Guam and the Philippines.

INVISIBLE HIGHWAYS

Long-distance transmission no longer depends on the undergound cable alone. Radio waves above 1,000 MHz. called *microwaves,* are used to transmit telephone, telegraph and television signals.

Microwaves behave like light waves and travel straight as line-of-sight over a flat terrain. Microwave signals usually travel up to 80 km from normal antenna heights, without being obstructed by the earth's curvature. The actual distance, however, depends on the nature of the terrain and propagation factors. Repeaters are needed to transmit them over long distances. The repeaters receive the signal through the antennas and transmit it after amplifying it. The usual repeater spacing is 40 to 50 km. but it can be longer, depending on the line-of-light condition. For example, the hop between Tiger Hill and Katihar in north-east India, is 186 km long.

The use of microwave links followed the deployment of radar during the Second World War and the development of antennas and related radio equipment. The commercial use of microwaves in the United States began in 1984 for the transmission of TV and telephone signals.

A 240-channel telephone system was first commissioned between New York and Boston. Subsequently, one video channel for television was also provided. By 1962, most of inter-city video circuits and a little less than half the long-distance telephone circuits in the USA were carried on microwave links.

The capacity of the microwave channels increased considerably after solid-state components became available. It was possible to transmit on one radio bearer channel 2,700 telephone circuits as against 240 in the early days. With the same antenna, several radio channels can be transmitted, though at different frequencies. In the USA, more than 20,000 channels are used in each direction on a single antenna, using different radio frequency bands.

In India, microwave systems capable of carrying 1,800 telephone channels or one colour TV programme on a single radio frequency channel have been installed. Systems of similar capacity have been developed and are under production indigenously.

Direct and Reflected Waves

When energy is transmitted at microwave frequencies from one point to another, there 'may be four different types of waves. There are surface waves and sky waves, which are not important for mircrowave transmission. While microwaves generally go as direct wave signals, reflected waves are also important in some cases. In a point-to-point system, the antenna's beamwidth is such that reflections from the ground are always present.

While land acts as a rough surface, still water presents a smooth surface. If the surface is rough, the energy is dispersed and less not affect the transmission. whereas water can reflect the signal (Fig. 21).

Compared with the direct signal, the reflected signal may be weak or even absent. But when it is strong, it may either add to the signal strength or cancel it completely. It all depends on what is known as *phase difference*. When the two signals are in phase with each other, they may be added. If they are of equal strength, the combined signal will be twice as strong as either of them. If, on the other hand, they are on phase opposition, they may cancel each other.

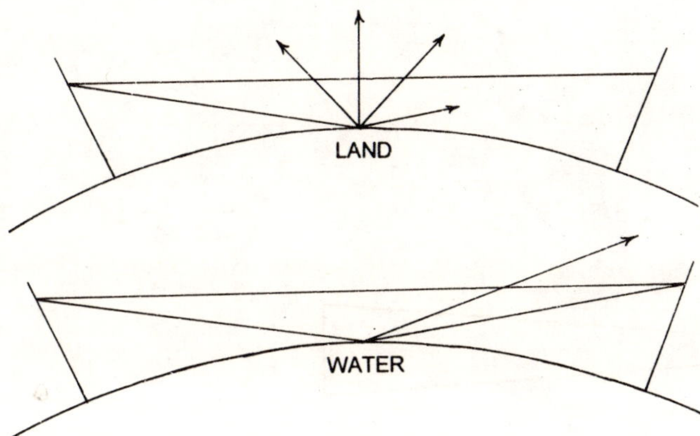

Fig. 21: Land acts as a rough surface and disperses the energy, whereas still water can affect transmission by reflecting the signal.

Studies indicate that reflectivity is acceptable up to 130 per cent If water is to be crossed, the height of the antennas should be adjusted to avoid reflection from water. Calculations have to be made to ensure correct relation-ship between the direct and reflected signals at the receive-end.

Microwave signals spread as they advance, like a torchlight beam. A one-degree beam, spreads to about one km at a distance of 50 km. Theoretically, the beam does not remain just one but tans out as an infinite number of beams. Each component of the wave has its own path subject to reflections and refractions. Also the power of the transmitted beam gets reduced as it travels along. The received signal is feeble and hence the output from the transmitter has to compensate for it. A power amplification of 10,000,000,000 is necessary.

The Problem of Fading

The received signal fluctuates in intensity and hence special steps are necessary to minimise fading. One way of doing it is to send the same information either on two paths or on two frequencies. It is safe to presume that both will not fade at the same time (Fig. 22).

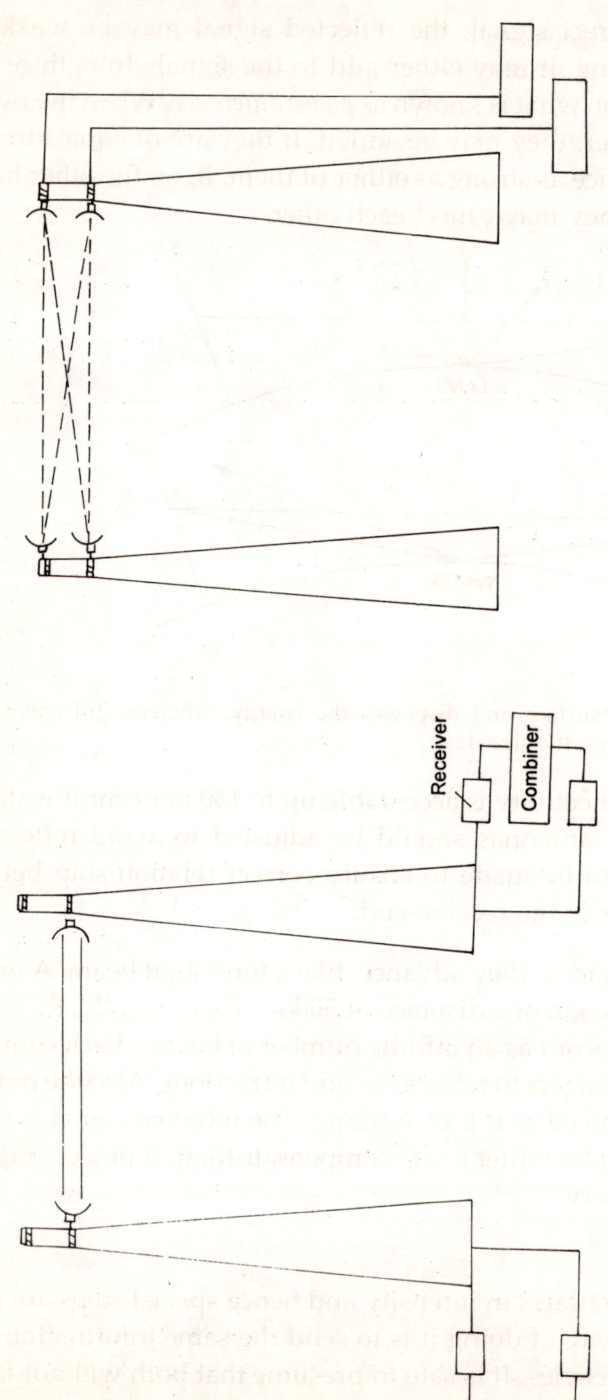

Fig. 22: Two methods of ensuring reliability of microwave signals in transmission. Frequency diversity method (left) employs different frequencies to send the same information, while the space diversity technique has two more paths of transmission on the same frequency.

Where there are two paths of transmission, the technique is called *space diversity*, while the other method is known as *frequency diversity*. In space diversity, the same frequency is used but there are two antennas, separated vertically Transmission and reception of information are over two paths. In frequency diversity, two different frequencies are used to send the same information. This technique is less expensive and simpler to operate and maintain. However, the number of frequencies available for use is a limiting factor. Different frequencies have to be spaced out in order to avoid mutual interference as well. This depends on the antenna capacity and the frequencies used.

Space diversity is used in some cases, where economic and operational advantages are in its favour. The provision of two antennas in this method and the related items in duplicate will, of course, add to the cost. The vertical spacing of the antennas has also been studied, since increase in tower height costs more. It appears that vertical spacing of the antennas can be reduced as higher frequencies are used. For example, at 2 GHz, a spacing of about 20m to 26m is necessary, while at 11 GHz, the spacing need be only 18m to 10m.

Space diversity can be done only on a per hop basis. In other words, every repeater station must provide for two antennas and each individual radio frequency channel must have its own diversity. Since both the channels are used for the same message, occasional use of either of then for transmitting other messages cannot be made.

Whether the same message is received through two different antennas or on two frequencies, the incoming signals are received separately but combined together for output. Suppose the paths of transmission vary in length the signal will not be received properly. At 6 GHz. for example, a difference of just about an inch will make the two signals out of phase. Hence provision has been made to sense automatically the distortion, and correct it.

Ensuring Reliability

Reliability of the signal depends on many factors. They include the height of the path, the length, the terrain, the weather and the frequencies used. In the Calcutta Belmuri microwave section, for example, humidity and temperature often affect the propagation of the transmission waves. Even when there is no interference from other channels, there could be thermal noise intrinsic in the system. Again, when two-or more frequencies are mixed, there could be intermodulation noise and there could be interference by another signal. The long wave guides, which conduct the signals from the antenna down to the equipment room, can cause noise.

In order to ensure reliability of the link, it is usual to provide for a hot standby, which comes into operation immediately in case of failure of one channel group. For example, the main microwave route between Delhi and Bombay has two groups of 1.800 telephone channel capacity each, while a third group of similar capacity acts as a standby. It has what is known as *protection switching*, which senses the failure of the traffic- bearing channel group and automatically switches on the standby. While doing so, it can be programmed to give priority to message traffic or to TV transmission. A no-break power supply is provided for at the repeater stations and remote supervision is done. The master control in the system knows what is happening all along the Line.

Dropping Signals

Sophisticated systems have been developed to carry the microwave signals over short and long distances. Different techniques have been evolved, depending on whether the signals are required to be 'dropped' en route at repeater points for interconnecting with the local telephone or TV network, or needed only at the final destination. Accordingly, there are two types of repeaters, called *baseband repeaters* and *intermediate frequency repeaters*. Each of them provides a different way of modulating the microwave carriers (see Appendix 2 for details).

The incoming signal at a repeater station is sent out at a slightly different frequency so as to avoid the problems of interference. A difference of at least 100 MHz is kept between the incoming and outgoing signals. If the repeaters are kept in a straight line, the signals from repeater A meant for B, may over-reach to repeater D. To avoid this the location of repeaters is carefully planned. In a six-hop link, for example, the microwave signal is received and transmitted six times from one modulation station to another.

The present bands allocated to fixed microwave links are in the range of 2 GHz to 13 GHz and are generally around 2,4,6 and 7 GHz. If frequencies higher than 10 GHz are used, repeater stations have to be placed closer because of the attenuation of the signals by rain.

VHF Links

Where broadband channels are not required, radio links can be used on Very High Frequency (VHF: 30-300 MHz) and Ultra High Frequency (UHF: 300-3,000 MHz) bands. The lower limit is around 30 MHz, where the ionosphere does not play a part in reflecting the signals. The upper limit lies below those frequencies for which microwave systems are used, In practice the upper limit is 1,000 MHz.

In the VHF, up to 24 channels and in the UHF, 60 to 120 channels are possible.

Where television is not required, there could be a choice between VHF and UHF. Such links could be provided between local and the bigger exchanges, when they cannot be satisfactorily or economically connected by fixed junction cables.

In the frequency spectrum of 30 MHz to 1,000 MHz, the bandwidth requirements for these links are small. At lower frequencies, severe reflections can still affect the signals, even over rough terrain. UHF links, generally providing 60 telephone channels, are installed on routes that are yet to pick up traffic. When warranted by traffic needs, a full-fledged microwave system is provided on such routes. UHF links are ideally suited to routes covering rugged terrain. Such systems working on 400 MHz are part of the national VHF links and can also be used in the countryside for contacting adjoining villages, without laying underground telephone cables or overhead wires An Indian equipment, called the Rurafone, can convert the telephone speech signals into VHF radio waves to be beamed to another antenna in a nearby village or town. There it can terminate or be linked further into the telephone network. A village near Allahabad can, for example, contact a village near Delhi in this manner. The call will go through the Allahabad and Delhi exchanges. Essentially Meant to cater to low traffic areas. VHF links can be— economical in some, cases.

Bharat Electronics Ltd. has developed and manufactured equipment for civil users in the VHF, UHF and microwave ranges. The products include receive-only antennas for television reception from the satellite, VHF runnel-to-train communication system for the Calcutta Metro Railway, digital radio relay equipment for the Railways, oil and gas pipeline communication, power networks and the police and wildlife boards.

Troposcatter Link

Radio waves at microwave frequencies are normally used for line-of-sight communications. But there are regions where the repeater towers required for microwaves cannot be located. Mountains or lakes or inhospitable terrain are such places where microwave links cannot be established. Normal radio communication is of course possible but it is subject to fluctuations of the ionosphere.

In such areas, another way of establishing communications is followed. Instead of making use of the ionosphere, this method will utilise the region below it, called the *troposphere.* This is the region in the earth's lower atmosphere. The turbulence in the troposphere scatters the microwaves and some of the waves bounce back towards the earth. These waves become 'visible' to aerials far beyond the horizon. It is like the glow of a searchlight, even though its beam is not visible. The tropospheric scatter communication demands a powerful radio signal. Even then its usable return signal gets reduced in strength by one hundred million, million, million times! They can still be detected by special techniques to provide good quality communications.

The first recorded investigation of troposcatter was reportedly made by Marconi in 1933. A practical tropo link was proposed in 1952 by Bell Telephones. Its first application appears to be for defence purposes. The capacity for a tropo link is generally limited to 120 channels, while some systems have 300 channels. Tropospheric links can span up to 800 km without repeaters. Typical spans cover 240 km. Very high power transmitters are necessary. They vary from 200w for low capacity to 1 kw to 10 kw. Fifty or 100 kw may be used for long spans up to 800 km. In order to cope with the increasing power transmission demands, special billboard antennas are put up for tropo links. High-gain parabolic antennas, with a diameter of 10 m to 40 m are used.

A low-noise receiver is put up at the receiving end. The receiver gets several paths of signal. One radio path alone may be risky as it is subject to fading. A combiner is kept so as to combine the different signals and give the best output.

High reliability of the system is ensured by a process known as *quadruple diversity*. This is a method of sending the message signals simultaneously by four independent paths, using two transmitters and four receivers. The signals at the receiving end are continuously combined to give a steady output. The turbulence of the received signal level causes fluctuations and rapid fading of the signal. Since a large number of signals arrive at the receiving point, studies can be made on the impact of noise on the signal.

Space and frequency diversity methods can be used to transmit the message. In space diversity, the receive-antennas should be kept sufficiently apart to allow for proper reception. In the case of frequency diversity, separation of frequencies is required.

The system is planned in such a manner as to minimise the scatter angle, thereby reducing the loss of the signal. In selecting the sites for locating the high-power transmitters, great care has to be taken to avoid radiation hazard. The transmission frequency could range from 800 MHz to 2 GHz. Some of these frequencies may affect the normal line-of-sight microwave communications. This fact too has to be kept in view. One way out would be to go in for space communication, provided a satellite and ground facilities are available.

Across the Himalayas

A troposcatter link has been established by India with the Soviet Union across the

Himalayas. There are ground stations on either side, one at Chari-Shariff, 23 Km from Srinagar and the other near Dushanbe in the Soviet Union.

The terrain is such that normal microwave links are not feasible. However, even the normal troposcatter link is not found suitable. Hence the engineers evolved what is known as *double diffraction tropo.* In this method, two peaks in the Himalayas, about 5,000 metres high, diffract the microwaves beamed from one side towards the other. In this way, the long distance involved, viz. 700 km, is covered without any intermediate repeater.

The antennas have the shape of large parabolic billboards. At each of the ground stations, two antennas of 30 by 30 metres, are set up to ensure proper reception. The transmitters have high power amplifiers of 10 to 15 kw. There is simultaneous transmission of two frequencies with each frequency having three transmissions. Both frequency and space diversity methods can be used. As many as 12 paths can be used to derive the signal and there is provision to get the best signal output. The link gives 12 voice grade circuits of international standard. It can be used to put through telephone, teleprinter and telex messages. The channels are connected to New Delhi and Moscow. The International calls are switched through the gateway exchange of the Overseas Communication Service in Delhi. In the UK, tropo link is used for contacting oil-drilling platforms located 150 to 300 km away from the mainland in the North Sea. The men working on the oil and gas platforms can use the public telephone service by direct dialling to places throughout the UK and to many places abroad. It is called *trans-horizon microwave radio.* In India, the Institute of Technology. New Delhi demonstrated its capability to set up a tropo link with Pilani, in Rajasthan. It was a successful experiment. Bharat Electronics Ltd. has developed a digital mobile troposcatter system.

Microwave Links in India

In India coaxial cables were first used since their power requirements were less than those of the microwave systems. In the early 1960's the availability of semiconductors in the microwave systems reduced the power needs drastically.

The need for reliable communication links with the border areas was keenly felt in the beginning of the sixties. The terrain in the north-eastern areas is not ideal for coaxial systems. It was therefore decided to import some microwave systems, while development within the country was initiated.

The Telecommunication Research Centre (TRC) of the then Post and Telegraphs Department was entrusted with the development of microwave systems. A 300-

channel narrowband system was taken up in the 7-GHz band. A link set up in the laboratory covered hardly 25 metres between two rooms. Yet, like all beginnings, it was a small but significant and proud moment for Indian technology. The first field link was set up in 1966 between Calcutta and Asansol.

Soon the 7-GHz narrowband system was made at the Indian Telephone Industries Limited in 1968. The first results were not satisfactory but gave quite a few lessons for improvement. Though the system was not capable of working on long distances because of noise limitations, it was satisfactory for short links. The problem of proper power supply was solved with the help of silicon power transistors.

Later, broadband (over 960 channels) systems were tried. It soon became evident that the performance depended on perfect subsystems. An analysis made in the early seventies showed that in addition to the increase in services and routes, the needs of defence, railways and the satellite would justify a development programme of microwaves. After a survey of the practices abroad, new methods of construction were adopted and R & D decisions taken to make wideband microwave systems. In addition to systems for services, equipment for satellite and troposcatter communication was also made.

Progress of Links

In the first phase of microwave links in the north-eastern region, there were both wideband (high capacity such as 1,200 telephone channels) and narrowband (low capacity such as 300 channels) systems with imported equipment.

A wideband system linked Calcutta and Asansol, while a 240-channel narrowband system connected Asansol with Katihar. Tiger Hill, Cooch Behar. Shillong, Jorhat Dibrugarh and Tinsukia. Similarly, on the northwestern side, Jalandhar and Srinagar were linked by a narrowband system.

In order to gain time some trunk routes were linked by radio systems imported from Canada and Hungary. The Canadian system covers the 'northern triangle' connecting Delhi. Bombay, and Calcutta. The Delhi-Bombay link, totalling 1,080 km. goes via Jaipur, Kota, Indore, Dhulia and Thana. Dhulia is a cross-over point to Calcutta via Nagpur, Raipur, Sambalpur, Jamshedpur, and Kharagpur. The Calcutta-Delhi route has two phases, one via Kharagpur, Asansol. Patna. Gorakhpur and Lucknow, and another via Lucknow, Kanpur, Etawah and Agra.

These links have TV transmission capacity also. The provision of large blocks of circuits alongwith alternate paths by way of coaxial cable gave for the first time the facility to diversify traffic, in case of failure of any one medium. On several occasions, the microwave system had taken over, when the coaxial cables on the same route were snapped, without the knowledge of subscribers. In addition, traffic can also be diverted through alternative routes. Traffic from Delhi to Bombay can be partly routed through Calcutta, if need be.

Indian equipment has been used on the 960-channel Pune-Secunderabad (540 km). Indore-Bhopal, Ahmedabad-Nadiad and other routes. The last mentioned route has TV transmission capacity: More links, with TV handling provision built into them, have been set up.

Standing as silent sentinels of progress in telecommunications are the microwave towers with their saucer-like antennas, overlooking dense forests, desolate deserts, snowbound peaks, lush green hills and busy cities. They transmit through free space thousands of telephonic conversations and telegraphic messages across vast distances with a clarity which could not have been imagined in the days of the open wire.

The success of these vital links depends on continuous and dedicated effort on the part of hundreds of engineers and technicians. The maintenance men often work in the early hours of the day, when traffic is light. Several of the repeater stations are situated on hill tops, tar away from human settlements. With inadequate water supply and bad approach roads, it take hours of climbing to reach some of them. Strong winds and snow blizzards hamper the work in places like Jammu and Kashmir. where the workers go up to 3.000 metres to clear the snow blocking the microwave reflectors.

Varied Uses of the Radio Spectrum

Broadcasting news or entertainment is only one of the uses of the radio spectrum. Telecommunication engineers use it to establish phone and telegraph links with overseas centres. The high frequency portion of the spectrum is also used to maintain vital links with ships, remote areas, oilfields, project sites, mines and dams and to get data on the weather and readings from distance gauges and instruments. Other parts of the spectrum are used for mobile communications for the benefit of cars, taxis, ambulance and the police. Persons on the move can also be contacted with the help of radio waves.

Coastal radio stations handle a wide range of messages, from distress calls to intimacies exchanged between sailors and their friends on shore. Besides putting out weather reports, the stations help in connecting the vessels to various places in the world through their national network.

There is an agreed order of priority for radio communications relating to ships.

SOS, the familiar distress call, will be attended to first. It has a code 'May Day'. Frequencies have been reserved for such messages in both telegraphy and telephony. This is followed by urgent and safety messages and those relating to radio direction finding, navigation and other traffic.

Round-the-Clock Vigil

The telecommunications coastal stations in India broad-cast weather-in-general messages and navigation warnings regularly. They keep a round-the-clock vigil on the distress frequency, viz. 500 KHz on wireless telegraphy and on 2.182 KHz for radio telephony. The distress messages are promptly picked up and passed on to the naval and port authorities for arranging rescue operations. The stations handle telegraph and telephone traffic between ships and shore stations. Ships belonging to various nations avail themselves of these services. Contacting ships is facilitated by long-range radio telephony. Bombay has a 20 kw transmitter for the purpose. It can contact ships even in the Atlantic Ocean. Calcutta and Madras have long-range transmitters on the high-frequency bands. Other stations offer medium frequency transmissions that can reach up to 160 km.

Modern ships provide radio telex facilities on board. Messages containing detailed orders, change of route instructions for cargo handling are flashed and printed on shore. The equipment is so perfected that it can automatically detect and correct errors. Ships with suitable equipment can also establish instant links with the INMARSAT maritime/satellite system.

For short-range communication near the coast, VHF channels are used to provide radio telephone facility. The facility is generally available up to 64 km and besides big ships, yachts and leisure craft avail themselves of it.

Snow, Goats and the Wireless

High-frequency radio waves are used for maintaining communication links with remote and inaccessible places. Over 200 such wireless stations are working in India. Most of them are in snowbound areas such as Leh, Kargil, Bharmour, Pooh and Kalpa in the Himalayas. The wireless links provide the only means for the people in the area to remain in touch with the outside world.

One such place is Keylong in Himachal Pradesh. Situated at a height of 4,000 metres, the place can be reached though the still higher Rohtang Pass. Kilar is another high spot and mountain goats are used to carry provisions through the 5,000-metre high Sach Pass. The operators walk for a few days on glaciers to get there.

BIRDS IN ORBIT

Advances made in microwave transmission encouraged engineers to use satellites as reflectors in space to relay signals. Several advantages of satellite technology were perceived.

No repeaters are needed between a station and the satellite and signals are not lost because of the curvature of the earth. A satellite can 'see' a much wider area than a transmitter on a hill. Remote areas can be served, and difficult terrain or water will not pose problems in providing a direct link with a satellite. The quality of the links is excellent, subject only to the efficiency of the land-based links between the signal reception station and the end user. The satellite medium can provide diversity in a national telecommunication network which has microwave and coaxial cable links. A satellite system can provide new services such as nationwide television, high-speed data transmission, teleconference and computer interworking. International satellites provide clear links for voice, vision, and data transfer across continents. The satellites 'assemble' the biggest ever world audiences for witnessing important events simultaneously. The British Royal wedding, for example, was seen by an estimated 700 million people at the same time!

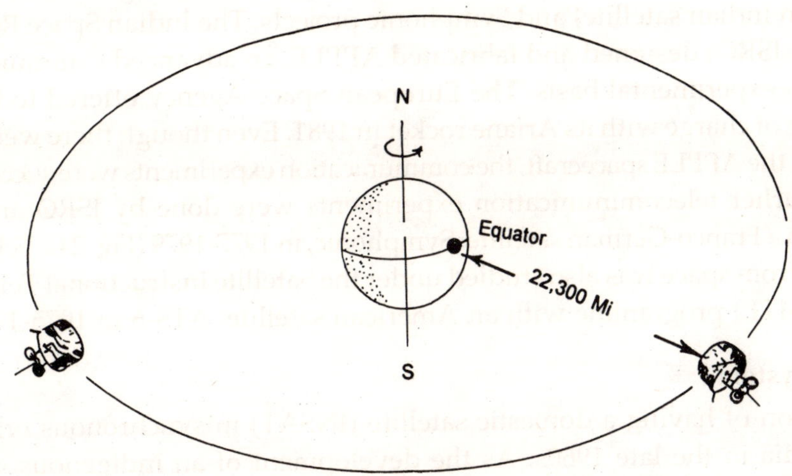

Fig. 23: Synchronous Orbit: A satellite in this orbit, which is about 36,000 km above the equator, appears stationary from the earth.

The idea of telecommunications through satellite became a reality in less than three decades. In 1945, the well-known science writer, Arthur Clarke proposed the use of the synchronous orbit for placing the communication satellites. Bigger rockets were developed which placed satellites in the desired orbit. The invention of the transistor of 1947 led to the production of lighter and more reliable equipment to amplify signals. In recognition of his contribution, the synchronous orbit is also called the 'Clarke Orbit'.

A communication satellite is generally in synchronous orbit about 36,000 km above the equator (Fig. 23). It is also called *gee-synchronous satellite,* which was developed by Harold Rosen. It appears stationary as its speed (10,360 km per hour) is synchronous with that of the earth (about 1,620 km). The satellite rotates in the same direction as does the earth, once every 24 hours countering the earth's gravitational attraction. A satellite is spun like a top to keep it steady: it could also be stabilised by other techniques. Onboard systems correct its path, while communication equipment handles the calls. A transponder on board a satellite receives the signal from the earth, filters it, amplifies it and retransmits it to a different point on earth. A transponder can generally carry 1,000 telephone conversations or one colour television channel. New frequencies are necessary as traffic increases. Space communication began with C-band (6 GHz and 4 GHz) and is also using K band (10 GHz-36 GHz) in addition.

Indian engineers acquired considerable experience in working satellite links in the APPLE (an Indian satellite) and Symphonic projects. The Indian Space Research Organisation (ISRO) designed and fabricated APPLE, an advanced communication satellite on an experimental basis. The European Space Agency offered to boost it into space free of charge with its Ariane rocket in 1981. Even though there were some problems with the APPLE spacecraft, the communication experiments were successfully conducted. Earlier telecommunication experiments were done by ISRO and P&T engineers with a Franco-German satellite. Symphonic, in 1977-1979 (Fig. 24). Television broadcasting from space was also studied under the Satellite Instructional Television Experiment (SITE) programme with an American satellite, ATS-6 in 1975-1976.

The INSAT System

The question of having a domestic satellite (INSAT) in synchronous orbit was studied in India in the late 1960s. As the development of an indigenous satellite would take time, it was decided to purchase a satellite from abroad and pay for its launch as well.

Normally, three separate satellites would be required for handling telecommunications, television and weather monitoring. Indian engineers suggested a three-in-one satellite to save money and to solve the problem of finding a suitable place for three separate satellites in space (Fig. 25). Accordingly a US firm (Ford

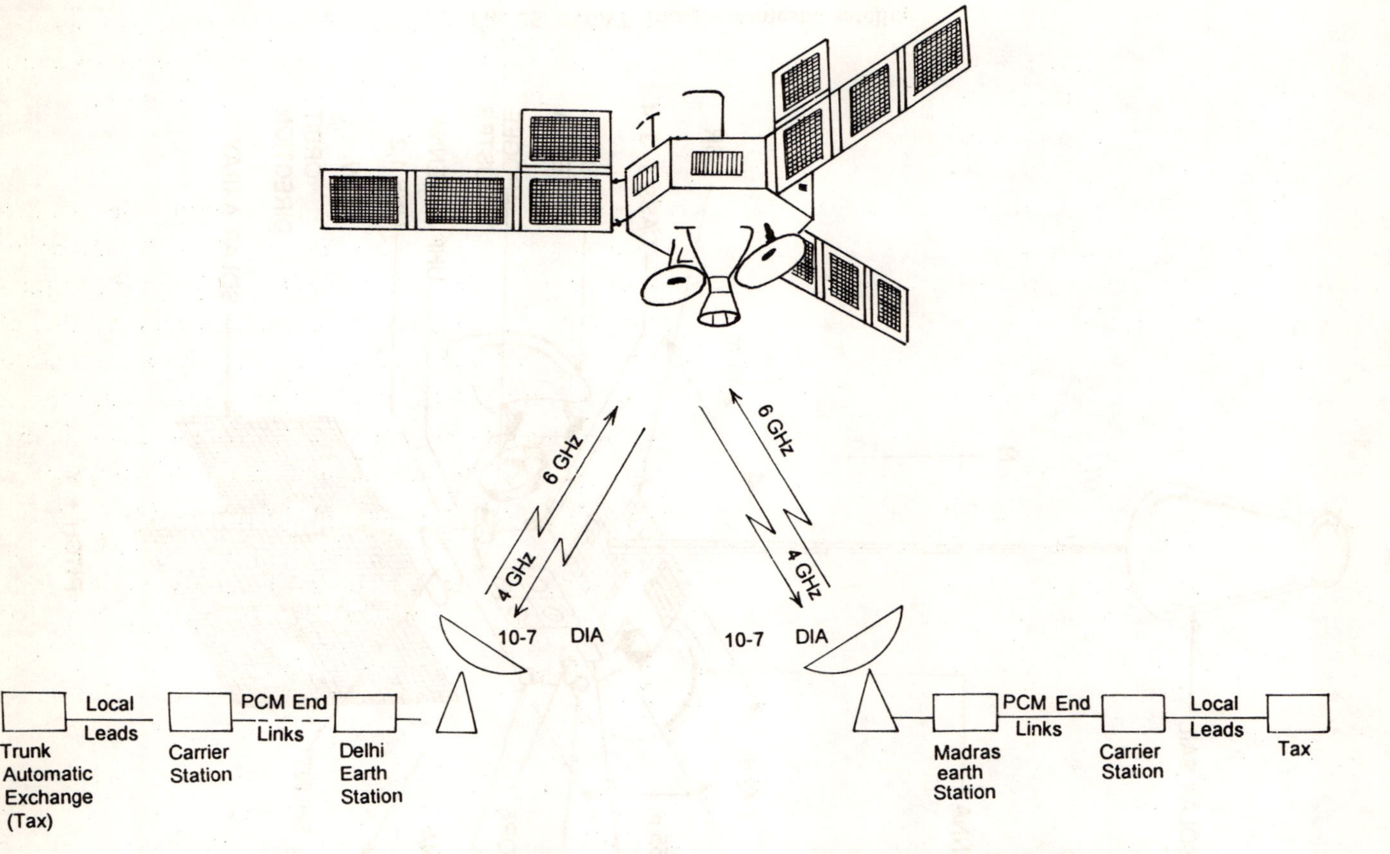

Fig. 24: A series of Indian experiments were done with the Franco-German satellite, Symphonle. In one of them, satallite circuits carrying trunk telephone calls were integrated with the automatic exchanges in different cities.

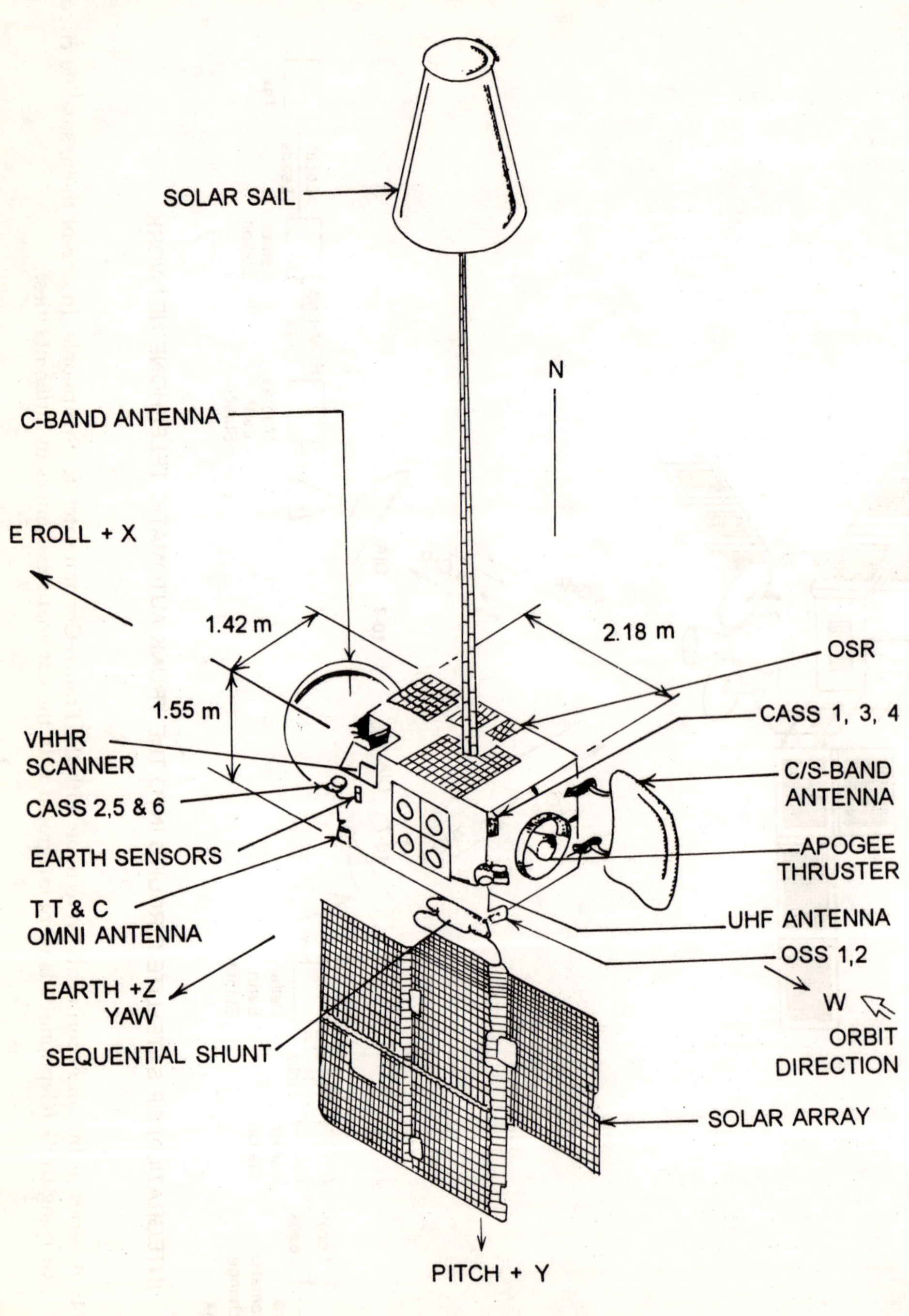

Fig. 25: INSAT: India's domestic satellite.

Aerospace) agreed to make the satellite. The US Space Agency, NASA, was given the contract to launch it. A Master Control Facility was set up in Hassan near Bangalore, from where Indian engineers can command the satellite and maintain it.

INSAT 1A was launched on 10th April 1982, but the C-band antenna of the satellite did not open. All the communication receive-equipment was connected to it. The next major snag came when the solar sail and its boom, designed to balance the spacecraft, did not open. Some thrusters were also blocked. Much of the fuel was lost in corrective manoeuvres. Though C-band was deployed later, and TV a d telecommunication services were operated for some months on a restricted scale, the satellite lost its earth lock during an eclipse (when the sun was hidden by the earth for some time) and subsequently, all contacts with the satellite were lost in September 1982.

An analysis showed that the basic three-in-one design was not to blame for the unexpected development. It was decided to make suitable modifications in the spare satellite INSAT 1B, which was taken aboard the US Space Shuttle. Challenger, and deployed in space by a team, of astronauts on 1 September 1983. There was some delay in getting it to its slot in space because of a temporary problem with the deployment of the solar array. After some anxious manoeuvres, an hour's heat soak in the sun unfreezed the solar array unexpectedly and normal deployment was resumed.

INSAT I B had indentical payload as INSAT 1A. Its communication equipment consisted mainly of 12 transponders (a receiver-cum-transmitter) which together gave roughly 4,300 two-way telephone circuits. Each transponder also handled up to two TV distribution channels. INSAT 1 B functioned well into its sixth year. INSAT 1C, launched in July 1988, had a power problem and only half its TV and communication capacity could be used. INSAT 1 D was launched in June 1990, and put into operational service.

Under the second generation INSAT 2 series, two test spacecraft (INSAT 2A and 2B) are being designed and built by India. Three more INSAT— 2C, 2D and 2E have been approved. The time-frame for orbiting the second series is 1993-1995. Each of the three will have significantly larger service capability than INSAT 1. (Some 28 C-band fixed satellite service transponders, two S-band broadcast satellite service transponders, a very High Resolution Radiometer with 2 km resolution in visible and 8 km resolution in infrared channels and facilities for weather data relay and for satellite-aided search and rescue missions).

The uplink from the ground stations is at a frequency of 6 GHz. while the

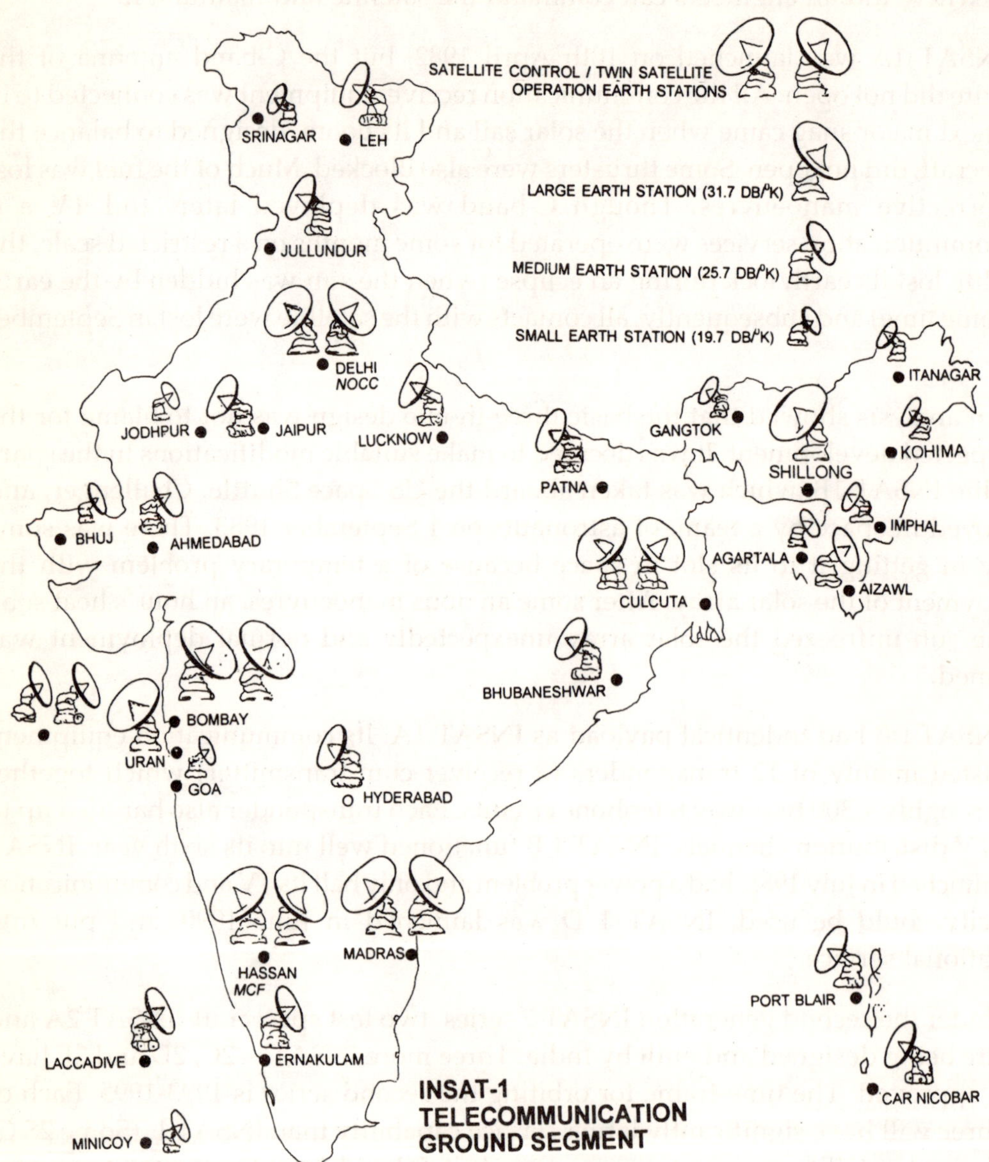

Fig. 26: INSAT Ground stations for telecommunications.

downlink is at 4 GHz for telecommunications. The ground segment, consists of 28 fixed telecommunication terminals, for linking three of the Oil and Natural Gas Commission terminals (one onshore at Uran and two offshore terminals, for linking the oilfields in the Arabian Sea) and three transportable stations (Fig. 26). The main telecommunication stations are in Delhi. Calcutta, Shillong. Bombay and Madras. The Network Operations Control Centre for monitoring and control of the earth station operations is co-located with the Delhi earth station situated in Bulandshahar district of Uttar Pradesh. The primary stations are mostly in State capitals. Smaller earth stations are located in remote areas such as Port Blair, Itanagar and Laccadives.

The Master Control Centre consists of two independent satellite control earth stations (with two 14m antennas) provided by the Space Applications Centre of the Indian Space Research Organisation and a satellite control centre, the equipment for which is provided by Ford Aerospace. SAC has also built all the earth station electronics. The Electronics Corporation of India Ltd. has supplied the reflectors while the Bhabha Atomic Research Centre has supplied the servo control system for the antennas.

INSAT provides two nationwide TV broadcast channels for direct transmission from satellite to augmented community TV receivers or to any of the TV stations. The 2.5 GHz transmitters can beam TV to any part of the country. The beam can be directly received by augmented television receivers. It can also be received by a TV station which can in turn rebroadcast the programme to normal, unaugmented TV sets within a specific area.

The initial scheme was to use direct satellite TV broadcasting service to clusters of selected (three) contiguous districts each in Andhra Pradesh. Bihar, Gujarat, Maharashtra, Orissa and Uttar Pradesh, using 8,000 direct reception sets, with an uplink facility to support. In addition, it was planned to start with four rebroadcast transmitters at Gorakhpur, Nagpur, Rajkot and Ranchi and provision of 6,600 community TV set besides provision of uplink facilities from Delhi and Shillong, a satellite TV receive-only terminals at all TV transmitting stations for relaying common programmes. The TV broadcast service has expanded rapidly.

There is growing demand for the use of Very Small Aperture Terminals (VSATs) working directly with a satellite, bypassing the terrestrial networks. VSATs have become essential for businessmen to get strategic information on finance and marketing without delay. The establishment of National Informatics Centre's VSAT Network, called NICNET, is in response to the needs of enterpreneurs.

INTELSAT—A Symbol of Progress

Even before INSAT, India became familar with operating global satellite links by its participation in the International Telecommunications Satellite Organisation (INTELSAT) set up in 1964. INTELSAT is a commercial not- for-profit cooperative of 119 member nations that owns and operates a global satellite system used worldwide for international as well as domestic communications. The world's first commercial satellite. INTELSAT 1, known as Early Bird was launched in 1965 and provided service over a single path between Europe and the USA. Today, global service is provided to almost 180 countries, dependencies and territories. A total of 15 satellites (1990) provide transoceanic telephone and television services besides international video, teleconferencing, facsimile, data and telex.

Fig. 27: INTELSAT VI, the latest in the series (above) and INTELSAT VII, due in 1992.

Each generation of INTELSAT has introduced significant innovations (Fig, 27). INTELSAT 1 was launched amidst doubts and uncertainties about the whole venture. However, it proved the concept technically with 240 telephone circuits. Though there was no multiple station access, its design life (18 months) was exceeded and it operated satisfactorily in continuous full service for over three-and-a-half years.

INTELSAT II introduced (1967) multi-point communications capability between earth stations. The next generation. INTELSAT III (1968) weighing four times as much as Early Bird—had 1,200 circuits or four TV channels or combinations thereof. It could transmit all forms of communications simultaneously—telephone, telegraph, TV, high-speed data and facsimile, it provided TV service without interrupting that of telephone or message service. INTELSAT III started the technique of stabilised antennas which could point at the earth precisely. INTELSAT IV (1971) increased the capacity to 4,000 circuits and 2 TV channel capacity. White it had two global transmit antennas, it had two steerable spot beam transmit antennas to serve the areas of high traffic density. It also provided links to smaller traffic routes on a demand assigned basis in places where full-time circuits are uneconomical INTELSAT IV A (1975) had 6,000 (two-way) circuits plus two TV channels. The additional capacity was obtained by the two-fold-re-use of in the C-band (6 and 4 GHz) by geographical separation into east and west beams. The next series, INTELSAT V, was the first three-axis, body stabilised (the earlier satellites were spin stabilised) spacecraft. It had solar arrays which can be deployed in orbit and provision for frequency re-use. Higher frequencies (14 and 11 GHz) were used in addition to the C-band. The capacity went up to over 12,000 circuits plus 2 TV channels. Digital techniques introduced onboard the satellite can send (if configured in an all-digital mode) one gigabit (1,000 million of information in a second. At that rate, the equivalent of the *Encyclopaedia Britannica* can be sent across the Atlantic some six times a minute! The satellite has increased capacity that would provide digital based business services, viz. high-speed text, data and facsimile and audio and video teleconferencing. INTELSAT VI (1989) has 500 times the capacity of Early Bird. Launched in 1989, INTELSAT VI has a capacity of 24,000 telephone circuits and 2 TV channels or up to 120,000 circuits with digital circuit multiplication equipment (Fig. 27). The satellite can transmit the equivalent of some 3.5 billion bits per second, which is enough to send the *Encyclopaedia* about 20 times every minute! Five INTELSAT VII satellites are scheduled for launch between 1992 and 1994.

It is noteworthy that over two-thirds of INTELSAT membership and one-third of its ownership belong to developing countries. Almost 40 countries rely on INTELSAT to meet domestic telecommunication systems. India too availed itself of the system for communicating with remote areas, prior to INSAT operation. Smaller earth stations were built for the purpose.

Two Earth Stations

For the international links through INTELSAT, two big earth stations, one in Arvi near Pune and the other near Dehra Dun, have been set up. They are identical, though more of indigenous equipment has been used in the Dehra Dun station. Both work with the Indian Ocean satellite of INTELSAT. At each station, the same antenna, about 30m in diameter, transmits and receives, the signals. The signals are transmitted at a microwave frequency in the 6 GHz band to the satellite in a very narrow beam. Dehra Dun is linked to New Delhi, while Arvi is connected to Bombay by a chain of repeater stations with antennas on high towers 'facing' each other on the 'line-of-sight' route.

The earth station's antenna can be steered plus or minus 270° and minus 1-1/2° to 90° in elevation so as to contact the satellite in space. The main dish is made up of a number of panels of cast aluminium alloy with a good surface accuracy. Although the antenna weighs 240 tons, it can be rotated rapidly and can track a satellite, about 36,000 km away to within one-fiftieth of a degree. It can track automatically *as* well as in a manual mode. Before commissioning the antenna, engineers performed a test to see whether the antenna was capable of receiving signals from a radio star, quite far away from the earth, unlike the satellite which is relatively nearer home.

Since the signals are very weak, they have to be cooled, using gaseous helium. This would reduce the noise and the signals are then carried by waveguides to the equipment room. The entire spectrum received from the satellite is available for 16 receive-chains. They can select 16 different carriers transmitted by as many countries. The receive-chains consist of down-convertors which convert the 4 GHz carriers to an intermediate frequency of 70 MHz and demodulators to get the baseband. The relevant portion due to the earth station is recovered. It can also send and receive TV signals from other countries in the world. One receive-chain, which is a standby, receives TV sound during a TV reception.

For transmission of messages and programmes, Dehra Dun has three transmit-chains, consisting of a baseband unit, modulator, up-convertor and high power amplifier. The baseband carrying traffic is received from the main station in Delhi Bombay.

Large antennas of 30-metre diameter are known as Standard *A* stations, with full versatility for receiving and transmitting all types of telecommunications. As the power of the satellite increased, small earth stations became economical. In 1976, INTELSAT, adopted a second earth standard requiring only a 10-metre dishshaped antenna with limited steerability. They use a transmission technique suited to make optimum use of the satellite in areas of moderate traffic and for operating domestic links. A standard B earth station can avail itself of one transponder to provide either a colour TV channel or 500 telephone circuits or a combination of black and white television and a limited number of telephone circuits. A dozen or more centres can be served by it.

Small Dishes

INTELSAT has outlined the specifications of 11 other standards for earth stations of varying diameters (including 3.3 m and 4.5 mi and capacity. Meanwhile, smaller antennas (3m, 5m or 7.7m in diameter) have become popular. Quite a few of the small dishes are on rooftops linking directly with the satellite. INTELSAT has provided a full-time private digital data service for collection and distribution of data, that need small terminals. Known as Intelsat Business Service, the facility is offered over the three ocean regions.

Small dishes have made a big difference in international communications. The small-dish satellite business communications service was first started between the UK and Canada in 1984 and was later extended to the eastern States of the USA. In India, another earth station (7-8 m in diameter) will be set up to work with an INTELSAT Atlantic Ocean region satellite. This will provide telecommunications diversity and flexibility for serving both Atlantic and Indian Ocean region customers.

INTELSAT has completed 25 years of service. A remarkable fact is that the reliability of INTELSAT operation has been 99.9 per cent continuously. Moreover, there has been more than a 30-fold decrease in the costs of using the INTELSAT system. The system has provided the first globally available international digital services. The system has also been pressed into service to aid the restoration of disrupted submarine cables.

Technological Progress

The technological progress made by communication satellites is remarkable in the early days of space links, the beam from a satellite covered one-third of the globe, and the energy (called Effective Isotropic Radiated Power or EIRP) over a wide ellipittcal area 'illuminated' by the satellite was stronger in the centre and weaker at the edges. This type of beam is still send by satellites. In order to catch the signal, huge earth stations are needed (such as the one in Arvi). As larger satellites could be deployed, more powerful signals could be generated on board and antennas could be steered to cover closely defined regions. Signals for specific geographical areas can be sent as spot beams. It is possible to re-use frequencies as different spot beams can use the same frequency. Larger satellites can put narrow but powerful beams which, can be received even by small rooftop antennas.

As the communication bands initially used (6-4 GHz) were also utilised by terrestrial microwave links, efforts were made to try higher frequencies, which were useful in sending more data. Some countries tried 11 and 14 GHz while some others such as Japan successfully tried 20-30 GHz. The problem with higher frequencies is that they are affected by rain. Generation of higher frequencies became possible with the development of a device called the *travelling wave* tube, which increases the input signal typically by 10,000 times.

The frequency available in a satellite can be used in different ways. Each repeater on board the satellite has its own assigned frequency range, which is divided into discrete bandwidths to serve various types of traffic. As in a terrestrial system, the space within the frequencies can be shared by different users. In one method, the power and bandwidth of the satellite are allotted on a fixed basis and are in constant use irrespective of the number of voice channels actually used. In another method known as the Single Channel Per Carrier (SCPC), the carrier is energised only during the actual speech and cut off during pauses in speech. If one person is speaking, only one carrier is energised. This method is useful for stations operating international public switched service in light traffic areas, whereas the normal pre-assigned method can serve medium traffic levels. The SCPC system can use a technique called Demand Assigned Multiple Access (DAMA), where the frequency is not pre-assigned to a station. The channel to be connected is assigned to any available frequency. This results in a virtual switch in the sky and the capacity of the satallite is effectively used. Widely scattered terminals can be served by this method without wasting a frequency on any lean station. In another technique, different earth stations can time-share a frequency. This is known as Time Division Multiple Access (TDMA). 'The system is suitable for medium and heavy traffic. Digital transmission techniques are used for it. Speeches are sampled and coded pulses corresponding to the samples are sent on the same frequency but sequentially in a 'burst' form rather that continuously. At 8,000 samples a second (with a 8-bit coding of each sample), there will be 64,000 bits per second per channel and for 30 channels there will be 2 Mega bits per second (Mbit/s). The satellite receives individual 'bursts' and broadcasts them back to all terminals, each of which divides the information frame into its component parts and selects the desired signals.

The communication payload on the Indian-designed and made geostationary satellite APPLE, operated for over 5,000 hours. Advanced communication technology experiments included Time Division Multiple Access (TDMA), Spread Spectrum Multiple Access (SSMA), Small Communication Terminals (SCOT), and TV with multiple audio. In the SSMA experiment, it was possible to provide for simultaneous access by more than one station to the entire bandwidth of the transponder of the satellite; the wanted signals are derived with the help of identifying codes. Yet another experiment done was Digital Speech Interpolation (DSI). This works on the principle that the telephone channel needs to be activated only when a person is speaking which is normally only 40 per cent of the time. The speech will be sampled at 8,000 pieces of a second and each sample given a digital code. This method can compress, for example. 240 channels into 120.

In addition, a computer in Bombay was routinely connected to another in Ahmedabad through the satellite enabling both ends to interact with the computer. The Bank of India conducted an experiment to speed up transactions between its offices in Bombay and Ahmedabad. Towards the end of the mission, a course on robotics (use of robots) was beamed through APPLE simultaneously for scientists in Bangalore, Madras, Ahmedabad and new Delhi. The signals were received in Bangalore through a transportable earth terminal. It was designed to receive and send one video and up to eight audio channels, with its own diesel generator for use in unelectrified areas India has developed a software expert programme, a new industry for computer operations. The programme can he exported electronically, with the assistance of Videsit Sanchar Nigam. India's signatory to INTELSAT.

Time Delay

The satellite transmission path is 71,000 km long andsignal propagation takes about 270 milliseconds. A user waits for the reply for 540 milliseconds (over half a set ond). This delay does not matter in terrestrial telephone signalling, but it becomes significant where what is known as *compelled multi-frequency register signalling is* the national standard. In this case, two round trip travel missions are required to confirm that a digit has been sent so that the next digit may be transmitted. The trunk automatic exchanges, which will handle the satellite traffic, will have to be adjusted to accept the signals from space and handle them. Tone detection time takes almost 1.2 Second or more to transmit. More time is needed to send automatic number identification information. All this results in long post-dialling delays. Several steps have been taken to shorten this delay. Semi-compelled signalling can be used by modifying the logic in the equipment in which, the return signal can be short pulling instead of continuous one. It will reduce digit transmission time from 1.2 to 0.8 second. Compelled signalling itself can be changed by another technique. To prevent hearing one's own voice, echo suppressors are provided. When a person talks, voice from the other end is blocked and released only when the other person finishes talking. Both cannot talk at the same time. The delay may be of little consequence to voice or broadcast traffic, though it can pose problems for computer to-computer communication or in calls routed through more than one satellite.

Besides INSAT and INTELSAT, there are several domestic as well as regional satellites in orbit. The USA, Canada, the Soviet Union, Europe, Japan, China, Indonesia, Australia and the Arab States have domestic satellite services. In April 1990, Asia's first privately-owned communications satellite was launched by China.

When INSAT proved inadequate, ARABSAT and a Soviet satellite were used to distribute domestic TV service in India.

Role of INMARSAT

Satellites have made maritime communication facilities quite reliable and readily available. No longer do the vagaries of the Ionosphere affect calls to ships at sea. Crowded radio channels need not pose a problem. Calls can be made to ships without delay. The organisation which has brought about this change is INMARSAT (International Maritime Satellite Organisation). It began operations in 1982 and several countries have acceded to its convention. Thousands of ship earth stations have been commissioned. These stations are installed on a wide range of vessels including oil tankers, cargo and container vessels, passenger ships and seismic survey vessels, besides oil drilling rigs. Several coast earth stations are in operation to provide links to national networks. Exploration and production of oil in the sea can greatly benefit from the new system.

INMARSAT provides high-quality telecommunication services round-the-clock to and from ships virtually anywhere in the world. In addition, it provides for distress alerts, group calls, data communication, facsimile and leased circuits with ships and coastal stations equipped for the purpose. In the ship-to-shore direction, high speed data service at 56 kilobits per second is also available. Ship-to-shore calls are automatic for both telex and telephone. Satellite telex is generally less expensive than Morse telegram.

For the first time, huge volumes of data relating to cargo, etc. can be made quickly available for use on shore.

The ship terminals use the L-band (1.5-1.6 GHz) mari-time frequencies and the coast stations use the C band (3.6-6.4 GHz) for communications. The communication subsystems Provides two Independent links for ship-to-shore (250 voice channels) and shore-to-shore (125 voice channels). The ship earth terminal-one metre in diameter-is stabilised adequately to 'look' at the satellite all the time even when the sea is rough.

The Crowded Orbit

The synchronous orbit is getting crowded. Since the orbit is about 36 000 km away, the earth's equatorial circumference at this distance is 300,000 km long. At present the satellites are placed 3° apart, creating a total of 120 positions. If the satellites can be brought nearer and located at an interval of 2°, 60 more positions can be created, reducing the distance between any two satellites from the present 2,200 km to less than 1,500 km This would require earth station antennas to produce" narrower beams, as otherwise they could spread so wide by the time it reached the orbit that it could interfere with nearby satellites. As the diameter of the ground antenna dish decreases, the beamwidth increases. But a new generation of small dish aerial developed by British Telecom International can reflect a beam (at 14 GHz) which is only 336 km wide when it reaches the orbit. The antenna has a parabolic dish reflector (5.5 m dia) The design is based on the geometry of an optical telescope invented by James Gregory, a 17th century Scottish mathematician.

The problem is complicated because the emission power and the received signal power very from satellite to satellite. There could be an overlap of high-power and low-power signals. Basically, interference arises because of the radio frequencies popularly used. viz. 6 and 4 GHz They are in demand as their propagation features are well known and as higher frequencies may not be technically possible in all cases. Also certain segments of the orbit are crowded as they are ideally suited to serve the countries below. The are over the Indian ocean is a popular place for locating several satellites. One consideration in deciding the location is the occurrence of eclipse which is invitable as it is caused by the earth's rotation around the sun. During the eclipse period, the satellite's onboard batteries have to supply the power needed. There is therefore a tendency to locate satellite over longitudes as far west as possible, so that the peak of the eclipse period occurs during midnight or near that time when not much traffic is expected. If an Indian Ocean satellite is located at 80° E longitude, for example, the peak of the eclipse period will be during midnight in India. The other consideration for location of satellites is the spread of its signals which can overspill into other countries. Interference can also arise as the bandwidth allowed for users (generally about 500 MHz) is almost always fully utilised by every satellite so that not much margin is left between satellites.

The solution to orbit congestion lies in negotiations among interested countries and organisations about the location, making adjustments in the technical features of the satellites involved. India's INSAT IB was at 74°E longitude, a place obtained after consultations with other parties concerned. For INSAT 1 D, India had notified its intention to locate it at 83°E, In practice, however, the trend has been to occupy the orbit on a first-come, first-served basis, except in a few cases. Developing countries feel that orbit slots must be reserved for a reasonable time till they are in a position to occupy them. India is of the view that access to the synchronous orbit and radio spectrum should be consistent with the requirements of a country, economic factors, technology status and effective use of the orbit and spectrum providing maximum benefit to all countries.

ITU has recognised that frequency assignment does not confer any permanent right or priority for anyone and that all countries have equal rights in the use of both orbit and radio spectrum. ITU holds international conferences periodically to solve the problem.

A SOUND AND LIGHT SHOW

The latest mode of transmission is provided by optical fibres. In 1966, two British scientists, K.C. Kao and G.A. Hockham, suggested that if pure glass could be drawn into thin fibres, information tarried on light could be sent over long distances. Within eleven years, the first fibre optic link was in operation in the UK carrying about 2,000 telephone circuits. The potential of optical fibres for use in telecommunication is enormous as in the higher frequency bands of the electromagnetic spectrum, larger bandwidth is available. The frequency of light is more than 1,000 times that of the highest microwave band in use. Telephone calls are conventionally sent pulses of electricity on normal telephone wires. Using optical fibres. pulses of electricity are turned into pulses of light, and the signals are transmitted and reconverted into electrical signals at the other end.

Three Types of Fibre

A bundle of optical fibres can easily pass through the eye of a needle Basically, an optical fibre is a very fine glass tube, consisting of a core and cladding. Both visible and infrared radiation can be transmitted. Total internal reflection keeps the radiation within the fibre. Basically two types of fibre are used: multimode and monomode (or single mode). Multimode fibres have relatively large diameter (50 micrometres) and their core and cladding have different densities. Light rays which are not absorbed by the fibre, *zigzag* their way by as many 250 different paths Depending on the angle of their entry into the fibre. The rays travelling longer take more time to pass than those going down the core of the fibre and pulses of radiation spread out. The time interval between the arrival of pulses should not be more than that allotted for the different bits of information.

In order to reduce the dispersion of light pulses, a graded index fibre is used, in which there is no fixed boundary between the core and the cladding. The glass in the core varies in density and its refraction varies continuously from high, in the core to low in the region away from it within the fibre. The light travelling the longest distance goes at the highest average speed. The arrival time of different rays is almost the same.

The other fibre, which is a second generation device, is called *single mode* (also known as *monomode)* as its core is so small (5 micrometres) that it allows only one ray path or mode and light travels straight. There is no loss of energy and the signal goes further.

A monomode fibre works best only with the coherent light from a laser, while a multimode fibre can use incoherent light sources such as Light-Emitting Diodes (LED). Semiconductor lasers or LEDs respond quite fast to handle the millions of pulses needed for transmission of information. A typical diode detector can handle a hundred million bits of information per second. Its scope can be imaged when we recall that a colour TV transmission needs only 90 million bits. A laser beam can transmit as many as 100,000 telephone conversations simultaneously or 100 different colour TV programmes. Infrared. generated by solid state lasers, is used because the glass used conducts it well, and laser light can be tuned sharply.

Ultra-Pure Glass

Optical fibres need ultra-pure glass. Even the best optical glass in the market is not suited for it, as it has impurities in the form of hydrogen and oxygen atoms that obstruct light. Even if one part of impurity in 100,000,000 parts of glass is present, it will absorb light. Glass of extra purity is therefore made for the purpose. It is,made from high purity silica, boron oxide and sodium carbonate. It takes about ten grammes of pure glass to make one kilometre of fibre. A common coaxial cable of 8 pairs measures about five centimetres (cm) in diameter, whereas a cable of 20 to 100 glass fibres would have a diameter of only one cm. Further refinements are under way. The most obvious quality of fibre is its transparency. A slab 20 km thick would transmit as much light as an ordinary window glass does!

Even a fibre system with pure glass would gradually absorb light. Light gets dispersed into its component wavelengths which arrive at minutely different moments. A small discrepancy of 5 billionth of a second, for instance, is enough to distort high-speed data message over a distance of 160 km. Silica fibres disperse the least light when the latter's wavelength is 1,300 nm.

It was also noticed that rays with longer wavelength travel further in the fibre allowing the installation of intermediate repeaters to boost signals further apart. Lasers were designed to transmit light at a longer wavelength. With monomode or single-mode transmission, repeaters became necessary only at every 30 km Instead of at every 10 km earlier.

New Records

In 1982, British Telecom in UK transmitted optical fibre signals without intermediate amplification over a distance of 102 km. The light pulses were sent at a rate of 140 million a second (140 Mbit/s) corresponding to 2,000 simultaneous phone calls. It was then the world's longest transmission on an optical fibre at that pulse rate, using the technology of long wavelength operation. The pulses transmitted were soon increased to 650 Mbit/s the same year (1982) but over a short distance of about 31 km in a test, while another record was set by installing the world's longest optical fibre line running 204 km between London and Birmingham. British Telecom has since developed and installed monomode fibre technology and is implementing the world's most comprehensive, optical fibre network in UK. Another feature worth noting is the introduction of optical fibres in the junction network interconnecting local exchanges. Those light lines' can carry four times as many calls as their copper wire equivalents do. Optical transmission is done at 1,300 run in graded index fibre.

Optical fibres are in use in other countries also. In the United States, the first commercial application of the new technology was tried in 1977 in Chicago. The test was made on 2-6 km cable, which had 24 fibres that could handle 7,000 phone calls. Today optical fibres are used not only in high-density metropolitan areas but also in office complexes and sports arenas. A commercial light wave system was announced in 1984 at the highest bit rate ever offered, viz. 1.7 Gbit/s (billion bits per second). In 1985 Bell Laboratories disclosed that they had developed an optical fibre system that would transmit 2 billion bits (2 Gbit/s) over a 1,128-km route.

Japan introduced in 1983 optical fibres on long distance lines (operating at 400 Mbit/s with a capacity of 5,760 telephone channels). The same capacity cable connected a large part of Japan with a route length of 3,400 km (including two submarine sections) in 1985. Additionally in the subscriber loop area, optical cables have been introduced for video transmission and high-speed digital leased circuit service. The next targets are development of 1.6 Gbit/s system for long-haul transmission and the multipurpose application in subscriber loops.

In India, the first optical fibre system (140 Mbit/s) has been set up between Ahmedabad and Baroda. More links are under way.

Many Advantages

Optical fibres, once described as science fiction, are now a commercial reality. The advantages they offer are far in excess of what is considered feasible with electrical signals. Their capacity to carry speech and data is virtually unlimited. In theory a single wavelength of light can carry 30 times as much traffic as a copper coaxial cable does. The optical fibre would eventually replace copper. A typical half-inch optical cable with 144 fibres can support more than 40,000 two-way voice channels. Optical fibres are the basis for high-speed digital networks being set up in several countries.

Besides improving the quality of transmission, the optical fibres would facilitate the introduction of advanced services such as video-conference, and computer links. The fibre technology is ideal not only for heavy traffic in cities but to suburban traffic also. What is more, local networks can have their benefit, while junction cables can increase the quantity and quality of inter-exchange traffic within cities.

There are other benefits from the new technology. Optical fibres are immune to electrical interference with no cross talk or noise or disturbance from nearby power or railway lines. A big saving will be on the reduced number of repeaters. A conventional coaxial cable needs repeaters every two kilometres. The optical fibre on a trunk line in Japan has repeaters every 40 km. The cost of optical fibres shows a downward trend unlike the cost of copper. Moreover, repeaters in an optical system need not be located under the ground with manhole access: they can be placed in buildings along the route. Further more, repeater spacing does not depend on bit rates, thus making it easy to design the system.

Another attractive feature of the optical system is called Wavelength Division Multiplexing. Different wave-lengths can be transmitted through one fibre. It is possible to use one for an analogue system and another for a digital system. Capaçity can be multiplied without using another fibre.

In an experimental transmission in 1989. British Telecom sent light at different frequencies simultaneously along the same optical fibre and increased the capacity of the system by 13 times from 1920 telephone channels to 24,960 channels, over a 94-km route without regenerators for amplifying the signals. Four lasers at different frequencies were used, one being modulated at 140 Mbit/s and the other three at 565 Mbit/s. All four outputs were multiplexed onto a single fibre and separated at the receive-end.

Some basic research is under way to further improve the optical system. The Japanese are Trying to reduce impurities in the glass to one part in a billion. Work is also being done on evolving a new type of fibre optics which has germanium additive that would carry light signals up to 300 km without repeaters. Another field of research lies in evolving better lasers that would give off infrared light in the longer wavelength of 1.5 micrometres—considered ideal for long-distance transmission in this area.

Japanese engineers are also examining a novel idea. At present the relays convert light into electrical signals before passing them on as light again, a process not considered optimum. Experts are trying to make a semiconductor which would directly,, amplify the light signal without electrical conversion. This raises the question of developing an opto-electronic chip that can process light signals just as an integrated circuit chip handles electronic signals in a computer. The search is on to find materials that would handle both electricity and light. Scientists may discover or make a fibre that absorbs so little light that it could work without repeaters!

The search for new materials is going on. One approach is to replace silica with new materials that use light farther into the infrared spectrum (over 2 micrometres in wavelength). Mixtures of zirconium, barium and aluminium with flourine and chlorine are tested to see if they could be more transparent than silica is to light.

MOBILE PHONES

Mobile communications had an exciting start. Marconi himself demonstrated mobile radio in 1898 when he reported a regatta from a tug for a newspaper. Wireless telegraphy was brought to the popular imagination from a ship on the high sea, when in 1910 a criminal was arrested on board a ship after its captain flashed a secret message. The first attempt to operate a mobile phone link was reportedly made in 1926 in Germany. Radio from automobiles was tried in the 1920's During the second World war, frequency modulation of radio waves was found reliable by the allied forces in Normandy. After the war, vacuum tubes were replaced by solid-state devices which reduced the size and weight of mobile communication devices.

Most two-way mobile radio systems (walkie-talkies) are simplex and so one has to operate a push-to-talk button before speaking. Generally, mobile communication has a limited range. The frequency spectrum (generally VHF and UHF) is limited but the uses are increasing. Radio is also used, for example, to operate machines by remote control.

The VHF range is ideally suited for mobile communications, as the energy radiated by UHF waves becomes weak much more rapidly than in VHF transmission. Only after the advantages of VHF were perceived, good progress was made in the use of mobile radio. Today, taxi caps, police, ambulance fire fighting vehicles and a growing number of services, both public and private, are equipped with radio telephones. The first commercial mobile telephone service was started in St. Louis in 1946. It connected moving vehicles to the telephone network. Since the 1940's, railroad and river vessels have been using the radio in the United States.

A mobile service in the UK enables people to make and receive phone calls in their cars. Customers can avail themselves of the service, when they are within the range of any of the radiophone service areas. The subscribers can directly dial from cars to any of the telephones in the UK as well as to all phones on international direct dialling. Calls from the UK can also be received in cars. Several other countries including Japan, the USA, and Sweden have a similar facility. In India also, mobile telephones are used to a limited extent. While cellular radio telephony would be in demand in urban areas by mobile users, the technique can serve India's villages in a fixed mode with high reliability.

A Honeycomb of Cells

The problem which prevented the widespread use of mobile phones was a shortage of radio frequencies. Often in a metropolitan area, one high-powered base station would serve an entire city and its suburbs and each channel can handle only one call at a time. The cellular system is meant to solve this problem by using low-power base station transmitters and receivers linked to the public wire-line telephone network. Every area equipped for cellular telephones will be divided into a honeycomb of geographic areas or 'cells', each of which will have its own transmitter receiver and a computer control (Fig. 28). When a cell's capacity is reached, it is divided again and new cells are created. Neighbouring cells would have different frequencies in order to avoid interference, but cells separated by long distance can use the same frequencies. Computers allot different radio channels to incoming callers. Fixed telephones can also be reached through the computer's direction. By splitting cells,

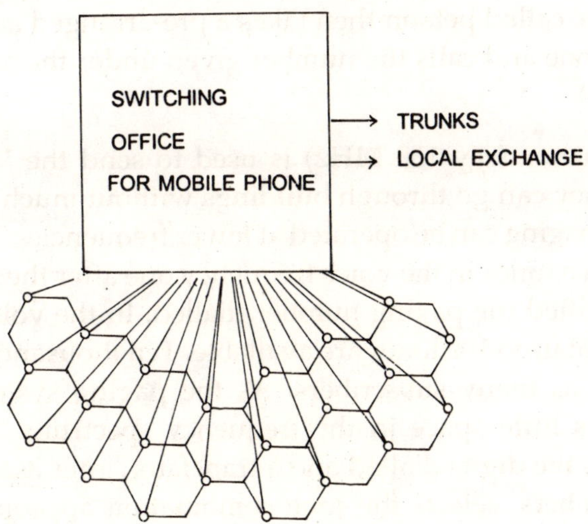

Fig. 28: *Cellular Mobile Radio Telephone:* A territory is divided into cells each using a different frequency from its neighbour. Each cell has a radio station linking It with a mobile switching office. When a car picks up a frequency, the station allots another frequency for others. When the car moves into another cell, a different frequency is allotted automatically.

a carrier can serve over 100.000 customers in one area. The system operates around 800 and 900 MHz bands which are allotted to cellular service. The system's data processing equipment determines the base station that will handle the call and will promptly reassign every frequency.

Air-to-ground communication for private users is also possible. Japan, for example, is developing a fully automatic direct dial operation for an aeronautical public telephone system. A fully automatic coastal maritime telephone service has also been provided in Japan as in a few advanced countries. Recently, skyphones were introduced by a few airlines to enable passengers in flight to talk to people on the ground.

Paging People

In a recent application, mobile devices are used to contact people on the move. Doctors, salespersons, reporters and workers in the field can be contacted while they are away from their phones, provided they have a small pocket-device that could be triggered by remote control. Such technique is known as *radio-paging*. It is a one-way *selective* signalling. Anyone who wants to ring a person covered by radio paging should dial an access number, followed by a paging number allotted to the individual. A control terminal processes the call and initiates a calling tone to the paged number through a transmitter. The called person hears an alerting signal which sounds. "Bleep, bleep!" The called person then takes a pre-arranged action such as going to the nearest telephone and calls the number given under the arrangement (office or home) (see Fig. 29).

A carrier frequency (say 150 MHz) is used to send the Very High Frequency (VHF) waves as they can go through buildings without much loss. In limited areas such as hospitals, paging can be operated at lower frequencies. The carrier frequency is modulated by two tones in the voice frequency one after the other. A combination of two tones identified the paging number dialled. In the voice frequency band of 300-3,400 Hz, sets of upto 100 tones are available. Ten thousand combinations can be obtained to serve as many subscribers. As the paging system does not involve speech, it occupies little space in the frequency spectrum. The control terminal receives and stores the digits dialled and a translator, after ascertaining the validity of the dialled numbers, selects the tone combination appropriate for the wanted number. All the receivers will detect the VHF signals, while the tone filter in a receiver will pass only a specific tone and reject other. There can be provision in the receiver to store the calls and ring only when switched on. Doctors who may not like to be disturbed while examining patients would find it useful. The signal can come as a touch-sensitive vibration. There could also be a group alert which would call a selected group like police or repair workers.

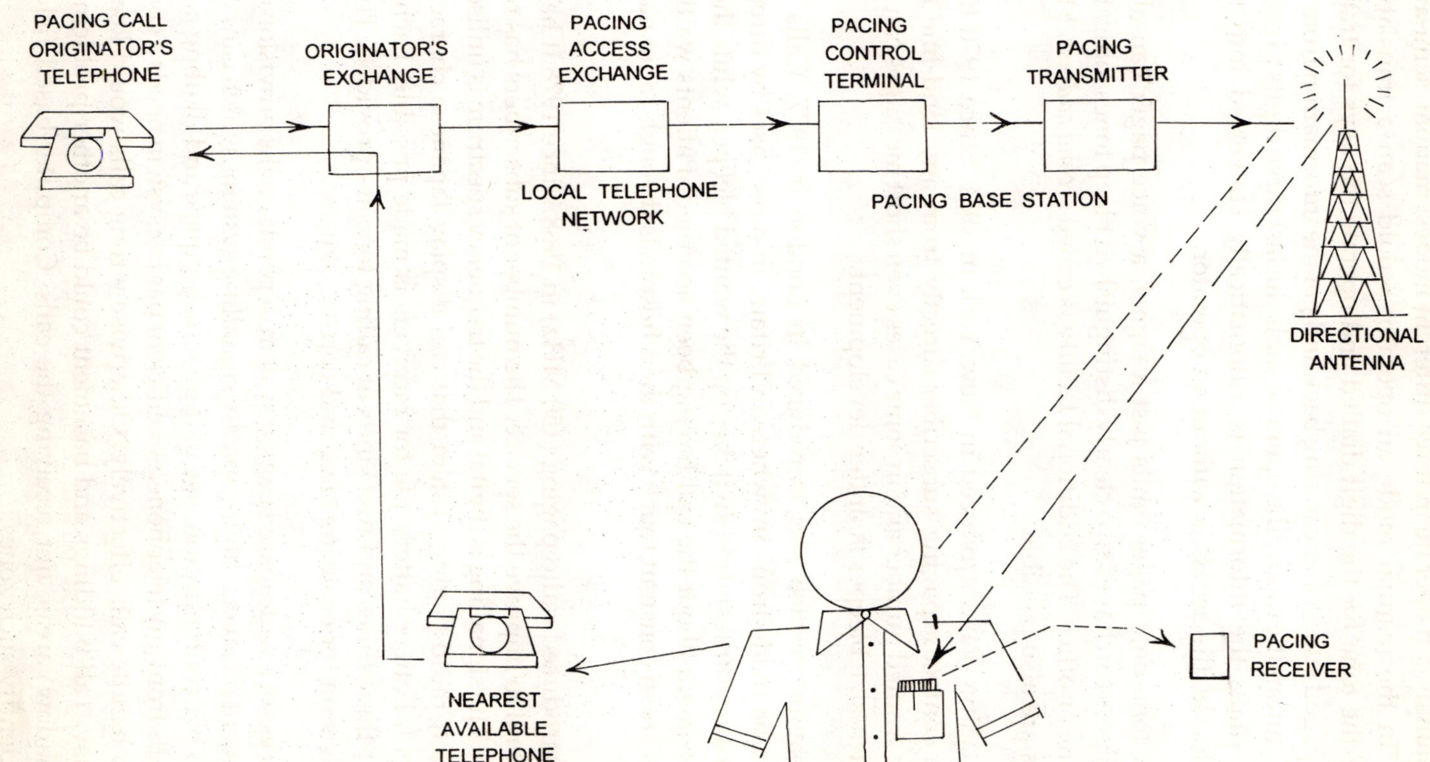

Fig. 29: Radio paging is a method to alert people on the move. First, a person gets access to the paging exchange in the local telephone network and his request (in the form of dialled numbers) is processed and transmitted to contact the paging receiver carried by the person who then goes to the nearest telephone to get further information.

The terminals can operate in three different modes: manual, semi-automatic and automatic. In the manual mode an operator would scan a translation chart for identifying the tone for the digit dialled and operate the keys for transmitting the tones. The paged subscriber can ring back and get the information from the operator. In the semi-automatic mode, the operator dials the last three digits to call a subscriber and as he dials, the information is automatically converted into tones. In the automatic mode, the access is without an operator.

While a tone-only pager emits just a signal, a voice pager can allow voice to follow. Bleepers can have" two clearly distinguished bleep tones indicating if the call is from home or office. The additional facility is called *second address.* More than two bleep tones are also possible.

Radio paging was introduced in New York in 1951. Since 1970 it has become possible to contact a paging subscriber directly from any land-line telephone by dialling the wanted number and in some cases even short messages can be conveyed. A wristwatch-size bleeper is under development.

Radio-paging service was introduced in London in 1977. Calls to pagers in London can be made from anywhere in Britain, in most cases by direct dialling. A computer-run central station switches on the wanted bleeper. while the caller hears an announcement about the call having been accepted. Patients waiting for organ transplants are in constant touch with their hospitals through radio pagers given to them free.

Japan introduced radio paging (150 MHz) in 1968. Since 1978 it has utilised the 250 MHz band to improve the service. The number of subscribers has reached about two million. The signalling is digital and the frequency spectrum is utilised efficiently. An advanced radio paging system that can display Japanese characters is under development. Longer battery life for receivers is made possible. Each call will put out an alert three times and two kinds of calling tone are provided. The system has inbuilt provision for ensuring clear and correct signals,

The success of a widespared paging system depends on the provision of economical and convenient receivers, high-capacity signalling systems which can cover a million subscribers per configuration, use of digital techniques, and dialling access codes to facilitate calls from any telephone. An efficient paging system needs a good Telephone network to handle calls effectively. Otherwise wrong calls would keep the paging register busy. Tall buildings and basement could be another problem as they may lead to 'shadow' areas, not receiving the calls. Computer-based field studies are done to indentify such zones.

Portable Phones

Paging may soon yield to a revolutionary innovation—truly portable telephones. It would mean people with portable telephones can make or receive calls while on the move. The new telephones service is known as *cellular mobile radio.* In the new system, a telephone can be freely carried about and used anywhere in its service area. In this 'cordless' telephone system, the indoor portion of a subscriber line is replaced with a radio so that the telephone set can be taken anywhere within its service area. The phone can ring from a briefcase and you can talk as you walk!

Japan began the cellular radio system in 1980. The service area in Tokyo is divided into 12 different radio zones to eliminate interference.. Each cordless telephone can search idle channels from among multiple radio channels during waiting time, set up speech paths on the selected channel and detect interference from other cordless telephones. The system can handle 45 speech channels for 50 subscribers in a 300 m by 300 m area.

In the United States, demonstrations of the cordless telephone began in 1977. Today there is keen competition among firms to sell cordless phones. In Britain, the cellular service started in 1985 is expanding rapidly. According to a British expert, a low-cost, light-weight portable telephone, the size of a pocket diary, will be commonplace before the end of the century. What is needed is an innovation that would improve the battery and reduce its size. The mobile communication revolution would be assisted by the production of inexpensive, large integrated circuits and adoption of international standards for cellular transmission.

In Automobiles

The cellular method of using the radio frequency spectrum has been tried in the automobile telephone system in Japan. The new system was introduced in the Tokyo Metropolitan Area in 1979. It provides for fully automatic call setup and high quality service covering about 40,000 subscribers in Japan.

Each radio zone—5 to 10 km in radius—is served by a comparatively low-power transmitter that enables the re-use of frequencies at 25 to 30 km intervals without interference. Each mobile radio unit can tune to any of 600 radio channels in order to facilitate communication using any idle radio channel. The mobile radio unit also advises the base station of its location as it crosses zones. This means only the relevant zone will be paged. When an automobile crosses a radio zone during a conversation, the call is automatically transferred to a new base station channel. The system handles a large number of control messages.

Railway telephone services are also operated in some countries. In Japan, the service was started in 1964 on one line and in 1982, on another. Service on the recently added line places originating calls to customers in the public switched network and to the weather forecast office on the automatic mode. Calls from customers in the public switched network are manually placed to connect travellers. Besides calls from telephone exchanges, automated maritime and land mobile radio telephones can also be connected with that of the train.

Future trends in mobile communications aim at improvement of service quality and effective use of frequencies. Research is necessary in miniaturising the mobile units and lowering their power consumption, in using very large-scale integrated circuits, and in integrating the automobile, maritime and aeronautical communication system. Another way improvement of mobile communications is by using the digital technique by which a voice signal can be converted into digital information and transmitted at a slow digital rate using less bandwidth than required for analogue transmission.

New Features

While mobile phones, which can be 'worn' by everybody, are yet be perfected for widespread use, several innovations have already improved and enlarged the use of the telephone. Automatic answering telephones give out a pre-recorded message to callers, while there is also provision to record the incoming messages. A 'catch phone' allows a person talking on the phone to answer an incoming call without disconnecting the first party. An auto-dialler helps to dial numbers frequently used by pushing the appropriate key and provides abbreviated dialling. A loudspeaking phone leaves the hands free, while instant privacy can be restored if desired. Digital telephones can also display the caller's phone number, a feature that will discourage abusive and prank calls.

Privately operated national and international trunk dialling booths are a common sight in several Indian cities. Coin-box phones are undergoing a big change in many countries. It is possible to insert coins of different denominations in the same slot and get back unused coins. Coin-boxes can be used for making both inland and international calls. Other designs allow the caller to use personal credit cards both specially made for the purpose and the normal one. There is provision to indicate in the special card the number of calls made already. Some pushbutton models can also be operated after an identification number is verified automatically by the exchange. Cashless public phones will be the best answer to fight coin-box thefts!

Special provisions are made to help the handicapped. The world's first talking electronic office telephone exchange, developed in the UK, is specially designed for blind operators. The device tells blind operators the number being called and other information on display. It is a modified version of British Telecom's private automatic branch exchange. Another telephone terminal has been developed for deaf people. Coloured flashlights indicate that a connection has been established and users type the messages. Yet another device helps speech-impaired people to communicate. At the touch of a button, it enables disabled people to select words and phrases which are transmitted by the equipment's built-in voice. There are in addition red emergency buttons to call the fire service, police or ambulance, automatically giving the caller's home address. In other methods, the pushbutton telephone can also be adapted for people suffering from hand tremor A frame is placed on the digits to ensure that only the right buttons are pressed. Where it is a dial instrument, bigger finger holes or larger dials may help. Various designs have been developed to operate the telephone even with one's breath, foot or elbow.

The phone is not for conversations alone. It provides a variety of information services—such as telling time, scores in a cricket match, election results and answering directory enquiries. In some countries, 'dial-a-disc' and dial-a-story services entertain callers. But if the lines are faulty, one may hear music without asking for it!

INSTANT DATA

"If I travel tonight from Bombay to Paris, can I catch a plane from the French capital to New York, allowing for a stay of five" hours in Paris?" This query of a passenger made to an airline in Delhi no longer involves sending messages on teleprinter to various centres and delay in getting the reply. The question is answered within a minute or two. The answer is displayed on a video panel at the reservation counter in Delhi. The terminal consults a master computer and updates it after every reservation. This real time application has become possible because of data transmission facility.

There are innumerable applications involving data transmission. Data from various firms, banks, supermarkets, industries and technological institutions can be transmitted quickly, leading to benefits to businessmen, executives, and customers. Trends in production and distribution of essential goods can be communicated without loss of time.

In India, an experimental link was set up in 1976 connecting terminals in Bombay to a computer in Rome through the INTELSAT satellite over the Indian Ocean. A feature of this link was that it went through the Bombay telephone network. Scientists at Bombay were able to get the latest data on scientific and technical matters within seconds from a computer in Italy. The data were displayed and, when required, a print-out also made available. Following the successful experiment the demand for data transmission facility—steady increased, especially with the use of more and more computers.

If data transmission is to benefit a large number of customers, the costs of transmission should be lowered. Certain facilities are necessary to achieve this object, including multiplexers, concentrators, multi-drop and multi-point data sets.

Most of the devices operate at speeds below 300 bits/s. Low-speed data terminals include tele-typewriters and paper tape-readers. Instead of using a separate circuit for long distances for each terminal, it would be more economical to bring several terminals to one point and multiplex them for transmission over a high-speed, long distance circuit. For this purpose, well conditioned speech highways can be provided with multiplexers.

Again, most terminals do not transmit messages all the time. A concentrator can be set up to make better use of the highway by storing incoming signals and sending them in a more economical way. Thus, a larger number of low-speed terminals could be handled. Multi-drop and multi-point circuits mean several terminals being connected to the same line. Two terminals on a multi-drop line cannot transmit and receive at the same time, but have to take their turn. This arrangement would be more economical than lease of separate lines.

In-Built Limits

The telephone network has an in-built limitation. The maximum speed of data possible on a well-maintained telephone switched network is normally 1,200 bit/s and can go up to 2,400 bit/s. Only low-speed traffic can go through the switched telephone network. The call set-up time is rather long, ranging from 6 to 15 seconds on trunk lines. On the other hand, the time in which the message is actually transmitted for data calls is much shorter in general than that for telephone or telex calls. At present most data calls are supposed to have a communication time of 10 to 20 seconds. If data speeds increase, the time for transmitting the messages would be still less. Thus, the call set-up time becomes relatively more than the actual call duration. The computer is occupied in an inefficient manner. Moreover, the transmission of speech can tolerate a wide margin of noise, interruption and other defects but data transmission cannot. The telephone network consisting as it does, of various switching and transmission systems, uses one of the many alternative routes to establish a call. The transmission quality naturally suffers.

Besides, data transmission can cater to a wide variety of services. In addition to messages and voices, it can transmit colour TV. facsimile and even electrocardio graph

In order to handle increased demand for data transmission, a dedicated digital network becomes essential In such a network, there is no need for modems, which are otherwise needed to convert digital bits into a continuous range of frequencies. The transmission path will be digital. Such a network can operate at higher data transmission speeds with lower error rates.

Special Networks

Special networks for data transmission are necessary as computing power gets distributed widely in a country. Till recently big computers called *mainframes* were in service and in view of their cost and complexity, they were located in a small number of places that had special skills to operate them. The mainframes were linked by phone lines either privately leased or connected to the public phone network. Nowadays, increased availability of mini and micro computers has made it possible for a large number of people to own and operate computers. This has opened up several new applications such as electronic filing and electronic mail. Banking and financial institutions, airlines and travel agencies, data banks, computer companies, research institutes ana industries have started using computers. It has thus become necessary for the computers of different capacities and types to communicate with one another as well as with centrally stored information pools. This demands a special network that would overcome the limitations of the traditional telephone network. Indian Railways, Indian Airlines the State Bank of India and Computer Maintenance Corporation are among the increasing number of institutions that have their dedicated telecom links,

The answer is the emergence of public data networks. Essentially, there can be two ways of switching calls in a data network. One is called *circuit-switching* and the other, *packet-switch.* In a circuit-switched mode, as in a telephone conversation two people establish an end-to-end connection to their exclusive use. The present telex network is also circuit-switched. During the call period, no other call can be made or received.

Packet-Switching

In order to increase the utilisation of the communication channels, packet-switching was introduced. In this method, a message is split into packets of fixed length (say 1,000 bits each and forwarded separately with an address code and assembled at the destination. The length of the packet is independent of the length of the message. Thus, parts of the message will go in different packets, interposed with other messages, taking different routes from exchange to exchange. There is provision to detect error in any packet and to call for repetition of the packet. The user will not notice all these operations! The packets are handled quickly (like hot potatoes!) and so the lines are used to their maximum.

What are the advantages of packet-switching? There are several. A large number of terminals can link up to a computer over single capacity highway. The range of devices that can communicate is increased. Transmission costs are lower, particularly at higher speeds of data traffic. The links are simpler to set up, quicker to connect and more reliable to operate. The provision for automatic retransmission taken care of errors. The sender and receiver need not operated at the same speed or use the same character code.

Packet-switching adds value to the telecommunication network. The *value-added network,* as it is nowadays" described, is likely to handle more and more data. First proposed in the mid 1960's the technique became operational in the early 1970's. Growth in data traffic is four times that of speech as business firms utilise data network to communicate electronically. Data rather than words seem to predominate the networks of the world. The use of satellites seems to increase data transmission.

In UK and Japan

It would be interesting to see how two countries which recently introduced packet-switched network are running the service. Commercial operation of the public data packet-switched network in the UK, began in 1981, and has been steadily growing, as customers use it for information retrieval from computer data banks within the UK and overseas, credit card validation, automatic clearance of bank payments between clearing houses, customs clearance of air freight and inventory control. Future uses will include electronic funds transfer at the point of sale and new message transmission methods through sophisticated devices such as *teletex.* The growth of packet-switching data, it is claimed, has made it a well-established service comparable in status to the traditional telephone and telex services.

It is noteworthy that customers who use commonly accepted transmission rates up to 1.200 bit/s, for sending their data do so with 'character' terminals. Data from them are converted into packets by a special unit at the local packet-switching exchange. Customers can dial the units first and then send their data. Where higher speeds of transmission are involved (such as 2.4. 9.6 and 48 kbit/s), 'packet' terminals are used and these accept data only in packet form and link them with the dedicated data line. Full duplex synchronous communication is possible. The requirements of most computer terminals (in the UK, for example) can be met by the data speeds of 2.4 to 64 kbit/s, while large volumes of information need higher speeds (48 and 64 kbit/s and 2 Mbit/s). Packet-switching requires the observance of international rules and procedures collectively known as *protocols,* which are followed automatically. The protocols are recommended by the International Consultative Committee for Telephone and Telegraphs (CCITT).

In Japan, packet-switching service started in 1980. Circuit-switching was established a year earlier. In operating these modes. Digital Data Exchanges (DDX) are used. Latest digital technologies are used in switching and transmission lines. Packet switching uses a store-and-forward switching system to hold and transmit information in 'packets'. Widely distributed data terminals will play an important role in bringing together the various users and the systems.

In India, a packet data switch has been commissioned in Bombay to handle international electronic mail. This is especially needed because of the low completion of incoming international calls—about 18 per cent for telex and 28 per cent for telephone. The Videsh Sanchar Nigam has plans to provide facility for the electronic storage of information coming from abroad. A packet-switched net-work connecting most of the major towns is being planned. In order to cater to the information needs of industrial and business sectors, digital PABXs are being planned with limited networking facility. Later it is proposed to connect them to the digital public exchanges forming part of the integrated digital network. Several private enterprises would find it cost-effective to use domestic packet-switch network on a "pay as you use" basis rather than own a 24-hour dedicated facility.

Improving Teleprinters

Even as data transmission needs are increasing, the traditional device for sending and receiving recorded messages, the *teleprinter,* has undergone several improvements.

A teleprinter, which has nearly 2,400 components, is a printing telegraph apparatus to transmit and receive messages. It is used by the public telegraph services, newspapers, news agencies, railways, airlines, banks, factories and offices. A keyboard, similar to the one in a typewriter, is operated to send messages.

The teleprinter can send messages through any medium, be it open-wire, underground cables, radio links, or carrier telegraph lines. They can work on a point-to-point basis or in a network with switching facilities, like the teleprinter exchange system. The wanted teleprinter can be dialled and connected.

There are teleprinter models, which will only receive messages, without the facility to send them. There are *page teleprinters,* winch will get the messages on a page 210 mm wide instead of on a 100 mm tape. If it is a Devanagari script page teleprinter, the send-unit has special features like automatic emission of the shift signals and character storage. Special arrangements take care of the formation of combined characters by the use of more than one typing operation. If it is an Arabic script, the typing basket will move from right to left, instead of from left to right.

In order to cut the transmission time, tape transmitters are used. There is a send-receive apparatus, which prints and simultaneously perforates the messages on a tape, which is later used for transmission. A transmitter attachment can be tagged on to a send-receive teleprinter and used for transmission as an alternative to operation of the keyboard.

An automatic tape transmitter is used to achieve the full theoretical sending speed. This scores over manual operation as it uses the available circuit-time to the maximum. There are units for use in working into telex exchanges. Facilities are provided for punching messages, when the machine is off the line. It is possible to work on a full-duplex basis, i.e. send and receive messages at the same time. These items are among the 30 varieties of teleprinters and ancillary equipment made by the Hindustan Teleprinters Ltd., Madras.

An electronic teleprinter has been developed indigenously. It is an improvement over the electromechanical model. It has a lighter and faster keyboard. The conventional models can send only 66 words per minute. The new model can store words given at higher speeds and transmit them. The changeover from letters to figures has become smooth by operating an automatic shift.

An electronic keyboard reduces the minimum distortion of signals from the present three per cent to one. With the electronic equipment, longer communication channels can be operated with less errors. The receive equipment can accept 48 per cent distortion due to disturbed line conditions as against 40 in the electromechanical versions. An electronic tape teleprinter for use in public telegraphy is under development.

A bilingual teleprinter has been developed for printing in English or Devanagari. In an English teleprinter. There are 54 keys. 26 for the alphabets and an equal number for numerals and punctuation marks, besides two functional keys. The bilingual teleprinter has 84 keys. There are 32 keys for Devanagari 28 of which will cause the printing, one for spacing and three for functions like shifting. Each key can print an English letter or a Devanagari letter or a numeral or punctuation mark.

In order to ensure that distortions in a teleprinter or a telegraph circuit are within the prescribed limits, special devices have been developed. These include a device to introduce distortion (besides the signals) and another to measure the distortion.

Microprocessors have added several new features to teleprinters. A fully electronic teleprinter can provide for automatic calling, message editing, storage and other facilities. Stored messages can be selected for transmission without further operator action. Repeat attempts will be made when the other terminal is busy. Messages can be addressed to more than one destination. The teleprinter can be programmed to remember up to 25 frequently used numbers and call them automatically in answer to a two-character code.

Telex and Teletex

Teleprinters are inter-connected to provide a telex service. The number of the machine at the receiving end is dialled, and after the machine is connected, the message is typed. Messages are often prepared in advance. The typed message is turned into a pre-coded punched tape which is fed into the teleprinter and the message is sent out at about 70 words a minute.

The pre-coded tape is not needed in a new device called *word processor* which puts the typed messages into an electronic memory. A disk with a large capacity for holding messages is used. The page is visually displayed and an operator can see it and alter characters or even entire lines, rearrange the page at the touch of a key or two and give several instructions to edit the matter. A print-out can be quickly obtained. The stored page can be automatically sent out at 400 characters per minute to a receiving machine, even as Incoming matter is recorded.

Yet another technique sends messages typed on tele printers over private or special circuits to a *message switcher* (a form of a computer) which routes them automatically to the desired teleprinter. If the distant machine is busy, the switch can store the message until it can be delivered. This flexible message-switching service can be connected to the public telex network also. Civil aviation, meteorology, police and defence can have special networks for handling messages.

Another new device is *teletex,* which is a telex with more sophisticated functions. It is working in Germany, the UK and the Scandinavian countries. The text is transmitted page by page at a speed of 2,400 bit/s. Some countries offer teletex services based on packet-switched public data networks or on public telephone networks.

While a normal telex exchanges, messages in telegraph form, teletex transmits documents containing characters and symbols in page form. The desk-to-desk, high-speed text transmission by a telex takes only ten seconds per page, which is about 30 times faster than a standard telex. The information may go either over the telephone lines or on the data network. The transfer of text from memory-to-memory by teletex heralds a new age of the electronic office.

VISION UNLIMITED

The development of radio and telephone communications kindled the imagination of man to transmit pictures as well. The photoelectric cell encouraged him to try new methods in this regard. The cell would transform light into electricity. And electrical signals could be changed into light again.

A picture can be sent on telephone lines to another city. A newspaper page itself can be transmitted for reproduction at the remote end. It is also possible to transmit a legal document or a drawing urgently to another place.

The technique which does it is known as *facsimile* or *fax* for short. It is the transmission of an exact copy of document over a distance. Its principles were outlined in 1843 by Alexander Bain in a British patent.

Facsimile works like this. The copy to be transmitted is wrapped around a revolving arum. A narrow beam of light scans the copy, as the drum revolves and registers line by liner the image. The received light pattern passes through an optical system to a photoelectric cell, which in turn converts the light impulses into an analogue signal pattern. The transmitting and the receiving drums must be rotated in synchronisation. White spots produce more current while the electrical output is the least for the black.

For low-speed transmission, a speech channel band-width is enough. For high-speed transmissions {for newspapers), a larger bandwidth is necessary. A group of 12 channels (48 KHz) is used with an appropriate carrier. Both grey-scale and black-and-white fax can be transmitted over common channels.

If a good quality picture with a wide range of grey tones is necessary, several tones have to be transmitted. Depending on the light Intensity of the copy, the amplitude of the wave form will change in direct proportion. This is an *analogue fax system* and requires broadband facilities. If more lines are scanned, the definition of the picture will be better. The modern practice is to scan 50 to 100 lines per inch.

A simpler system does not transmit any shades of grey, but only black-and-white portions. The wave form has only two values corresponding to black and white.

It may be noted here that transmission bandwidth and transmission time are inversely related. As the bandwidth is increased, the time is decreased and vice versa. If the resolution of a picture has to be doubled, the bandwidth required has to be increased four-fold.

Several techniques are being employed to reduce the bandwidth and time—for transmission. One idea is to transmit only, the black letters in a page which is mostly white. Known as a *compression technique,* its use can reduce costs.

Transmitting Newspapers

Newspapers can be transmitted for remote printing and delivery. The first operational newspaper page facsimile system was developed in England in 1958 for the London edition of *Manchester Guardian.* When the newspaper decided against going in for the system, the manufacturers sold the device to a Japanese newspaper.

In India, *The Hindu* started-facsimile service in 1969, when its pages from Madras were transmitted to Coimbatore. 480 km away. Later, the paper started its second facsimile edition from Bangalore in 1970. A 12-channel telephone circuit through the coaxial system is used for the transmission. It is also possible through a microwave circuit.

The page proof is mounted on a drum of the transmitter and an electronic scanner moves from one end to the other. A page with only type-matter can be transmitted faster than a page with half-tone pictures. As the drum revolves, the whites and blacks on the page are converted into electric impulses. A special film receives the image of the page. It is later processed for printing. The transmission of each page takes about six to nine minutes, depending on its contents (all-type or half-tone picture). The page is ready for printing at the other end in about half an hour.

Besides newspaper pages, new applications of facsimile are coming up. The police can use it to transmit fingerprints. It will help them in the quick identity of persons. Banks can also use facsimile.

Several countries have started public facsimile service between their cities. The customer's document is transmitted over the telephone network. At the receiving end, copies are delivered to the recipients.

Television and Teletext

Techniques have been developed to transmit information alongwith the television signal. TV transmission does not utilise all the 625 lines for a picture. There are 25 lines in each transmitted field (50 for each picture) which do not carry any picture information. Several of these lines are used to carry test signals. A special decoding unit in the TV receiver converts the information into visual pattern. The British Broadcasting Corporation (BBC) developed in the early 1970's a system known as CEEFAX. for utilising the unused portion of the video signal. A page displayed 24 rows of 40 characters each. In fact, the technique was an extension of the 'sound in sync' system developed earlier for carrying the sound of TV in digital form, between the studio and the transmitter, instead of in a separate sound channel. The Independent. Broadcasting Authority in the UK. evolved a similar system called ORACLE (Optional Reception of Announcements by Coded Line Electronics} named after the ancient Delphic Oracle in Greece, which was sought by-people in doubt. The modern version, of course, gives only facts!

The service, known as 'teletext, is developed countries also. It is known as *Anttope* (France). *Telidon* (Canada) and *Keyfax* (USA). These services are essentially one-way devices. The user has no real control over the information provided and cannot interact with the machine.

VIDEOTEX—A Unique Mix

A new facility, known *as videotex,* has been developed to combine television, telephone and computer services. Videotex is a two-way system giving its user 'talk-back' facility so that interaction with the computer is possible. The system allows a user not only to choose the information required but also transact business based on feedback of data. The information that can be retrieved is not confined to texts only but to images and graphics even in colour. A vast range of information including news, sports, arts and commerce is displayed on the domestic television screen through ordinary telephone lines. The examples include *Prestel* (UK). Vista (Canada). *Teletel* (France), *Viewtron* (USA) and *Captain* (Japan). The system provides essentially for a host computer data entry; 'transmission display and retrieval through a hand-held decoder (Fig. 30).

Videotex in the UK, developed by the British Post Office (now British Telecom) and known as Prestel, was commercially launched in 1976 as the worlds first device in this field. Prestel allows users to talk back to computers with an inexpensive adapter to the TV set. By pressing a button on the control unit (without lifting the phone), the display of information will start and change as selected. When not used, the telephone can function normally. The information stored is on a wide variety of subjects including news, sports and commerce. A Prestel computer has a capacity for about 320,000 'frames' or pages of information, provided by over 1.200 agencies. Through further linking with other computers in the country, a Prestel user can have access to the full potential of computer-based data. The user can by interaction with the Prestel unit buy goods and do banking business, besides choosing the

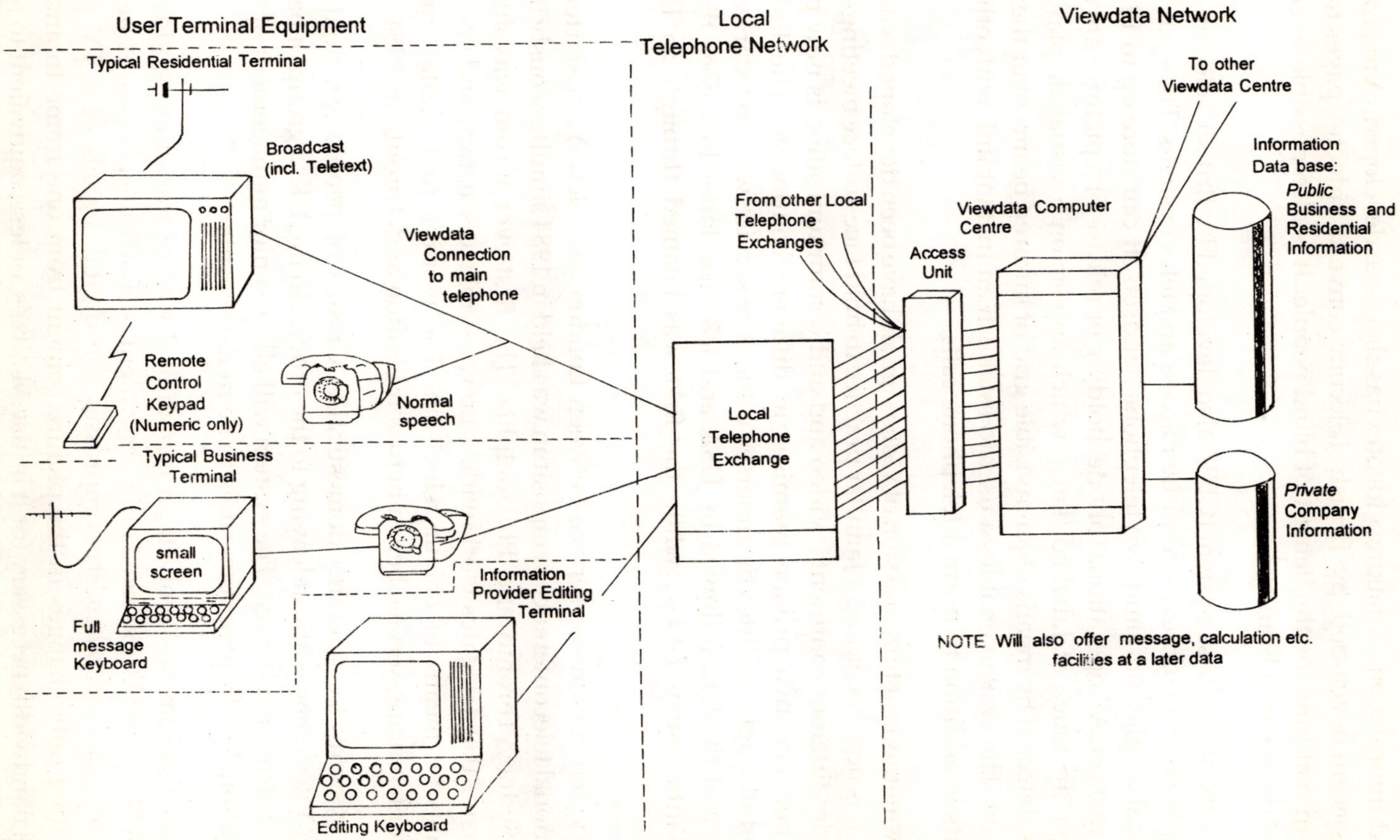

Fig. 30: An outline of VIEWDATA, showing user terminal equipment, local telephone network and the computer banks.

required information. A talking videotex has also been developed, A microprocessor-based system developed by British Telecom converts videotex pages to synthetic speech in real time for the benefit of blind people. It is also possible to convert the text of videotex into Braille.

The City of Business System (CBS), also developed by British Telecom, combines the telephone, data retrieval, computer access and telex systems. The system consists of a visual display unit and two telephone handsets. It can store up to 10.000 pages of information. All operations (phone, holding or release of a picture) are controlled by finger tip touch of labelled 'keys' which appear on a visual display unit. The touch is detected by means of an invisible grid of infrared beams over the surface of the screen. The system enables a user to establish an Instant link with other dealers or clients in addition to normal telephone calls.

New methods of transmission of video signals have been developed with amazing results. It is now becoming a famillar practice to hold face-to-face meetings of people located in different continents. Video and audio communication is now possible in colour between two private premises in different continents. The links can be operated through satellites or undersea cable. The service was first started between Canada and the UK. followed by USA and UK. The latter link goes through the transatlantic cable. TAT-7, while the first was beamed through an INTELSAT Satellite.

The video conference service between London and New York started after an international teleconference symposium was held in 1984 simultaneously in London, Tokyo Sydney Toronto and Philadelphia. The first-ever forum was attended by more than 2,000 delegates worldwide who were able to see, hear and speak to their colleagues by means of colour television. The world's first digital transatlantic video-conferencing service began between London and Toronto in 1984.

The system also operates domestically. Groups of people can hold meetings through TV screens without leaving to the offices. In the UK, a group of bankers has started utilising the service. The system will allow senior management of a firm and its operational staff in various cities to be in daily contact.

British Telecom has evolved an economical way of transmitting video signals. Normal TV transmission needs the equivalent of 1,000 telephones. A new device, known as *video coder/decoder*, compresses the digital signals of a TV picture by transmitting only changes in the picture content from one frame to another. The reduced bandwidth necessary for it is just M bits/s, or less, equivalent to fewer than 30 telephone lines, but with good quality.

In Japan

Experimental use of picture transmission through broadband transmission lines has been started in Japan. A Video Response System (VRS) is created when a video and sound file centre is connected to a home terminal such as the home TV set, video terminal or pushbutton phone through broadband transmission lines. This system allows a user to receive various kinds of information guides and study services on request. VRS is connected to terminals by a 4 MHz broadband transmission line which sends diverse types of information including characters, figures, photographs, moving pictures and sound information. The *CAPTAIN* system is an interactive video information system which provides a user with character and graphic information on a TV screen through telephone lines. The CAPTAIN system will be developed to include computer services such as seat reservation, bank account balance, and tele-shopping. Another growing area of application is facsimile, which makes use of the telephone network.

Telematic services in France are provided through electronic digital exchanges that have devices for offering special services. The subscriber to this new range of services has a terminal supervisory device to control the access to new services. The electronic exchange (E 10) is designed to communicate with these 'smart supervisors'. The method is already in use for computerised telephone directory, videotex, mobile cellular radio telephone and satellite links for inter-company communications.

Singapore has devised its own videotex service called *Teleview* which makes use of both the telephone network and high-frequency radio. Instructions given on the telephone line and the desired information are returned by very high frequency radio.

Telewriting is another type of service, which offers voice and drawing or handwritten information simultaneously using the telephone lines. An electronic note-pad and a visual display unit are used for transmitting information. This is used in the Netherlands.

Facsimile, teletex videotex and telewriting are also known as *telematic services,* and as their use increases, international standards become necessary to operate them efficiently.

Cable Television

A new form of television, which may also change lifestyles, is *cable television.* It was started to provide TV to places which are difficult to reach by normal means. Cables take the signals to homes.

Such cables can be augmented. As against a bandwidth of 3,000 Hz provided for telephone conversations to homes, a bandwidth of over 300 MHz can be made available. The increased capacity can transmit 20 TV channels, thus providing a choice to viewers. What is more unlike the present TV system, cable TV can be a two-way process. It is also called *interactive* TV giving initiative to viewers not merely to select programmes but also to call for data of their choice.

Over-the-air television is limited to a small number of signals as otherwise they would interfere with each other. Cable television would be able to give more channels. The range of services possible with cable TV seems to be unlimited. School Instruction, adult evening classes and correspondence courses can be arranged. Just as the telephone has changed the pattern of working life, cable TV may give new opportunities to conduct business from home. Viewers may have dedicated newspapers according to their tastes displayed on the TV screen. (Some do not like the idea)! They can also get more information than what is presented in the first instance by pressing a few buttons. In other words, the information available is not filtered by the editor. They can have access to a wider store of information. Access to libraries, rail and air reservations, transactions without cash, information on entertainment are some of the other features of cable TV services.

Restricted viewing is possible. Executives can hold conferences, not seen on other TV sets. Likewise, doctors can have consultations with patients. On the entertainment side, special films can be screened on TV, as a feature exclusive to those who pay for it.

Certainly, some of the possibilities look too sophisticated and perhaps a little too much, viewed against certain priorities. But the lines of communication that could be technically made available to anyone or a group will indeed strengthen a democratic society with free expression of opinion. Certain groups of people may rent time to air their views, ha feet, video conferences between the elected representatives and their constituents in their home may give a new means of keeping in touch with people and their problems. Ultimately TV by coaxial cable may complete a revolution in communication started by TV over the air.

THE DIGITAL AGE

Information-handling is undergoing a profound change because of the digital technology in telecommunication. The technique is increasingly used in areas such as signal encoding, bandwidth reduction, switching and storage of information. Digital technology has improved the reliability of the system considerably.

The telephone network has been developed to handle speech as analogue signals.

The network is unable to cope with the high bit rates needed to transmit data from computers which are growing in number and complexity. Separate networks for telex and other non-voice services have been developed. Since it is now possible to reduce all information—be it voice, data, text, facsimile or television—into streams of binary numbers, they can be handled more efficiently in one integrated network where transmission and switching and processing can all be digital and integrated to handle all traffic. Known as Integrated Services Digital Network (ISDN), this technique has become the most popular innovation in telecommunication (Fig. 31). Many countries are planning or implementing some sort of ISDN system. India is also introducing digital technology in a phased manner. The Consultative Committee on Telephone and Telegraph (CCITT) of ITU has provided a set of specifications (running into 10,000 pages) agreed on as international standards for a digital telephone network architecture. The bulk of the ISDN plan was adopted in 1984. It calls for regular telephone lines which carry analogue signals to be converted into 'pipes' for digital streams, comprising both high speed channels for voice or computer data and low speed channels for data or signalling information. Moreover, a sophisticated signalling system will allow telephone switching centres to talk with one another. As a result, the telephone network will handle voice and data equally efficiently without, the need for devices such as modems to convert the signals from analogue to digital or vice versa or special wiring for computers. The network will offer several new features to customers.

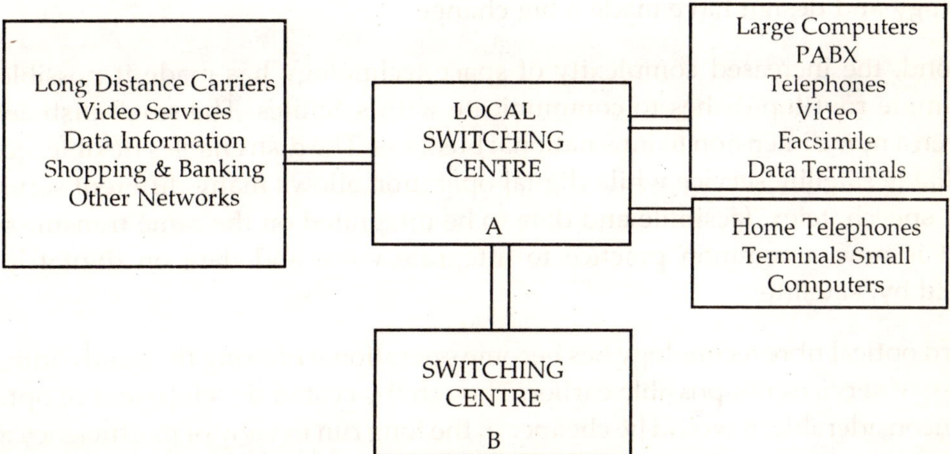

Fig. 31: *Intergrated Services Digital Network:* The standardised network of the future wherein the regular telephone lines will be converted into a network of digital bit streams to handle voice and data without the need for converters or special wiring for computers. The network can provide several new services such as data and information. Sophisticated signalling: links switching centres.

In order to have a single multipurpose network to handle all information in digital form, digital exchanges will be necessary to provide electronic circuits in place of electromechanical switches, controlled by computers. The British experience is an example to illustrate the variety of services possible with digital exchanges. Four data services are in operation known as *Switch Stream, Mega Stream, Kilo Stream* and Sat Stream. Switch Stream is designed for non-voice communication and can handle 48,000 bits of information per second. This facilitates quick verification of credit cards on line retrieval of data and remote order processing. Mega Stream is a point-to-point service for private business exchanges and can handle a combination of voice and data or a video conference (at the rate of two million bits per second). Kilo Stream provides lower bit rates: 2,400 bits per second for teleprinter, 4,800 bits for slow-scan TV and credit card check, 9,600 for high-speed facsimile. 48,000 for high-speed data and 64,000 for voice channels. Sat Stream offers private satellite links to firms using small dish aerials; This point -to-multipoint service is useful to newspapers to bring out simultaneous editions in different cities in various continents and to banks and other organisations in need of data transfer to several points.

Three Factors

Three major developments have given a tremendous fillip to digitalisation. First, the development of large-scale integrated circuits has vastly increased the power and complexity of electronic switching, data communication, signal processing and control of terminal devices. Large-capacity memories based on state-of-the-art processor technology and design have made a big change.

Second, the increased complexity of space technology has made it possible to have simple roof-top dishes to communicate with satellites. The small-dish aerial has given a new dimension to international business. The dish enables flexible, quick and reliable satellite service while digital operation allows many different services such as speech, telex, facsimile and data to be integrated on the same transmission path. It is now a common practice to integrate voice and data on digital links provided by. satellites.

Third optical fibre technology has become operational offering the bandwidth for a variety of services not possible earlier. Though the cost of development of optical fibres inconsiderable; it would he cheaper in the long run in view of its efficiency and capacity.

Just as the telephone has steadily enlarged our field of communication, the advent of visual devices is enriching our experience of the world indeed, television is proving to be more effective than the printed word in communicating ideas in several areas. The transition from limited audio transmission to visual transmission will mark a new age. Several new services will then be possible: interactive video information; computer-aided education: electronic banking and tele-shopping; teleconferencing; electronic mail and newspaper; security surveillance and video entertainment.

The future scenario does not mean that digital technology is not needed for meeting today's needs in developing countries, In fact, digital technology is described as the appropriate technology for rural areas as well. This technology offers a chance for the rural areas to leapfrog into the modern communication network.

Emerging Trends

Experts have noticed some broad trends in this fast-growing field. The most prominent change will be in the switching technology, where the present predominance of electromechanical systems will yield to electronic systems controlled by computers. Digital electronic ex-changes based on time-division switching will take over from those working on space-division method. The increasing role of the computer in switching will enhance the flexibility, reliability and efficiency of exchanges and lead to better management practices and new levels of consumer satisfaction.

In accordance with the change-over in switching technology, transmission systems too will increasingly become digital. Pulse code modulation on more and more short routes will be introduced. Research is also going on with a view to increasing the bandwidth of coaxial cable system (presently working up to 60 MHz carrying 10,800 telephone channels) on a frequency division basis. Similar efforts will be made to increase the capacity of microwave systems which can today carry up to 2,700 voice frequency equivalent channels. Subscriber lines in certain areas may be given wideband capacity. Satellite transmission will be increasingly employed to serve the needs of lean traffic areas also. Network operators will have the means to switch over to satellites to divert or augment traffic, when necessary. Satellites too may not continue as mere reflectors of transmitted signals from point-to-point but may carry out some switching as well.

Communication terminals will sport new innovations, as a result of new methods of switching and transmission. Telephones as wrist watches may not remain a scientific curiosity for long, given the trends in portable phones and mobile communication. Cellular radio has solved the basic problem of congestion in frequencies in operating such links. The telephone service itself may incorporate several new services such as abbreviated dialling (easily up to 80 numbers for each subscriber line); stored call facility when called parry is busy: automatic wake-me call that can be booked a day in advance follow-me call for those going out of their office or home; malicious call tracing; alerting a talker to a waiting call; and restricted access. The television screen may serve as a new source of instant information in addition to providing entertainment, with the emergence of two-way communication between users and media operators. New services such as on-line reservations in air and train services, banking inventory and production control will be done in an entirely new fashion with fantastic speed and accuracy. Office working and business communication will have new gadgets that make transmission of documents including graphics and drawings, quick and accurate.

Is ISDN Necessary?

Even though the idea of ISDN is welcomed in principle, several observers ask whether there is a risk of creating artificial needs. Someone has called ISDN as Innovations Subscribers Don't Need! Is it necessary to provide 30 channels of TV? What will the ordinary customer do with the enormous capacity being offered?

Part of the challenge lies in assessing realistically what the market wants. In vast areas in the developing world there is no basic telecommunication service. Here the emphasis has to be not only on increasing the tele—phone density but also on increasing the access to basic services. At the same time, the needs of a growing economy cannot be ignored. In several developing countries there is a growing demand for new services such as teletext, interactive networks for banking, rail/air reservations, laboratories, computer links, and video transmission. The region has shown its willingness to go into the new Digital Age, despite being saddled with obsolete technology. Any new technology must have high reliability under the climatic, power and other conditions of the developing countries. New techniques should not be rendered obsolete too soon. No wonder, therefore, for a majority of the developing countries, the old and the new must coexist efficiently. A complete and quick change over to new technologies such as ISDN is not feasible for most of them. The evolution of ISDN in the developing world can only be progressive, extending through the next few decades rather than the next two or three years.

The change-over need not be prolonged. The ongoing revolution in micro electronics has resulted in a declining cost curve of many a device used in telecommunication, even as its capacity expands exponentially. An ITU study (1986) has pointed out that keeping the provision of telecommunication services on a commercial footing in developing countries would be conducive to development. With rising revenue curves, most telecom administrations would do well to aim at financial self-reliance, subject to selective assistance from outside. In fact, several developing countries have started de-regulating the telecommunication sector and encouraging private enterprises to take over several areas of services and production. The results have been generally encouraging.

Role of ITU

Technological progress is moving fester than the pace of decision-making by the managers of technology. In promoting the right, decisions, ITU, as the United Nations specialised agency for telecommunications, plays, a crucial role. ITU is one of the oldest international organisations. It was formed in 1932 when it succeeded the inter- national Telegraph Union established in 1885.

Today, ITU has three committees the International Telegraph and Telephone Consultative Committee (CCITT), the International Radio Consultative Committee (CCIR) and the International Frequency Registration Board (IFRB), which regulates the use of the frequency spectrum. In 1947, ITU became a specialised agency of the United Nations.

The purpose of ITU is essentially threefold, viz. to maintain and extend international cooperation for the improvement and rational use of telecommunication of all kinds; to promote the development of technical facilities and their most efficient operation with a view to improving the efficiency of telecommunication services, increasing their usefulness, as far as possible to the public; and to harmonise the actions of nations in the attainment of these common ends.

In accordance with these aims, ITU, along with UNDP, extends assistance to various countries. A notable example is the setting up of the Advanced Level Telecommunications Training Centre (ALTTC) in New Delhi, to promote the spread of modern techniques appropriate to the needs of the region. Under the auspices of ITU, India provides experts to various countries and offers training facilities to engineers from other countries.

ITU's specific objective of promoting the acceleration of universal telecommunications development is a big challenge. As the report of the Independent Commission for Worldwide Telecommunications Development. *The Missing Link* (ITU. 1985) states. "Of the 600 million telephones in the world, three-quarters are concentrated in nine countries. The remainder are distributed unevenly throughout the rest of the world. While telecommunication is taken for granted as a key factor in economic, commercial, social and cultural activity in industrialised countries and as an engine of growth, in most of the countries the telecom system is not adequate even to sustain essential services. In many areas there is no system at all"

APPENDIX - 1

USE OF ELECTROMAGNETIC SPECTRUM FOR TELECOMMUNICATIONS

100 Hz-10 KHz

Telephone/Telegraph/Signalling
Dialing/Low-speed Data, Music

10 KHz-100 KHz

Radio Navigation Maritime
Radio Location
Radio Navigation

100 KHz-l MHz

Loran C
Maritime
Radio Beacons
Aeronautical
Radio Navigation
Loran D Mobile
Broadcasting

1 MHz-10 MHz.

Broadcasting
Communications
Loran Fixed Module Broadcasting
Mobile
Aeronautical
Maritime
Broadcasting

10 MHz - 100 MHz

Aeronautical (fixed)
Maritime (fixed)
Aeronautical
Broadcasting (fixed)
Land Mobile
Instrument Landing Systems

100 MHz-1,000 MHz (1 Ghz)

Aeronautical

Met. Satellite

Instrument Landing System

Radio Location

Radio Navigation Satellite

1 GHz-10 GHz

Aeronautical Radio Navigation

Radio Location

Radars Satellite Communications to Earth

M.W. Communications

Satellite to Satellite Communications

10 GHz-40 GHz

Radio Navigation

Radio Location

Fixed Mobile

Experimental part of the spectrum covers frequencies above 40 GHz.

APPENDIX - 2

MODULATING MICROWAVES

Baseband repeaters on microwave towers are generally used for short and medium haul. The baseband consists of the signals of different telephone channels or video to be transmitted. The baseband signal (say of 4 Mega Hertz) is converted into an intermediate frequency around 70 MHz for purposes of amplification. The signals of about 70 MHz would be amplified and upconverted into the microwave frequency (like *2,000* or 6,000 MHz) and amplified, if necessary, and transmitted.

The upconversion into microwave frequency is done by a process of generating microwave frequencies and mixing them with the intermediate frequency. For example, if 6,000 MHz frequency is to be transmitted, the microwave source will generate 5,930 MHz and it will be mixed with the intermediate frequency of 70 MHz to get 6,000 MHz. At the receiving end, the signals at microwave frequency are brought down to an intermediate frequency which is converted back into baseband signals.

At a repeater where the signals need not be dropped, there is no need to recover the baseband signals from the microwave carrier. Here a micro-wave source generates a stable frequency of about 70 MHz away from the incoming frequency and after mixing gets the intermediate frequency of about 70 MHz which will be amplified. This is mixed with the output from a second microwave generator to derive a microwave frequency for transmission.

Baseband repeaters are less expensive but the other type of repeaters (called I.F. for short) give a better performance especially for the long-haul system by minimising noise, as they pass the signals without demodulating them to the baseband.

APPENDIX - 3

C-DOT DIGITAL SWITCHING SYSTEM

Telephony services which can be provided in the systems developed in India:

Base Services:

— Subscriber Dialled Calls
— Pushbutton Dialling
— PBX lines (DID, Hunting)
— Service Quality Observation

Rapid Call Set-up Services:

— Hotline (timed. W/O time out, nailed-up)

Call Booking Services:

— Alarm Call.

Call Restriction Services:

— Incoming/Outgoing Call Barring

Absent Subscriber Services:

— Announcements
— Call Forwarding
— Follow Me

Call Completion Services:

— Automatic Call Back
— Diversion on Busy
— Call Waiting
— Priority Subscriber
— Trunk Offer
— Queue

Call Charge Services:

- Charging Information Services
  — Subscriber's Home Meter
  — Printed Record on Duration
  — Subscriber Meter Observation

APPENDIX - 4

- Charge Debiting Services
  - — Credit Card Call
  - — Freephone
  - — Coin Collection Boxes
  - — Collect Calls
  - — Non-Metered Lines

Information Services:

— Access to operators for special services, e.g. directory enquiry, maintenance, complaints

— Access to recorded announcements, e.g. weather forecast time, air schedules, results, programmes, fixtures

Multi-party Services:

— Conference Call

Administrative Services

— Interception of Calls

Miscellaneous Services:

— Emergency Call Services

— Malicious Call Identification

— STD through Calling Line Identity Verification

— Shared Service with Calling Line Identity Verification.

GLOSSARY

Amplitude Modulation — The strength or amplitude of the carrier frequency is varied in accordance with the amplitude of the input signal (see, Frequency Modulation).

Analogue — An electrical signal which is analogous to a changing physical quantity measured.

Bandwidth. — A 'path' required for the transmission of information, expressed in units of frequency. The difference between the limiting frequencies of a band containing the signal.

Baseband — The sum of frequencies (representing the total Information) which is transmitted.

Baseband Signalling — Transmission of a signal at its original frequencies, i.e. a signal not changed by modulation.

Baud — A measure of speed in telegraph/teleprinter operation.

Bits — Binary digits of 1 or 0 used to code information.

Broadband — Microwave/cable systems, which carry a large number of voice channels, generally above 300.

Canter — A single frequency which becomes a band of frequencies, when modulated to transmit information. An alternating current of a frequency, at least twice that of the highest frequency component in the signal is used to provide a carrier. A continuous frequency capable of being modulated or impressed with a second (information carrying) signal.

CATV — Community Antenna Television.

CCIR — International Radio Consultative Committee.

CCITT— International Telegraph and Telephone Consultative Committee.

Character — Letter, figure, number, punctuation or other signs contained in a message.

Circuit—A means of two-way communication between two points comprising associated 'go' and 'return' channels.

Circuit switching — A method of sending a message or data by establishing an end-to-end connection between the place of origin and that of destination.

Coaxial Cable — A cable basically consisting of a single wire in the centre of a cylindrical conductor, used for carrying a large number of telephone channels.

Crossbar Exchange — A telephone exchange with common control elements; the cross-points in the switch are made by the operation of two bars—horizontal and vertical

Data — Any Information usually sent in the form of binary digits.

Delta Modulation — One method of coding the speech signals simpler than the Pulse Code Modulation.

Digital Signal—A signal which carries the Information in the form of on/ off pulses.

Domestic Satellite — A satellite used for Internal communications of a country.

Earth Stations —Antennas and related equipment on the ground that are in contact with a satellite.

Erlang — Unit of traffic load named after A.K. Erlang of Denmark.

Facsimile — Technique which reproduces an exact copy of a document or a picture over a distance.

Frequency Dwersity —A method of using two different frequencies to send the same Information in microwave links. (The other method is called *Space Diversity*, where two or more paths of transmission are on the same frequency)

Frequency Division Multiplex — A common technique of combining various channels, frequency-wise, for transmission. The other technique is known as Time-Division Multiplex (TDM) where coded samples of conversations are stacked in time and various channels time-share a common transmission medium.

Gallium Arsenide — Ideally suitable as a semiconductor material for new telecom devices and optical transmission systems.

Giga Hertz — Billion Hertz.

Heterodyne Repeater — Used in long-haul microwave systems, these repeaters do not recover the baseband signal: they only amplify the processed signal and upconvert it into microwave frequency again. (A baseband repeater, on the other hand, is used on short-haul. where the baseband is recovered and generally 'dropped' to connect cities *en route*).

Hertz — A unit of frequency for cycles per second, named after Heinrich Hertz.

High Frequency Link — Shortwave radio links between 3 and 30 MHz.

Hybrid — An interfacing device which will convert a signal on a two-wire subscriber line into a four-wire line having separate outward and inward paths (The reverse process takes place for incoming signals).

Integrated Circuit (IC) — A chip of semiconductor material in which numerous electronic components are bonded together. Instead of being wired to one another.

INTELSAT — International Telecommunication Satellite Organisation.

Ionosphere —The radio-mirror in the sky (extending from about 100 km to about 400 km) which reflects the radio waves sent from the ground.

ISDN (Integrated Services Digital Network) — A digital telephone network of the future, that can handle voice and data equally well without modems or special wiring for computers and provide several new services.

ITU — International Telecommunication Union.

Laser — Light amplification by stimulated emission of radiation.

LED (Light Emitting Diode)—A semiconductor device that emits light when an electric current is passed through it.

Long Waves — Low frequency waves that travel along the ground for considerable distance.

MF — Medium frequency waves useful for transmission. At night they are reflected by the ionospheric layers.

Marker — A common control device in a crossbar telephone exchange, which hunts the available path and routes the calls.

Microwave — Radio waves above 1,000 MHz which travel straight as light waves, used for transmission of telecommunication signals.

Modern — A device used in data transmission over telephone lines. It will condition the signals containing data, so that they can travel on the telephone lines.

Modulation — The process of shifting the input signal containing information, to another frequency slot assigned for the purpose of transmission.

Morse Code — Telegraph code, designed by Samuel Morse, comprising combinations of dots and dashes for alphabets.

Multi-frequency Signalling — A signalling system used between crossbar telephone exchanges, where two out of six frequencies Inside the voice band are selected to convey the dialled digit information.

Multiplexing — *A* method by which several circuits are combined for transmission over a common transmission path.

Numbering Plan -- A plan to allot numbers to various regions in the country so as to facilitate National Subscriber Dialling.

Nyquist Rate — The rate of sampling a speech wave at 8,000 times a second, which is double the maximum frequency of the voice band. (Named after the expert who evolved it).

Optical-Fibres-— Extremely thin and pure glass fibres which are used to guide light waves without loss in transmission.

Out-of-band Signalling — A signalling method in which a frequency outside the normal voice frequency is used for transmitting signalling information.

Packet Switching — A method of sending a message or data, part by part, as packets of about 1,000 bits to be reconstituted at the destination (*see* Circuit Swtiching).

Processor — A special digital computer which masterminds the switching of calls in an electronic telephone exchange.

Pulse Code Modulation — A method of modulation, where the amplitude of the original (speech) wave is sampled and the values of the samples are converted into 1's and O's, positive and negative pulses, for transmission.

Quadruple Diversity—A method by which the same radio signal is received on four different paths as a precaution against fading on any one of them.

Quantisation — Pulse code modulation, when the amplitude of the sampled signal is rounded off to the nearest number in a set of discrete values.

Radio paging —A method using VHF radio waves to call people on the move with a 'bleep' signal.

Registers — A common control device in a telephone exchange.

Relays — Electromagnetic devices used to open and close electric circuits.

Scanning —The process of 'seeing' a picture or an Image line by line, to pick up the variations in the light pattern that will help in transmitting the picture over a distance.

SCPC (Signal Channel Per Carrier) — A method used by light-traffic earth stations to contact the satellite.

Sillicon— The second most abundant element on earth, widely used for making electronic components.

SPC Electronic Exchange (Stored Program Control Electronic Exchange) — Where the operational programs are stored in electronic memory.

Strowger Exchange — Telephone exchange named after its inventor. Almond Strowger, which sets up the calls on a step-by-step basis.

Switchings—The process of establishing connections between telephones, which are not permanently connected.

Teleprinter — A printing telegraph apparatus needed to transmit and receive messages.

Telex — *A* teleprinter exchange system. where the wanted teleprinter can be dialled and linked.

Terminals —Common names for the end equipment like telephones. TV and data display panels.

Troposcatter—Scattering of microwaves by the troposphere, the lower portion of the atmosphere.

UHF (Ultra High Frequency) — Radio link in the range of 300-3,000 MHz (generally used on low traffic routes till regular microwave stations come up).

VHF (Very High Frequency) — Links set up by radio waves in the range of 30-300 MHz. ideally used for mobile communications.

Videotex — A new service providing Information on the TV screen on demand from customers involving the use of telephone lines and computers.

Viewdata (Visual Data Access Services) — Available in Britain. Data on subjects, chosen by the viewers by pressing a few burtons, appears on the TV screen.

Voice Frequency —The range of frequency used in telephony, viz. 300-3,400 Hz.

Waveguides — A hollow cylindrical conductor which guides microwaves.

Wavelengths — Distance between successive crests in a radio wave, measured in metres.

White Noise Testing — An accepted method of testing a channel by simulating the maximum planned telephone traffic on a line to see how the signals are recorded.

5

NEWSPAPERS AND MAGAZINES

INTRODUCTION

The publishing industry in India is highly competitive. A large number of newspapers and magazines are launched every year for the readers and advertisers. As a result of this, competition in the industry has not lagged behind in absorbing modern technology. In fact, some of the first application-specific computers, the photo-composing machines, were brought in by this industry and the industry has also been quick to automate the various functions. Significant level of computerisation has been achieved by the leading companies. As example, the top five publishing companies, viz., *Times of India, Hindustan Times, The Statesman, Indian Express and Living Media* have a total installed base of 1000 PCs and 17 medium range computers. At an average of 200 PCs per organisation, it is clear that the industry is serious about mechanising so as to be able to provide services to the readers and the advertisers.

APPLICATION AREAS

The application of information technology in newspapers and magazines can broadly be classified under two areas — production applications and commercial applications.

(A) Production Application

Production applications are those which involve the editorial, design and production department of a newspaper or magazine. Computerising the bread-and-butter function of a media company gives tremendous competitive advantage to the company. The applications are as follows:

Text Entry

A large amount of text has to be processed periodically by any publication. A newspaper would be handling around 50,000 words daily. A magazine would have

100,000 words in each issue. This large amount of text handling makes this activity highly amendable to computerisation.

Text Editing

Any story has to be edited for spelling mistakes, syntax, readability, correctness, consistency, house style, editorial policy, etc. It might even have to go through more than one editor. For example, one pass might look only at spelling mistakes, syntax and readability. In another pass, a copy-editor might look for technical correctness, etc. A computer facilitates the task considerably.

Desk Top Publishing (DTP)

The stories have got to be pieced together in a readable format. The design department, working on a set of rules, will lay the story out. This process was done earlier by literally 'cutting and pasting'. Today, computers help the design departments to work out attractive pages with much more flexibility than what was available in the earlier system. For example, in case a story is not filling up the complete page and is a few lines short, the designer can increase the point size of the headline or the size of an illustration/blurb and refit the balance text.

News Network

Newspapers and magazines subscribe to a number of news agencies. Some have there own agencies which syndicate news to other smaller newspapers. The earlier systems of teletype were very slow Today computers, communication links and store-and-forward technology (SFT) is used by most publications so that there is a quick access to events occurring around the world. Publications also have to have their own networks so that news from the bureaus is available immediately.

Database

Publications need access to past stories by multiple keywords so that the background information can be compiled fast, when required.

(B) Commercial Applications

The three major commercial applications relevant for a publication are circulation, advertising and accounts, described below.

Circulation

Publications have to keep track of their readers so as to be able to understand the profile of the readers, ensure maximum reach and retain its reader base. Most periodicals are habit-forming and, therefore, publishers have to ensure that competition should not find an entry into their reader base. So, it is necessary to monitor stand sales and subscribers so that there are minimum complaints from the readers.

Subscribers' records have to be maintained, receipts, renewals, etc., have to be generated, to ensure a lock-in with the subscriber. Organisations have to work out right address-slips so that the publication reaches the reader without any problem.

Publications usually have a very extensive retail network. There are a large number of vendors who might be picking from very few to very many copies. Complete vendor accounts have to be maintained. Since a large part of the product is despatched through train, optimum-sized bundles have to be made. For example, if 54 copies of the newspaper and 5 copies of magazine A and 7 copies of magazine B are to be despatched, the circulation department has to work out the bundling procedure, since smaller bundles may get misplaced and larger bundles will create handling problems.

Advertising

Tie real revenue for a publication comes from the advertisers. A computer system keeps track of advertisement bookings, special requests, advertisement material, etc. After production and despatch, accurate records of each agency and client are to be kept to ensure best results for the company.

A publication may be a member of Indian Newspaper Society (INS). In this case, records have to be maintained for INS accredited advertisement agencies and certain specific reports are to be generated.

Accounting

Like all commercial organisations, a publisher has to keep a track of the accounts. Also, in case the publication wants newsprint quota, statements have to be generated to fulfil the requirements of the Registrar of Newspapers of India (RNI). Similarly, in case the organisation goes through Audit Bureau of Circulation (ABC), specific records have to be maintained.

ORGANISATIONAL OBJECTIVES

The basic objective of the publication in going in for computerisation can be described as follows:

(i) Reduction of lead-time between availability of news and printing. This gives a publication a competitive edge over rival publications. Incorporation of last minute changes and updates ensures enhanced sales;

(ii) Better readability by sticking to a house-style and ensuring that mistakes are kept to a minimum. Better readability is also ensured by having an attractive layout for each page;

(iii) Access to news agencies as well as to in-house information carried in past issues of magazine. Availability of news and inputs from other bureau offices;

(iv) Transmission of stories and pages in case of multiple editions;

(v) Lesser manual mistakes for subscription record, agents accounts, advertiser accounts, etc.;

(vi) Lean manpower; and

(vii) Timeliness of management information systems.

METHODOLOGY

(i) Editorial

The editorial matter is keyed in directly on the computer using standard word processing (WP) packages. Editorial matter may also come in through communication channels from news agencies, such as, UNI, PTI, Reuter, etc.; syndicate services such as Dev Features, Radiant Sport Management, etc.; and from bureaus located in different parts of the country.

After the information is available on the computer, it goes through multiple editing steps. Spellings may be checked using standard packages such as Spellchecker. It is desirable that the house style (whether to use the spelling 'program' or 'programme') is incorporated in the dictionary.

Various sub-editors, copy editors and technical editors might have to look at the matter to ensure high readability and correctness. This is achieved by using standard WP packages on which the text is edited. At this stage, the photographs are indicated which have to be incorporated in this story.

The editorial department also requires a let of background information very quickly. Past issues are put on a data-base accessible through keywords. There are no good packages available for this, especially since the keywords may not be obvious at the time the data is put on the data-base.

(ii) Production

Once the matter is ready, the page lay-outs have to be prepared. This is done in a number of units by using special photo-composing and lay-out machines. Increasingly, general a purpose computers are being used for this purpose amongst whom the

Macintosh has got a clear edge. A number of PC AT/386 type of machines are also being used. The packages preferred are Pagemaker and Ventura, depending upon the specific requirement of a publisher.

The pages are laid out using desk-top publishing (DTP) software. The designer gets a lot of flexibility and, in fact, can do things which were—almost impossible manually. For example, there can be an odd-shaped illustration and the text can wrap itself around it. After the design is over, the output is taken out on a laser printer and is checked for correctness. Changes, if any, are incorporated and the final output is taken out on a high resolution laser printer or on a photo-composing machine compatible with the DTP system.

In case there are no photographs or illustrations (except line drawings), the output can be directly taken out on films, thus eliminating one step, i.e., processing of camera-ready artworks.

(iii) Commercial

There are no standard packages currently available in India for the various commercial activities performed by an organisation. Most organisations have gone in for customised packages for mechanising subscription records, agent accounts, advertising agency records and financial accounts.

(a) *Subscription system:* This system comprises four sub-systems, viz., receipt of subscriptions, maintenance of lists, renewal systems and management reports. Upon receipt of a subscription, a subscription code is allotted, the payment is accounted for, receipts are issued and the subscriber's record is created. Periodically, lists/stickers may be taken out for despatch of the magazine. Stickers may be taken out in a geographic sequence to facilitate posting. Lists may also have to be taken out for direct mailing to specific type of subscribers, etc. The renewal system ensures a 'lock-in' for a publication. A number of reminders may have to be sent. It is also necessary to analyse the reasons in case renewal is not made. Lastly, the software must give MIS reports so that the readership profile is available which is vital for soliciting advertisements. Special reports may have to be generated for RNI & ABC purposes.

(b) *Agents system:* This system comprises updation, despatch and accounting. Agents send their requisitions or changes on a daily basis in a highly unstructured format by way of postcards, telegrams, oral requests, etc. This has to be updated very fast. For instance, an agent may ask for higher despatch on the day following the budget. The system must generate a demand report so that the print run can be decided. Despatching includes bundling and label-printing so that the publication can reach the agent without errors and loss. The accounting sub-system monitors the billing and payment receipts. Again, special reports might be required in case the publication has to send statements to RNI & ABC.

(c) *Advertising:* The advertising system comprises advertisement booking, accounting and MIS. Advertisement bookings, special requests and material availability has to be monitored. This system also provides links to the production system so that the editorial and advertising mixture in each page can be planned. The system also does pagination. Subsequently, bills are raised, payments are accounted for and party accounts are prepared. In case of INS, special reports for INS accredited agencies are generated. Management reports help the publication to define its marketing strategies.

(d) *Financial accounts:* Standard packages have been used by various newspapers and magazines for computerising this activity. However, for ABC, RNI or INS requirements, special programmes are required.

Benefits

The benefits of computerisation clearly emanate from the objectives defined earlier, which can be summarised on follows:

(i) The ability to carry news fast and to make each individual item highly presentable and readable gives a newspaper/ magazine a competitive edge over rival publications;

(ii) Quick and extended accessibility of information from networks, bureaus, past stories, etc., helps a publication in better in-depth analysis of stories which again results in competitive advantage; and

(iii) Timeliness and accuracy of the commercial systems helps a publication to maximise reach and have satisfied readers, agents and advertisers;

Problems

The foremost issue is that the Indian computer industry has not responded to the needs of the publishing industry. In the process, they have lost a sizeable chunk of business which unfortunately has gone to imported systems. Looking at the size and maturity of the publishing industry, it is rather surprising that no computer manufacturer has looked at providing value added hardware which would have reaped rich dividends. This is not just a general sweeping statement but has a lot of merit as enumerated below:

(a) Presently, a publisher has to use a different system for text editing and production applications and a different one for commercial applications. There are excellent entry, editing and photo-composing systems but these cannot be used for general-purpose computing. Similarly, there are medium-range systems which would be able to handle the commercial applications but these can not be used for production applications because of lack of DTP software, language fonts-etc.

(b) As a result, a publisher has to go in for two different types of systems. A typical publication might go in for a number of steps: use PCs for text entry and editing, use Macs for DTP, take the photocomposed output on another machine and use a medium-range UNIX box for commercial work.

(c) The interesting thing is that the publishing industry is highly standardised and, therefore, it should be possible to offer a combined solution by doing a bit of system engineering. Unlike other industries, the method of operations for most publishers is identical. The degree of uniformity in the application areas is enormous. Yet the industry has to use multiple systems and has to keep on transferring data from one system to another. This is a waste of resources. The publisher would be very willing to pay for a CPU which could be useful as follows:

  (i) has entry/editing PCs, with WP software for required languages, hooked on to it,
  (ii) has communication abilities with other offices,
  (iii) possesses DTP software and full screen (19") monitors for layouts,
  (iv) hooks on to a Postscript-driven photo-composing unit with desired language fonts,
  (v) stores large amount of data for reference purposes,
  (vi) has terminals, disc space and software for commercial applications applications.

CONCLUSION

The publishing industry has had to pay precious foreign exchange for importing photocomposing equipment since their first priority was to automate the editorial applications. These machines have been of non-standard interfaces and, therefore, integration with other systems has not been possible. Only in recent times are standard Postscript-driven photo-composing engines available. The photo-composing industry has done this deliberately in the past so that high prices can be kept up, but no Indian manufacturer has ever attempted to take a lead in this area and come out with an integral solution.

The second major problem has been that of inadequate training. The publishing industry has tried to utilise existing manpower by training them in the use of computers. The people have basically learnt on the job. The knowledge-base, therefore, is inadequate. There are no specific programmes available where the users can learn how to utilise the technology available to them. The publishing industry has been a very rapidly growing industry and has the resources to pay, provided, proper training facilities are available.

It is not too late for the computer industry to tackle these problems. A solution will benefit the IT industry and the publishing industry both.

6

TELEVISION

INTRODUCTION

Doordarshan India is a vast organisation. It has programme-producing facility at almost all the State capitals, besides large set-ups at Delhi and other metropolitan centres. Presently, 528 transmitters have been installed across the length and breadth of the country, for providing TV coverage to about 62 per cent of the population.

Television is just not a leisure-sector topic and it cannot be treated at par with other agencies like newspapers. We consider that Doordarshan is a catalyst to social reformation. In the past decade, Doordarshan has influenced the lives of millions of people across the country in their attitude, thinking and behaviour, etc.

Even before Doordarshan contemplated computerisation, computer-based technology had seeped into the organisation surreptitiously and this has proliferated into all key areas. Now, contrary to the popular belief, Doordarshan has state-of-the-art equipment for its programme production and transmission. Many of these equipments are micro processor-based or computer-controlled. In Central Production Centre at Delhi, a very advanced lighting control system, based on micro processors, has been installed and is in use.

APPLICATION AREAS

Computers can be gainfully utilised in almost all spheres of Doordarshan's activities. It can be introduced at headquarters at Delhi in a big way and followed with a need-based systems at zonal offices, different kendras and the other associated set-ups.

(A) Project Monitoring

At the headquarter, the work of the planning and development (P&D) unit involves planning the television service, preparing plan document, project notes for studio transmitter and satellite services, equipment configurations, equipment list, equipment specifications, preparation of drawings, designing the air-conditioning system and preparation of estimates followed by procurement action for the equipment to be procured from abroad as well as indigenous sources. In addition, the headquarter is also responsible for implementation of plans, execution of different projects monitoring their progress and eventually completing the projects. Thereafter, the maintenance wing of the headquarter takes over. For the several activities listed above, the correspondence and the follow-up action is presently being done manually with all its attendant disadvantages.

It is proposed to computerise some aspects of the above activities like preparation of equipment list, cable schedules, purchase follow-up, monitoring of equipment receipts and diversion of equipment from one project to another, preparation of budget estimates, etc. *A* software package is being developed for this purpose. This should enable maintenance of necessary databases and back-up information, avoiding duplication of effort, so that all concerned agencies can have ready access to the information.

Computerisation is bound to improve the efficiency and helps in better planning and monitoring of the projects. One of the biggest problems likely to be faced is pertaining to entering data of the ongoing projects.

(B) Central News Room Automation

To just discuss another application area where computerisation is considered essential is the news room operation. Presently, the news room is connected to a number of wire agencies and the news fall is received through teleprinters. The clippings are circulated to concerned, for preparation of news stories deciding the visuals, deciding the run downs etc. Sometimes it may so happen that the person concerned to take action regarding the particular news items is not readily available to take immediate action. Beside, access to archives is not readily available at present. The news production and presentation at present is almost manual. This not only puts severe limitations in preparation of news bulletins, but also effects the presentation greatly. Many of the news organisations have computerised their operations and Doordarshan is also planning central news room automation.

All the news stories from wire agencies are entered directly into a central computer to which the news producers, editors will have ready access. This will help in systematic preparation of news bulletin, e.g., a sports producer will access his area in the computer to learn about the latest in the sports field. He will prepare these stories and contribute to the final bulletin. The News Editor may further work on these scripts if he so desires. He may also decide the visuals, the duration and the timing. The last-minute changes will be possible even while the news is on the air. Even the supporting equipment like teleprompter and videotape-recorders can be controlled by the central news room computer.

This will certainly make news production an enjoyable feat besides improving the presentation.

(C) Teletext

Teletext service was introduced by Doordarshan in Delhi in 1985. This service utilises the blank lines in the video signals for transmitting information in the form of magazines, each having a certain number of pages. With the help of a decoder, the viewer can view these pages.

The dedicated equipment in the teletext chain was based on computer technology. With the help of the National Informatics Centre (NIC), Doordarshan had introduced some utilities for editing the teletext pages. The software was configured around a MICRO-32 computer. The functions of the dedicated equipment have now been emulated on PCs. The entire set-up has been re-configured. The key equipment, the teletext broadcast controller (TBC), has also been emulated on PC. Dedicated PCs are now available for serving the different agencies utilising teletext service, like Indian Railways, Indian Airlines, etc.

(D) Central Archives

Another important area where Doordarshan wants to computerise is in the area of central archives. A large number of programmes have archival value and these are to be preserved in proper conditions for future possible use. These tapes will be required for play-back by Doordarshan and also to be made available for other agencies for their use. Proper cataloguing of these tapes and a query system has to be developed so that in the shortest possible time, we can access the relevant tape.

A computer system is being planned for the above applications. The software services of outside agencies may also be used in the development of this system. This system will also eventually support the news section, helping the news room staff to select the required tape, visuals, etc., with the help of an elaborate query system. This will help in retrieving the tape in good time so that the material can be used in the same day's bulletins. It is assumed that around 50,000 tapes may have to be archived. This also includes tapes of archival value which are preserved at individual kendras.

In the recently concluded elections for the special telecast of election analysis and special election news bulletins, computers and NIC-NET were extensively used.

These programmes were produced jointly by Doordarshan and NDTV. Computer hardware configurations and support software were developed by NDTV. A brief description of the system installed for the purpose is given below.

INFORMATION SYSTEM FOR ELECTION ANALYSIS

The election information system was used for collecting, processing and presenting election results during the election analysis programmes of Doordarshan. It consisted of the following three components:

(a) Data Collection

The election results from various constituencies were received through NICNET, UNI and PTI and hotlines;

(b) Studio Network

A network of super-ATs was installed in the studio for compiling and processing information coming from the above sources;

(c) Results Output

The output consisted of graphics for broadcasting, reports on monitors and printers;

(i) NICNET

NICNET, as we know, is a satellite-based network installed by National Informatics Centre that links over 450 districts to a mainframe computer at New Delhi. These district centres were feeding election results to the central computer after every round of counting. This included both the fast-track information, i.e., which party has won or is leading in a given constituency and the detailed information containing votes polled by the major candidates and the total valid votes. The NICNET mainframe was connected to the studio network through a DoT line for automatic downloading of these election results.

(ii) UNI and PTI

UNI and PTI were sending election results through teleprinters installed at the studio;

(iii) HOTLINES

The studio was also connected to various State election commission offices through hotlines.

STUDIO NETWORK

The studio-network consisted of four PC-ATs-(IBM-compatible 386 machines). There were two master computers, one of which was storing fast-track information and the other was storing detailed votes information. VT100 terminals were connected to these for entry of results coming through UNI, PTI and hotlines. One PC-AT was connect to NICNET central node at the C.G.O. complex. It was retrieving information packets sent by NICNET district centres and routing them to the two master computers. Another PC-AT was connected to the two masters which served as the back-up. Automatic periodic backups of the two databases were being taken so that operation could be shifted to the backup computer in case of a master crashing.

The election data on the two masters were being summarised continuously to generate various kinds of reports (latest party positions with gains and losses, vote shares, Swings for various parties, turnout percentage, etc.). These reports were being fed through RS-232 cables to the following:

(i) Graphics

The graphics subsystem consisted of two IBM PC-ATs having add-on video graphics cards to generate video signals. These were running software for displaying broadcast quality anti-aliased animated charts and text. Updates, showing latest position, were coming from the masters and within seconds they could be presented in the form of growing bars. This was used for showing the vote shares, vote changes, party positions and headlines during the programme.

(ii) Analysis

Printers and terminals were linked to the master computers which could be used for viewing the latest reports. These outputs were provided for special election bulletins.

CONCLUSION

In addition, a host of other uses to which Doordarshan can put the computer are: pay roll preparation, (already implemented), inventory management, personnel management, training, conference, etc. In the years to come, Doordarshan should be one of the biggest computer-users in the country.

7

BOOKS

Introduction

The application of computers to enrich the quality of life remains mostly a dream, here in India and elsewhere. At the same time, the fact that computers have changed the quality of our lives is undeniable. Computer applications have always suffered from a lack of definition of success. It is not very clear if a computer application can be called successful if it does any of the following:

(i) Earns a lot of money for its originator(s),
(ii) Increases human productivity,
(iii) Changes the way certain things are done,
(iv) Results in the sale and use of more computers or software,
(v) Alters human power structures or the society,
(vi) Alters human behaviour,
(vii) Some or all of the above.

Lack of a clear definition of success naturally also makes it difficult to decide when a computer application is unsuccessful.

The success or failure of computer applications is viewed very differently in different segments of society. One could thus devise these alternative definitions for a successful application.

Successful Application

A successful computer application is defined as follows:

(A) One which is financially viable, that is, the cost of development and implementation is adequately less than the earnings from the application;
(B) One which is socially useful, that is, the application improves one or more

of the important parameters of human society such as prosperity, power, happiness, productivity, and so on;

(C) One which actualises one or more capabilities of current science and technology, that is, it converts an idea into an event: and

(D) One which causes an irreversible change in the world, that is, a world with this application is substantially and irrevocably different from a world without it.

A computer application which satisfies all of the above definitions would, of course, be called a rip-roaring success. They are very few in number!

Definition (A) is usually adopted by traders and businessmen. Definition (B) is supported by governments. (A) and (B) together are acceptable to "good" industrialists and progressive bureaucrats. Definition (C) is a scientists definition while (C) and (D) together are what excites those inventors who do not mind a bit of fame and glory. It is very rarely that one comes across developers who can create applications where all four definitions apply Edison, a rare example, was one such. In Table 1, we have tried to classify some important computer applications and also include some non-computer products to show how they compare.

TABLE 1

Important Computer Applications

Product	*DEF(A)*	*DEF(B)*	*DEF(C)*	*DEF(D)*	*Affects...*
Data-base management Systems	Yes	?	Yes	?	Many people
Computer Assisted Communication	Yes	Yes	Yes	Yes	Almost everybody
The: "Windows" environment	Yes	?	Yes	?	Few people
Computer - Assisted Medical imaging	Yes	Yes	Yes	Yes	Most people
The Electric lamp	Yes	Yes	Yes	Yes	Almost everybody
The Hydrogen Bomb	?	?	Yes	Yes	Almost everybody

For the purposes of this article, we propose the following definitions:

"The success of a computer application is directly proportional to the number of human beings it affects."

This definition is restrictive and perhaps unkind. It merely measures change as a parameter of success. However, Nature too does the same. Evolution proceeds merely through change and benefits (or the lack of it) are not considered important. It is because of this unfortunate point of view that the above definition equates the success of communication technology with that of the hydrogen bomb.

It is with this restrictive definition in mind that the rest of this paper should be read.

New Applications Development

Before undertaking to implement a new computer application, one would generally consider whether the new applications, (a) can be created, and (b) can be used. One could generally expand these considerations into a nine-element matrix, as shown in Table 2.

TABLE 2

Strategies for Development

	A *Market Needs it Now*	B *Market does not Know that there is Need for it*	C *Market does not Need it New, but will in Future*
1. Products Exist	— Become a distributor — Make a better one — Leave it atone	— Create awareness — Create a need Become a distributor	— Hoard it — Plan marketing — Include in strategy
2. Product does not exist but can be made	— Build it fast — Don't try anything fancy — Keep track of competition	— Get marketing advice — Keep budgets low — Watch Competition — Create a need	— Build a low-cost research team — Keep track of university work — Include in corporate planning — Invest in research
3. Product does not exist and needs to be invented	— Invest in R and D — Invest in media and PR — Get funding	— Get government funding — Start low cost R and D — Invest in marketing	— Start Low-Key need-building — Participate in conferences and publish

In India, most industries operate in the A1 area and hence most industrialists prefer to be middlemen selling someoneelse's technology. At best they may venture into B1 or C1 but seldom anywhere else.

The government, on the other hand, prefers to remain in the C3 area where accountability is low. At best, if they are adventurous, they enter B3, and usually fail. One may well recall the laudable, yet suicidal plunge of C-DOT into the A2 area.

It is interesting to note that most creative and ambitious students would like to work in areas A2, A3, B2, and C2, which are unattended in this country. Hence they leave. The ones who remain tend to vegetate in A1 or C3.

Struggles with Indian Applications

Computers are now applied in many facets of Indian life. However, a list of these would neither be comprehensive nor throw much light on the application process. Instead, in what follow we present three case-histories of applications where we were involved in the conception, development and implementation. We hope this limited experience will provide some insight into the general area of computer applications for common man.

(A) The "Partners" Project

In 1984, we developed a system which used about a hundred rules to attempt automatic matching of men and women in the Indian "arranged" marriage format. The rules here are fuzzy and depend significantly on social parameters (e.g., caste, colour, etc.) not generally considered significant in other countries. The system seemed to produce good results and a businessmen attempted to set-up a service agency with it. This did not prove to be viable because the cost of educating the market and getting them to accept a non-human system proved to be too expensive. In the end, the product was sold to the *Times of India* and the *Hindustan Times* newspapers, both of which continue to use it as a value-addition to their matrimonial columns. In the last eight years or so, unofficial estimates from these organisations indicate that over 25,000 marriages have taken place using the output of this system. The Partners system has significantly affected the lives of 50,000 persons and, when it was developed, fell into the B2 category of Table 2. However, apart from meeting its development costs, it has not directly produced any money.

(B) The "Jobads" Project

In 1984, we were involved in purchasing and implementing one of the first LAN's in the country. This was a Convergent Technologies B-22 LAN driving a pair of Autologic APS-micro5 CRT typesetters. The user organisation was United India

Periodicals, publishers of Patriot newspaper. After the system was implemented, we began development of software which would enable operator-independent typesetting and pagination of databases. This was a time when desk-top publishing was unknown and we published some of results. Subsequently, this work led to a concept where employment advertisements from various newspapers were abstracted, classified and paginated automatically into a tabloid magazine called JOBADS. The entire magazine was produced by a single operator and two terminals. It reached a circulation of 8000 in Delhi. However, the massive increases of newsprint prices and distribution costs (fuel) in 1987-88 made the publication unviable. Subsequently, the concept changed its form to where several existing publications used an abstracted jobs section as value-addition to their readers. During its publications, about a million copies of JOBADS were sold, and while it is only possible to guess from readers' letters, at least 5,000 persons obtained employment using the information from its columns. In the framework of this article, in 1985, JOBADS was a B3 type project and should perhaps have been taken up by the government.

(C) The 'Yellow Pages" Project

In 1985, the Department of Telecommunication (DoT) produced their "Blue Book" of officers using the database publishing technology developed for JOBADS. The data was ported from their PDP-11 to the B22 LAN and typeset automatically in just a few hours. This generated interest within the DoT in the area of telephone directory publishing. Telephone directories were published from DoT databases by entering the information all over again on typesetting systems. This caused great inaccuracies and delays. In 1986, TCS who were contractors to the government for telephone directory production used the Patriot LAN and we developed directory-typesetting software for them and paginated the Delhi telephone directory.

Subsequently, the government awarded a contract to Patriot for the production of the telephone directories of Delhi, Bombay and Calcutta for five years. This was followed by similar contracts for Hyderabad, Coimbatore, Madurai, Salem, Trichi, Orissa circle, etc., covering over 70 per cent of all telephone directories in India. These contracts were unique since the government would get all these directories free of cost from the contractor and would, in addition, receive a hefty commission (over Rs. 30 crores) from them during the contract period. In return, the contractor would be permitted to produce a classified business section in the directory — "Yellow Pages" as they are called all over the world. The contractor would retain all revenues from advertisements in these directories and use this to defray their costs and pay the royalties. United India Periodicals (UIP) set up a new company — United Database India (UDI) to handle this project.

Production of yellow page directories require three main kinds of software: direct marketing software to guide a large direct marketing and telemarketing team; data-base software to maintain data-bases of over two million subscribers; and typesetting software for both regular ("white") and yellow page directories: This software was available from the USA for around US $ 500,000 to run on the IBM or VAX mainframe platforms.

At UDI, the software was developed on PC-LANs communicating with Convergent B-25 LAN's for typesetting. The effort was about 20 Man-years completed in about 10 calendar months. LANs were set up at Calcutta, Delhi, Bombay and Hyderabad and first directories of Delhi, Bombay, Calcutta, Hyderabad, and the smaller cities produced in 1987-88. Over 10 million people consisting of telephone subscribers, business houses and other buyers and sellers used the output of these programmes, and their calling, buying and selling patterns altered accordingly.

The turnover of UDI and UIP rose from around Rs. 3 crores in 1987 to over Rs. 30 crores in 1990. The management and ownership, reeling under these unaccustomed figures, went through massive transformations. UDI continues to be one of the largest yellow page publishers in the world and one of very few to have its own LAN-based marketing and publishing systems. The yellow pages project represents a A1 type project, purely in the commercial domain.

A Restrictive View of the Future

Any predictions regarding future applications of computers is an exercise in fantasy. However, it is sometimes possible to indicate broad areas where computers will be used. Our work and experience are restricted to the small computer/PC, MS-DOS arena and it is in this domain that we would like to hazard some guesses.

We would expect PCs to move out of EDP on to the streets (so to speak !) in a short while. For this to happen, many tools will be required in the areas of graphics (particularly bitmaps), voice, music and sound, animation, Indian language processing, expert systems and neural networks. Table 3 shows some of the position these technologies occupy in the application-development matrix as of now (August, 1991). Tables 2 and 3, consulted together, can easily produce application projects and strategies.

Conclusion

In India, in our limited experience, a new application takes a long time to be acceptable. It is much more easily introduced with piggybacking on some existing and accepted application. Funding for new applications development is almost impossible to obtain unless it is already ordered by an end-user. Consequently, new applications development is guided by the end-user's imagination which, in most cases, is dismal. There is not one India utility package in the world market (the last Indian conceptual invention was the zero). There is not one Indian game in the market (the last invention was chess).

TABLE 3

Positioning of Future Indian Applications (Non-exhaustive)

	A *Market Needs it Now*	*B* *Market does not Know its Need*	*C* *Market will Need it Later*
1. Products Exist	— Bitmap editors — Colour separators — Voice cards — Expert shells	— Video digitisers — Music systems — Transputers — Voice mail	— Indian language interfaces — Indian music — CD ROMS — Animation
2. Product can be made	— Graphics data-bases — Audio data-bases — Canned Indian expert systems — Technical training programs	— Indian language expert systems — Speech recognition — Process control for home use	— Neural net-work shells — Voice/image based medical diagonstic systems — Traffic and city planners — Real-time newspapers
3. Product has to be invented	— Ruggedised rural PCs — Electronic telephone directories — Indian games	— Energy management systems — Tax monitoring — Rural education — Applicat-ions for the handi-capped techniques	— Integration of voices, image, expert systems, neural net-works and process control — Image/data compression

8

IMPACT OF INFORMATION TECHNOLOGY ON SCIENCE INFORMATION SCENE

Information Technology (IT) is the coming together of computer technology and telecommunications. It has revolutionised the collection, storage and dissemination of information in the libraries.

Developments in computer technology have result in mini-and microcomputers which are used in information handling activities. These computers are efficient, reliable and work at high speed. Developments in telecommunications have resulted in Telex, Fax, Satellite and optical fibres by which it is possible to transmit information at distant places almost instantly.

Information Scene in India

Computers are widely used in the library and information activities, such as house keeping operations, net working, database activities, information systems, electronic publishing, document delivery, and micrographics, etc. Some examples of the use of I.T. in different situations are described below.

IT in Library Operations and Networks

A few scientific and technical libraries in India have started using IT in their library work. For example, DESIDOC and NISTADS have computerised their catalogues. INSDOC too has started computerising its latest collections. University libraries have also started using computers in their library operations. For example, Tamil University has started computerising its catalogue.

Information Technology is now being used to create networks through which it is possible to share library resources. The CMC Limited, Calcutta, has completed the feasibility study for having a network of Calcutta libraries, CALIBNET. A network of about 35 Delhi libraries has been conceived to from DELNET.

DELNET is a cooperative network designed to reduce outlay in library holdings, particularly serials in various ways apart from ensuring optimum use through sharing. It is estimated that the Network has saved Rs. 18 Lakhs by way of rationalisation in subscriptions to periodicals for the year 1990-91 in the field of physical sciences. In 1991, DELNET begain its operations with the introduction of E-Mail. Initially there were 10 libraries using the E-Mail facility. Later, 21 libraries were added to this facility. Thus Delhi became the first city in India to establish electronic link among its libraries making the beginning of a resources sharing venture.

Some scientific organisations are also to have their own networks. For example, CSIR has started a computer communications network, (SIRNET) for exchange of information among its laboratories. To provide information regarding scientific activities being carried out in CSIR national laboratories especially for the use of mass media, a complete database of scientists and their achievements has been launched. This database would form a part of the Quick Access Information System (QAIS) which has been set at CSIR headquarters in New Delhi and its 40-odd laboratories all over India.

ICAR is to have its own network, KRISHINET; DESIDOC is planning to have DESINET. VIDYANET is to provide rapid communication by linking computers of 30 institutions in India with a gateway to similar network like European Academic Research Net work (EARN).

Under the Information & Library Network (INFLIBNET) sponsord by UGC, it is planned to identify and modernise 45 university libraries.

The Government of India has established National informatics Centre (NIC) which has developed a satellite based Government information network (NICNET) to monitor the various schemes and assist in decision making process.

INDONET is a commercial computer network developed by CMC, Ltd., Hyderabad.

The Department of Telecommunications is developing a packet switched public data network, VIKRAM.

Database Creation

In order to create computerised databases, the Government of India established National Information System on Science & Technology (NISSAT) under the Department of Scientific & Industrial Research. The following 8 National Information Centres have been established to provide bibliographic support to an enquiry : *(i)* Leather Technology (NICLAI) at the Central Leather Research Institute, Madras, (ii) Food technology (NICFOS) at Central Food Technology Research Institute. Mysore, (III) Machine Tools (NICMAP) at the Central Machine Tools Institute, Bangalore, *(iv)* Drugs *&* Pharmaceutical (NICDAP) at the Central Drug Research Institute, Lucknow (v) Textile and Allied subjects (NICTAS) at the Ahmedabad Textile Industry's Research Association, Ahmedabad *(vi)* Chemicals (NICHEM) at the National Chemical Laboratory, Pune *(vii)* Compact-disk (NICDROM) at the National Aeronautical Laboratory, Bangalore, and *(viii)* Bibliometrics (NCB) at the Indian National Scientific Documentation Centre. New Delhi.

NISSAT has also planned to establish data centres with a view to acquiring, evaluating, integrating, condensing and analysing factual and numeric information. The following 3 data centres have been established so far: (i) Crystallography (NICRYS) at the Madras University, Madras *(ii)* Advanced Ceramics (NICAC) at the Central Glass & Ceramics Research Institute (CGCRI), Calcutta, and *(iii)* Research Centre on Software for Bibliographic application at the Andhra University, Visakhapatnam.

Besides the above Centres of NISSAT, efforts have been made by certain Governmental Institutions to produce computerised databases. For example, the Publications & Information Directorate, New Delhi, is bringing out a bimonthly publication, *Medicinal & Aromatic Plants Abstracts* (MAPA), with the help of a computer. The National Institute of Science, Technology and Development Studies (NISTADS) is creating a computerised database on *Current Literature on Science of Science* (CLOSS). INSDOC has brought out a *National Union Catalogue of Scientific Serials in India* (NUCSSI) using computer. INSDOC is also using computer to create a data base of *Indian Science Abstracts* from 1990. Database on Indian scientific periodicals has also been created. The National Institute of Ocaenography, Goa, has been generating a bibliographic database OCEANLINE with TANDY TRS-80. The Central Institue of Medicinal & Aromatic Plants (CIMAP) is bringing out *Current Research on Medicinal & Aromatic Plants* (CROMAP) using computer. Department of Biotechnology has set up Biotechnology information System (BTIS) and Department of Environment has set up Environmental Information System (ENVIS). Technology Information, Forecasting & Assesement Council (TIFAC), an autonomous body under DST, is providing TIFACLINE, a service designed to provide knowledge-based executive summaries for those who want to know about the world and Indian technologies from a commercialisable R & D.

NBPGR New Delhi is creating computerised database, Management of Plant Germplasm system ; Central Water & Power Research Station (CWPRS) and Central Board of Irrigation & Power/Central Water Commission (CWC), New Delhi, has created Water & Power Information System (WAPIS); National Bureau of Standards has created a bibliographic database of World Standards.

The National Data Centre, Pune, is developing a database regarding meteorological data. In the field of Patents, there is Patent Information System, which acquires patents from other countries and publishes them in the journal *Patent Information*. Patent documents of UK and USA are being purchased in microfilms. SDI research report is provided monthly in respect of currently published patent specification.

In addition to the above S & T Institutions which use computers in the creation of their databases, efforts have been made by various university libraries also to use computers. For example, SNDT University has created SUCHAK, a computerised database on MINISIS Software covering 400 Indian and foreign journals.

Tata Energy Research Institute has developed a computerised information system which include bibliographic databases on biomass, Indian energy literature, energy developments outside India, etc. CHEMTECH Foundation, Bombay is creating a databank 'Cheminfo'.

Database Searching

Foreign databases can now be accessed with the help of Compact Disk Read only Memory (CD-ROM), Magtape and Online. A Disk has a very large capacity to store information, it can store about 300,000 A4 size pages.

In order to promote utilisation of this technology, NISSAT has established a CD-ROM Information Centre at the National Aeronautical Laboratory (NAL), Bangalore, The Centre provides information on hardwarde and their suppliers, reference tools and databases corning on CD-ROM and technology trends, and guide Indian users.

INSDOC is subscribing to Science Citation Index on CD-ROM, AGR1S database is now available on CD-ROM at the Agricultural Research Information Centre, New Delhi; ICMR Centre is getting MEDLARS and POPLINE on CD-ROM. The National Institute of Oceanography (NIO) is subscribing to Aquatic Sciences & fisheries Abstracts databases, on CD-ROM.

The National Centre for Science Information (NCI) situated at the Indian Institute of Science, Bangalore, is providing SDI service to the scientists working in universities and other academic institutions of research work in their field. The centre covers the fields of physics, chemistry, biological sciences, mathematics and earth science. The database covered are INSPEC, Chemical Abstracts Service (CA Search), Bioscience Information Services (BIOSIS), American Mathematical Institute (MATSCI) and American Geological Institute (GEOREF).

The Bhabha Atomic Research Centre (BARC) sends its input for the INIS database and in turn gets full INIS tape for providing SDI service to its scientists.

Online Services

In Order to provide information services to scientists and technologists at par with those available to the counterparts in the developed countries, NISSAT has established online search facilities at the following 5 NACID Centres:

(i) Indian National Scientific Documentation Centre (INSDOC), New Delhi.
(ii) National Chemical Laboratory (NCL), Pune.
(iii) National Aeronautical Research Institute (NAL), Bangalore.
(iv) Central Leather Research Institute (CLRI), Madras.
(v) Indian Association for Cultivation of Science (IACS), Calcutta.

These centres operate on PSTN lines, local VSNL pad and the international gateway facilities created by VSNL.

The Centres will provide SDI services too on such databases for which the demand may not be sufficient to justify their installation on Indian Networks.

Bharat Heavy Electricals Ltd. is providing service through DIALOG Information Services, USA, and SDC using International Telex Network TELENT/TYMNET. DESIDOC too is having online search facilities.

DTP

Desk Top Publishing (DTP) has scotched the idea of a paperless society. It is a boon to the small press publisher. The production costs have come down and in addition they have direct control over very step of the production process. DTP will have a great impact on the publication of books as it would stimulate various authors.

Education and Training

In order to provide specialised pro-fessional training to the budding information scientists to cope up with the changing requirements of the society, efforts should be made to incorporate teaching information technology in their curricula.

Advanced information science schools like INSDOC and DRTC have already taken steps in that direction.

Courses run by the universities are bring revised to enable students to learn the use of new technological tools to browse, search and retrieve information. In the wake of new technological developments, library and information science professionals are now being trained and retrained to specialise in the methods of accessing or using information. Professional Associations like AGLIS, ILA, IASLIC, and SIS have been conducting courses on the use of computers in different parts of the country.

The technological developments which are taking place with a termendous speed in the scientific information activity have also necessitated the training of users. Their initiation in information search by online and CD-ROM is very much needed. In India, no such formal training has been organised for information users. However, with the increasing use of I.T. in library activities, it would be a good idea if such training courses are held periodically by library Associations and NISSAT etc.

Costs

The library services have so far been either free or at a very nominal cost. Any person could use the resources of library without fee. But the online services has changed the policy of free service. Many libraries are charging customers all or part of the costs incurred in online searches of bibliographic and non-bibliographic databases.

The charges for online service will be responsible for creating a new elitist culture in our society, those who can afford to pay would be able to get instant information through online and FAX whereas not so rich will have to search different printed databases and libraries.

Summary

It is now being increasingly used by various S & T libraries and information centres. Efforts are being made by NISSAT to from DELNET and CALIBNET. Emphasis is being made to create local databases and also to search foreign databases through online, magtape and CD-ROM. It has become possible to use DTP in the production of books which will stimulate book production. There has been increase in cost of library and information service. There is a need for training the information handlers and users.

Conclusion

New Information technologies have created changes far beyond the simple storage and retrieval of information. The information environment itself has changed. S & T libraries and information Centres in India have made a beginning by using computers for library and information activity. The country is making efforts to create indigenous databases and also to search international databases through online, magtape and CD-ROM. Production of publications with the help of DTP would increase.

REFERENCES

1. Accessing S&T Information: NISSAT emerges as a key component. *NISSAT Newsletter*. 9(2), 1990, 9-15.
2. Kuldip Chand, Biotechnology Information System. *SISCOM* 11 (10-12), 1991, 1-2.
3. Kuldip Chand, Environmental Information System, *SISCOM* 11 (6-7) 1991, 1-2.
4. Gupta, B.M. and Nathan, S.S. Handbook of Libraries, Archives and Information Centres in India, Vol. 7 Science and Technology Information Systems Centres. Delhi, Aditya Prakashan, 1990.
5. Kuldip Chand Impact of Information Technology on S and T Information Systems and University Libraries in India. Paper presented at the UGC Seminar on Information Technology and Libraries 2-3 February, 1990. Punjabi University, Patiala.

9

CREATION OF CRIPS: A BIBLIORAPHIC DATABASE

Introduction

In recent years, significant developments in microelectronics have considerably extended the range, of applications in information handling. The advent of personal computers has simplified many of the information handling activities, such as acquisitions, catalogue card production, circulation, information storage and retrieval, which were so far being handled by mainframe computers.

The advent of microcomputers in the 1970's and the availability of many standard software packages, which can now be used without any programming knowledge, have made the task of information processing simpler. In the past few years, quite a few microcomputer programs have been designed for bibliographic work, involving creation of catalogues, compilation of abstracting and indexing services, searching of databases, etc. One of the most versatile microcomputer based information storage and retrieval systems, knows as Mini-Micro CDS/ISIS has been developed and released by UNESCO. The package, CDS/ISIS (ver. 2.3) was acquired by Economic Botany Information Service, National Botanical Research Institute, Lucknow, in September, 1989. With the arrival of the package coupled with the interest shown by a cross section of the Institute's scientists, CRIPS Database was created in May, 1990. The publication of a monthly periodical entitled 'Current Research in Plant Science' (CRIPS) emerged out of this experience.

Current Research in Plant Science (CRIPS)

A monthly computerised Current Awareness Service (CAS) *viz.*, Current Research in Plant Science (CRIPS) has been started since June, 1990, by Economic Botany Information Service (EBIS), National Botanical Research Institute, Lucknow.

The CRIPS database, at present, contains approximately 19,000 records. On an average, 1,000-1,200 records are added to the database every month. The database carries the references of periodical articles from approximately 550 periodicals (received in NBRI Library) on the latest research and development work in the following fields:

Morphology, Taxonomy and Ethnobotany; Plant Wealth Utilisation; Floriculture; Environmental Sciences; Plant Biotechnology; Biomass/Energy Plants; Diseases and Pests; Genetics; and General (not covered elsewhere).

CRIPS satisfies the current information needs of plant scientists, in general, and the Institute's scientists, in particular. The service is available both on Diskette and Hard copies. EBIS also extends search facilities from the database to scientists, on request, for cumulative references.

Mini-Micro CDS/ISIS Ver. 23

CDS/ISIS (Computerised Documentation Service/ Integrated Set of Information Systems) is a menu-driven generalized Information Storage and Retrieval (ISR) system designed specifically for handling structured and non-numerical databases. One of the major advantages offered by the generalized design of the system is that the same set of computer programme is able to manipulate an unlimited number of databases each of which may consist of completely different data elements. The CDS/ISIS user is, therefore, freed from the expensive task of having to design and write computer programs each time a new project requires the use of information retrieval techniques. The software is user friendly and once the database is designed the system may be used by persons having little or no prior computer experience. The software can be used on different micro-computers operating on MS-DOS. A brief requirement of the hardware is given below: —

— IBM-PC/XT/AT compatible computers
— 512K RAM memory (640K recommended)
— floppy disk unit
— hard disk, capacity depending on the size of the database(s) to be created
— printer
— operating system should be MS-DOS 2.0 or higher.

In general Mini-Micro CDS/ISIS allows one to

1. Define databases containing user selected data elements.
2. Enter new records into a given database.
3. Modify, correct, or delete existing record(s).

4. Automatically create and maintain fast access files to each database in order to maximize retrieval speed.
5. Retrieve records from a database through sophisticated search facility which is based on Boolean operators, field level and proximity search operators.
6. Display the records according to one's requirements.
7. Sort the records in any sequence desired (in ascending order only).
8. Print partial or full records and or indices from any given database.
9. Exchange or merge the records of two or more databases that are in compatible formats.
10. Develop specialized applications using the CDS/ISIS integrated programming facility.

These facilities are provided through a set of 8 major services, classified in two broad categories: User services, operating on existing databases, and System services, designed for the database administrator to create new databases and perform various system tasks. User services require only a basic operational knowledge of CDS/ISIS, whereas system services assume an in-depth technical knowledge of all system components up to familiarity with computer programming.

The four user services provide for the following:

ISISENT —	data entry and record editing
ISISRET —	information retrieval
ISISPRT —	production of printed outputs
ISISINV —	inverted file maintenance and utility functions

The four system services provide for the following:

ISISDEF —	definition of new databases and/or modification of existing database definitions
ISISUTL —	miscellaneous system utility functions
ISISXCH —	facilitates for interchanging data with other systems and Master file utility functions
ISISPAS —	advanced programming facilities, which allow one to develop one's own application programs and integrate them with CDS/ISIS

Creating A Database

In order to create a database four steps are to be carried out in one work session. These steps are as follows:

1. Setting up of a Field Definition Table (FDT)
2. Defining Data Entry Worksheet (FMT)
3. Establishing a Field Select Table (FST)
4. Specifying parameters for at least one Display Format (PFT)

Field Definition Table (FDT)

The FDT provides information concerning tag, name, length", type, repeatability and delimeter. Each field can have subfields, identified by suitable delimeters.

Data Entry Worksheet (FMT)

The worksheet is user designed and can run into number of pages depending on the number of data elements and the length of each data elements. At no stage in the design of a worksheet, should the total number of lines per screen-page exceed 20—otherwise the system will be hanging. The default value can be assigned in the worksheet and help messages can be given for each data element that would help the data entry operator in entering the data.

Field Select Table (FST)

To retrieve records by the various access points (data items), it is necessary to create an inverted file using appropriate indexing technique(s). A Field Select Table (FST) defines a criterion for extracting one or more data items from a master file. An FST consists of one or more entries, each defining three items: a field identifier (i.e. tag number of a field), an indexing technique, and a format.

These items are then used to either create inverted file entries for the record for which they are extracted or for sorting the records into the desired sequence before producing a printed report.

The five indexing techniques which may be used in the FST are as under:

0 Indexes the whole element.

1 Indexes on each of the subfields of the data element.

2 Indexes the terms enclosed in angular brackets <....>.

3 Does the same processing as indexing technique '2' except that terms are enclosed in slashes /..../.

4 Indexes on each word of the field and eliminates the words listed in a "stopword file".

Display/Print Formats (PFT)

The software gives wide flexibility to display or print the output of a given query and/or print a range of records selected by the MFN (Master File Number).

Data Entry

The user service ISISENT is used to input data in CRIPS database. Data entry operators are provided with the data, that are to be fed, with specific instructions to be followed during data input. References are selected from the periodicals received in NBRI Library. The operator first uses the option 'D' to predefine the title of the journal, date of publication, volume and issue which are obviously going to be the same for all articles in that issue. Once defined, these fields will automatically be included in all records subsequently entered. After inputting the data, option 'X' is used to end the data entry. Inverted file is not updated at this stage. It is actually updated using ISISINV service at any appropriate interval or at the end of the day. Now the database creation is complete and it could be used for sorting, printing, searching, etc.

Sorting and Printing of the Main Text

Sorting refers to arranging data records in the database in collating sequence of one or more fields/subfields/combination of fields. First the records to be included in one issue of CRIPS are selected by specifying the appropriate MFN limits in the 'print worksheet' using ISISPRT service. As this 'print worksheet' is required every month, it has been stored using ISISUTL service.

In this worksheet all the values of different parameters have already been filled in and only the MFN limits, for each month, are modified. In the sort worksheet, the number of headings has been taken as 1 i.e. the Subject Status. Two sort keys have been used for sorting the records. The first sort key is 'Subject Status' and the second sort key is 'Personal Author(s)'.

The output file thus created is stored under CRIPS1. This file is now copied to Wordstar package for incorporating the Subject headings, superscripts and subscripts etc. After this, it is finally printed from WS package.

Sorting and Printing of the List of Journals Consulted

First the records to be included in one issue of CRIPS are selected by specifying the appropriate MFN limits in the 'print worksheet' using ISISPRT service (since this worksheet is required every month, it has been stored using ISISUTL services). In this worksheet all the values of different parameters have already been filled in and only the MFN limits, for each month, are modified.

In the sort worksheet the number of headings has been taken as 3. Three sort keys have been used for sorting the records. The first sort key is 'Title of the journal', the second is 'Year' and the third is 'Volume & Issue No.'

The output file thus created is stored under CRIPS2 which is then copied to Wordstar for making the corrections, if any. Now it is finally printed from WS package.

Searching

EBIS also extends search facilities from the CRIPS database to scientists, on request, for cumulative references. The database, at present, contains approximately 19,000 records. On an average, 1,000—1,200 records are added to the database every month.

The search language of CDS/ISIS is based on Boolean algebra, which provides a convenient way of expressing logical operations between classes.

Types of Operands—In formulating the Boolean expression, three types of class identifiers may be used:

Class Identifiers

1. *Precise access point*—It is any searchable element defined for a given data base, such as, subject descriptors, keywords, words in titles, author names, etc. It is used exactly in the same way as is known to CDS/ISIS.
2. *Right truncated access point*—Instead of specifying a precise access point, one may just give a root. Right truncation is indicated by placing a dollar sign (S) immediately after the last root character.
3. *Any term*—It is a collective term standing for a predefined set of access points. Whenever the term 'ANY' is used in the search formulation, the system will automatically access points of the cluster associated with that 'ANY' term.

Boolean operators—The three basic operators are:

1. Logical *"OR"*—It is the class union operator. The result of a logical OR between two classes is the class obtained by merging the two classes, retaining common elements. The symbol used to indicate the logical OR operation is the plus sign(+).

2. *Logical "AND"*—It is the class intersection operator. The result of a logical AND between classes is the class containing only those elements which are common to both classes.

   The symbol used to indicate the logical AND operation is the asterisk (*).

3. *Logical "NOT"*--It is the class exclusion operator. The result of a logical NOT between two classes is the class containing all the elements of the first class which do not belong to the second class. The symbol used to indicate the logical NOT operation is the not sign (^).

Limitations of CDS/ISIS

1. There is no provision in CDS/ISIS to assigns serial numbers to the sorted outputs (Hit file).
2. The printed outputs cannot be right adjusted.
3. Underlining, bold face or italics of specific terms in a given field is not possible. However, a whole field can be underlined, bold faced or italicised depending upon the printer.
4. The package does not support superscripts and subscripts.

REFERENCES

1. Chaudhury A.R. & Shukla M. Design and development of the bibliographic database INDEL using Micro-CDS/ISIS. *J Inf. Sci.*, 1988,14:159—70.
2. Kumar S".,' Lakshmi V.V. & Kundu S.R. Creation of the directory of participating institutions for NUCSSI using Mini-Micro CDS/ISIS. *Ann. Libr. Sci. Doc.*, 1988,35 (4): 178—88.
3. UNESCO—Mini-Micro CDS/ISIS 23 Reference Manual and CDS/ISIS Pascal Manual, Unesco, 1989.

10

DESKTOP PUBLISHING: ITS IMPACT ON LIBRARY AND INFORMATION CENTRES

Library and information centres and their services are changing rapidly these days due to the rapid development of information technology. Desktop publishing using library's microcomputer enables librarians to easily create newsletters and other printed publicity materials. With the arrival of desktop publishing (DTP), thousands of people are using computers to produce high-quality paper documents. Desk Top Publishing is a phrase coined by Paul Brainerd of Aldus Corporation, publishers of Page Maker, the best selling page layout program for personal computers. Page Maker was the first program to easily integrate text and graphics in 1985, incorporating the composition process in a what-you-see-is-what-you-get (WYSIWYG) environment.

DTP is commonly understood to refer to the production of camera-ready masters, incorporating text varying typefaces and fonts, graphic elements and display matter, with personal computers. DTP means connecting desk top computer to a computer (laser) printer, which produces professional-looking documents design with the aid of a sophisticated software package. DTP software and hardware makes it possible to produce high-quality documents easily and inexpensively.

The significance of the DTP is threefold. First, it provides the author with the tools to express thoughts and ideas in word, graphic and sometimes photographic form. The author has instant feedback in the appearance of the publication form. The paper output from the system is in finished form, ready for distribution to small number of readers or for further reproduction and subsequent mass distribution. DTP has found quick acceptance in most areas of document production within business, industry, government and education.

Need For DTP

The major advantage of using computer aids to lay out pages is in the reduction of the time taken to design and proof read documents such as brochures, catalogues, newsletters, reports and technical manuals. To improve the quality of our written communication in a library environment, the DTP is used. The possibilities by DTP are:

1. Possibility of less expensive and more attractive publications.
2. Possibility of affordable but small press runs.
3. Possibility of choice in publication quality.
4. Increased control over the publishing process.
5. Added convenience to designers.
6. Understanding of how to harness the real power of the computer.
7. Increased motivation to learn new technologies.
8. To communicate to the reader more easily and cost-effectively.
9. To produce the materials with various graphics, layout and type styles easily.
10. To have a complete publishing house on a desk or work table.

DTP Approach

DTP typically implies four key elements:

1. The ability to use multiple type fonts and faces in a single document.
2. The ability to combine text and graphics in a single computer-printed document.
3. The ability to define page layouts and "pour" or place previously created text and graphics into the layouts and.
4. The ability to see part or all of a page as it will print and modify the page until it has the desired appearance.

But in general the components of DTP are:

1. Input Devices
2. Page Processing Software and
3. Output Devices

1. Input Devices may be one of the following:

(i) ASCII word processor files
(II) Click art
(III) Paint programs
(iv) Draw Programs
(v) Digitisers
(vi) Scanners

2. DTP page processing software is the part of the DTP system that allows one to integrate text and graphics into composed pages for the laser printer to output. The page processing software could be of interactive, batch, Wysiwyg, non-wysiwyg with templates or style sheets.

In an interactive page composition, the designer digitally "places" elements on the page as displayed on the computer screen in a process much like manual text and graphic pasteup. An interactive process is relatively easy to learn for those who do not have typesetting or composition background because it is largely a digitisation of trial and error, with quick feedback on mistakes or success. Page Maker is a good example for this description.

A batch process, means that the user has embedded commands addressable by means of defined boxes (Quark Express), tags (Ventura) or codes (Just Text); these do not change immediately the display of the text on the screen. All the text composition is done automatically at one time by the computer system in one "batch". This is different from the piece-by-piece interactive method; it is usually faster for the system to output, and it is an excellent choice for texts with a large number of pages and a standard layout and design. Ventura works well where speed is required, and where a standard layout for many pages is used.

A WYSIWYG page processing software package would perfectly replicate typeface, leading, size, alignment and the like. A WYSIWYG approach requires a great deal of human designer interaction because each page must be formatted separately; there can be no batch processing of pages because both the content and format must be entered for each individual page.

3. In spite of the novelty and sophistication of the software, DTP would not have been a viable and marketable concept without the advent of the laser printer. The cost of the output devices, makes one system more expensive than another. The six variations of DTP system design are as follows:

System number	*DTP software*	*Output device*
1.	Font Generator	Dot matrix
2.	-do-	Hired laser jet
3.	Page Composition	Owned laser jet
4.	Page Composition using Post Scrift	Hired laser writer
5.	-do-	Owned laser writer
6.	Page Composition using Post Scrift or page layout language	Preview page on owned laser writer but produce final copy on service bureau linotronic type-setter

Why DTP in Libraries

Williams and Murr said that the real revolution of DTP as "Desktop Imagery" Where both text and graphics are combined to produce more effective communication. Bove, Rhodes and Thomas suggested that the next "revolution" in microcomputing will be the transmission of DTP documents electronically. The potential applications of DTP which might be used in libraries are classified as under:

Public Service Desks

(i) brochures
(ii) directional floor plan leaflets
(iii) bibliographies
(iv) catalogue of materials
(v) reading lists
(vi) new acquisition lists
(vii) bookmarks
(viii) questionnaires
(ix) newsletters
(x) range directory cards.

Display Materials

(i) signs and posters
(ii) display case descriptions
(iii) bulletin/display board information
(iv) program information
(v) personnel rosters.

Administrative Applications

(i) training materials
(ii) annual reports
(iii) grant proposals
(iv) organisational charts
(v) budgets
(vi) forms
(vii) calenders/schedules
(viii) floor plans/remodelling and.

Presentation Support

(i) transparencies
(ii) slides
(iii) onscreen slide/video programs
(iv) presentation notes
(v) workshop guides
(vi) audience handouts.

The list is by no means exhaustive, since almost any computer-generated printout can be improved using DTP tools. With the advent of DTP, it has become easier and more affordable for many libraries to produce near-typeset quality publications.

Available DTP Softwares

Apple's Macintosh

The Apple Macintosh is unique among medium-cost microcomputer systems in its ability to provide user-friendly text and graphics integration. The classic DTP system consists of an Apple Macintosh (512k) hard disk, Apple Laserwriter and software for text entry, graphics handling and Page layout. It is the first machine of its kind to combine many of the optimum qualities of a desktop typesetting and graphics system with an easy-to-use human interface, consisting in part, of a mouse and pull-down menus. One of the major factor that distinguishes the Macintosh from all other microcomputers is its typographic capabilities.

The Macintosh includes several typefaces and widely varied fonts in its operating software and hardware. The Laserwriter supports PostScript, a sophisticated language to describe pages and elements of pages. The program MacAuthor enables a style to be defined for all aspects of a paragraph or heading as a style editor. The program Page Maker enables master left and right hand pages to be created so that common design factors can be repeated automatically throughout the publication. It outputs to either the Apple Imagewriter or Laserwriter printer.

Xerox Ventura

Ventura is a DTP software package marketed by Xerox, which offers the most advanced capabilities. It can produce newsletters, reports, presentations and documents that are of outstanding quality.

The best way to approach Ventura is to select a canned style sheet that looks closest to the document you have in mind, then modify that style sheet to your liking. The style sheet works by dividing sections of your document into paragraphs, with each separate paragraph having different style attributes. The text for your document is generally taken from your word processor and loaded into Ventura for formatting and printing.

Ventura comes on 11 floppy disks; installation can be on an IBM PC or direct compatible with atleast 512k memory. The range of fonts and sizes that comes with Ventura is limiting. Ventura's page make-up features allow the provision of page headers, footers and page numbers, tables of contents, indexing, etc.

Quark Xpress

Quark XPress, produced by Quark Inc., a Denver, Colorado firm is a powerful easy-to-use program with many special features. It has one of the page layout program. It provides for easy insertion of graphics into a page of text. It permits fast flow of text throughout the pages of a document. It also provides commands to alter or change positioning of characters. Minimum system requirements to run Quark XPress are a MacPlus with 1Mb of RAM, system 5.1 or greater and a hard disk drive. It arrives in a large box containing three manuals and five disks. These disks are: a copy-protected program disk and backup, a data disk, a sample disk, and a disk containing the Bitstream Character and Provence typefaces. It can search and replace on style attributes - so that when the editor decides at the last minute to replace all 12 point Helvetica bold subheadings with 14 point Optima, it can be done. Typographic control is precise and sophisticated.

Quark XPress is built on "parent" and "child" boses which maintain defined relationships with respect to one another. The basic elements are text boxes, picture boxes and lines. An attractive feature of Quark XPress is its framing capability. A number of frame designs, suitable for surrounding a text or picture block, come with the package. It is certainly a good investment for any professional DTP business. It would be of top value for libraries and information centres whose need is to produce good-looking publications in more quantity.

Ready, Set Go (RSG 3)

It was developed by Martin Rosenberg and Kenneth Abbot. It uses the simple concept of blocks. A page clement may be one of four block varieties:

(i) a text block for copy
(ii) a picture block for illustrations
(iii) a frame block for ruled boxes or solid box for rules
(iv) solid window areas.

RSG 3 adds more than 35 new features. Some of them are:

(i) The "Put Text" option can be used to export formatted text out of RSG 3 for use in another application.
(ii) Characters can be set in condensed or expanded form.
(iii) The program supports multiple levels of Undo.
(iv) More than one publication can be open at a time.
(v) Graphics can be copied in a group, and entire pages can be lifted from one publication and placed in another.
(vi) Point sizes as large as *127* points can be set.
(vii) Global search and replace can be used to modify an unlimited number of linked blocks.
(viii) A single text block can have any mix of typographic attributes, including hyphenated/unhyphenated, justified, flush left, flush right, and centred, in alternate type faces, styles, sizs and line spacing values.

Pagemaker

During 1985, Aldus introduced the software program that revolutionised the publishing industry, i.e. PageMaker. It is of international standard for desktop publishing. It is more powerful. It has the link to more word-processing and graphics programs to a wider selection of computes than any other desktop publishing application on the market. The powerful new features are:

(i) Style Sheets — Applies repeatable, user-defined formats for headlines, subheads body copy, and other text. So one can save time and establish a consistent look for all printed materials.
(ii) Autoflow — Flows text over successive pages, without interruption, so that one can place long files quickly. Displays text flow on-screen to show progress and automatically creates additional pages for text overflow.

(iii) Text Wrap — Wraps text automatically around graphics in a variety of ways and retains text wrap specifications when graphics are moved. Provides user controls for white space (standoff) between text and graphics.

(iv) Spot Colour — Applies user-created spot colours to text and graphics. Supports a full spectrum of colour for colour monitor and provides separate page printouts (overlays) for each colour.

(v) Templates — Develops and saves PageMaker page formats and style sheets as templates for future publications. Also provides 20 complete templates to help and create and customise standard business communications for organisational use.

(vi) Replace — Replaces and inserts text and graphics without disturbing page format, so that one can update publications quickly and easily.

(vii) Image Control — Modifies the appearance of bit-map illustrations and scanned images with user-defined controls for lightness and darkness, object/background contrast, and angle and density of line and dot patterns for special effects.

There are many more DTP softwares like Fontasy from ProSoft of North Hollywood, California, which is compressed on two disks. The new Version has 25 new features.

ScenicWriter, a DTP software is designed to turn out camera ready pages for publication of newsletters, reports, manuals, books and many other types of printed material. Files in standard (ASCII) format can be used directly. The package includes a slow but adequate built-in spelling checker and indexes can be generated automatically.

SCO's Open Desktop (ODT) provides the graphical desktop idiom. ODTs objective is to be the software necessary to turn a reasonably priced 386 PC into a graphical UNIX workstation. ODT consists of a number of components, called Services. They are:

— ODT-OS—SCO's UNIX OS
— ODT-VIEW—X. Window, OSF/MOTIF, Desktop Manager
— ODT-NET TCP/IP, NFS, LAN Manager, Ethernet
— ODT-DOS Locus Dos Merge
— ODT-DATA — Ingres' SQL RDBMS

ODT-VIEW provides the graphical desktop interface.

Marketing

The market for desktop publishing is changing fast. A study reports in *Aslib*

Information that the use in the business and corporate markets has increased by a staggering 61%. Purchases of desktop publishing systems conform to the averages for purchases for other computer products; 82% of desktop publishing systems are sold through dealers or consultants with just 18% sold directly to the client by the manufacturer.

Advantages and Disadvantages of DTP

DTP has numerous *advantages* over traditional methods of publication. Some of them are:

1. Control of the publishing process is local rather than with publications designers, editors, graphic artists or typesetters.
2. Hardware is in-house and information is stored on the floppies (or) hard disks of the author, so any change can be accomplished quickly and effectively.
3. Data can be sorted, combined and restructured.
4. Files are easily tracked, updated, shared and combined more effectively during a project.
5. Even the simplest publications can be made to look professional by enhancement with graphics and laser printing.
6. DTP tools provide the capability and potential for more creative and productive work by staff members.

Some of the disadvantages are:

1. Quality is the most important issue in DTP. Laser printers such as the Apple LaserWriter offer only 300 dots-per-inch resolution. High quality output may have to be obtained from a printing bureau using more expensive and high resolution printers.

2. DTP technology only makes it easier for experienced writers and designers to complete their work.

3. Untrained desktop publishers often produce poor designs and violate company or institutional standards of publication.

4. DTP is not for everyone. Some basic graphics and design skills are required to produce a professional product. An understanding of page layout and typography is essential for designing an attractive and uncluttered page.

Maintenance of DTP Computer

The following points are helpful in the maintenance of the DTP Computer.

1. Do not keep turning the system unit on and off. Once on, keep it on for the entire working day.
2. Lower the brightness level of your CRT screen when it is on, to prevent "etching".
3. Do not install the PC in a room with vibration from a generator or other heavy motorised equipment.
4. Keep it clean, wash your hands before using, to prevent a built-up of dirt, grime or oil on the keyboard.
5. Keep all food and beverages away from the keyboard, PC, diskettes and printer.
6. Best temperature for the PC is between 60—80° F, with 50% humidity.
7. Don't use your PC during an electrical storm or at a time when a power failure seems imminent.

Conclusion

Setting up a DTP centre incurs considerable costs. Libraries do qualify for Apple Computer's Education Purchase Program, which offers considerable savings on hardware and software. After investing in a DTP centre, encourage the entire staff to use it. DTP can help people to produce more timely documents, with much more impact. DTP shows that paper is still the most potent way of storing and communicating information. In a library DTP should be used to produce bookmarks, flyers, new book lists, annual reports, posters, signs, bibliographies, reading lists, etc. New and future versions of page layout software are already beginning to include integrated tools such as drawing tools, greater speed and flexibility of word processing modules, import and export filters for a variety of programs, colour separation capability, spelling checkers, and network support. In future, voice, music and full-motion video as well as text and graphics will be manipulated and organised. The opportunities appear to be great for increasing effectiveness in library communications using DTP tools.

REFERENCES

1. Balas, Janet. Online help for Desktop publishers. *Small comp. in libs.* 1988; July/Aug, 28-31.
2. Beaumont, Jane. DTP: what does it mean for libraries? *C.L.J.* 1998; June, 141-4.
3. Bryan Denyer. The changing face of the DTP market. *Aslib Information* 1988; 16 (7/8), 183-4.
4. Cisler, Steve. DTP in libraries. *Online* 1987; Sep, 64-71.

5. Collier, Harry. Xerox ventura Publisher — Review. *Electronic and Optical Pub. Rev.* 1987; 7 (2), 86-9.
6. Crawford, Walt. Common sense Wordworking III: DTP and Desktop Typesetting. *Lib. Hi Tech* 117, 43-52.
7. Danziger, Pamela N. Xerox's Ventura Publisher. *Online* 1987; Sep, 66-7.
8. Dolak, F.I. Lowcost DTP made easier: the new version of Fontasy. *Lib. Software Rev.* 1990; Jan-Feb, 34-41.
9. Fast track to DTP enlightenment. *Bits and Bytes* 1990; April, 64-5.
10. Harriett & Richard Johnson. Mac, on your mark! Small comp. in Libs. 1986; Oct, 17-25.
11. Harriet and Richard Johnson — There goes another tree: DTP with Quark XPress. *Small comp. in libs.* 1988; July/Aug, 35-8.
12. John Brockmann, R. DTP. Beyond Gee Whiz. *IEEE Trans. on Profl. common.* 1988; 31 (1), 21-9.
13. Johnson, Quintin. ScenicWriter: DTP software. *Electronic and Optical Pubg. Rev.* 1987; 7 (3), 146-7.
14. Kleper, Michael L. The illustrated handbook of Desk Top Publishing and Typesetting, 367-563.
15. Mckenzie, Duncan J. DTP: Getting started. *Small comp. in libs.* 1987; May, 32-7.
16. McKenzie, Duncan J. DTP: its role in waging a successful referendum. *Small comp. in libs.* 1988; Dec, 22-5.
17. Nordgren. Layne E. Why use DTP tools ? *Small comp. in libs.* 1988; April, 27-32.
18. Orr, Bill. SCO open Desktop Unix gets "Look and Feel". *Bits and Bytes* 1990; April, 78-80.
19. Robert Jones. DTP: time to make it professional. *Aslib Information* 1988, 16 (7/8), 185-6.
20. Ruebens. Simon H. Desktop computer preventive maintenance. *Adm. Mgt.* 1985; Oct, 73.
21. Stubley, Peter. DTP on the Macintosh: six questions answered for librarians. *Program* 1988; 22 (3), 247-71.
22. Williams, James B and Murr, Lawrence E DTP: New right brain documents. *Lib Hi Tech* 117, 7-13.

11

DESKTOP PUBLISHING: A REVOLUTIONARY TECHNOLOGY

Information technologies can be broadly categorised as follows:

1. Oral;
2. Paper-or ink-based;
3. Electronic.

Oral communication plays a most crucial role in our day to day life. Life without it cannot exist. Many important developments in this medium have taken place over the centuries. Today we have highly specialised training courses for improving oral communication with and without a variety of external aids and systems.

Writing and Printing Technologies

Paper-and ink-based technologies include writing and printing, which are the two most significant inventions of all times. No words can ever describe adequately the impact of these technologies on our progress and development. I quote Galileo: *"But above all astonishing inventions, what loftiness of mind was that of the man who conceived of finding a way to communicate his most recondite thoughts to whatever other* person, *although separated from him by the longest intervals of space and time! To speak with those who are in the Indies, to speak with those yet to be born perhaps a thousand or even two thousand years hence! And with that ease! All through the various groupings of twenty simple characters on paper"*. It requires no further elucidation.

Guttenberg printed the Bible, the first European book with movable types in 1450 bringing in a new technology for much faster and durable communication. This technology is regarded as one of the major revolutions in our history. Since then, the printed word has been the most powerful communication vehicle for our advancement in all fields of human activity.

Emergence of Desktop Publishing

In recent times, the 'spin off of man to the moon and other far-reaching developments in microelectronics, microprocessors, computers, and satellite and telecommunication technologies have placed the mankind on an electronics information platform. The modern information technologies find the traditional Guttenbergian routes far too inadequate and slow to meet the rapidly growing challenges of information traffic. The proactive influences of the electronics industries and the reactive influences provided by the printing and publishing industries have led to the emergence of desktop publishing. This new technology has brought about radical changes in the conventional document production procedures and systems.

Origin of the Term 'Desktop Publishing'

The term *desktop publishing* is believed to have been coined either by Aldus Corporation or Apple Computer or both. But the credit for bringing publishing systems within the reach of a personal computer user goes to Apple. It is reported that by adopting certain desktop publishing conventions, the Apple Macintosh publishing system became the *de facto* leader, almost by default since little else was available. Now many systems with several configurations for a variety of applications are available in the market.

Quick and Wide Popularity

The desktop publishing was launched in 1986. Within five years, it has found quick and wide acceptance in most areas where some kind of document is produced. It is being used to create and produce all sorts of documents from labels to books. The authors, editors, journalists, designers, artists, and many other professionals, printers, publishers, corporate offices and government departments, business houses and industrial establishments, educational institutions, research and development organisations etc find it not only very useful but handy also in meeting their time-bound and other requirements at low cost in a professionally sound and aesthetically acceptable form.

State-of-the-Art of Printing Industry

The best way to appreciate a new technology is to understand the past and the present. It is an awful truth that the Indian printing industry in spite of its modernisation in recent years continues to be much backward as compared to the West. It is only the progressive daily newspaper industry and big print-shops located mainly in metropolitan cities, which have adopted the most advanced printing technologies anywhere in the world including transfer of made-up pages of full edition from Madras to New Delhi through satellite. The reference is to *The Hindu*.

Report of Printing Industry

According to the *Survey Report of Printing Industry* (1986), there are 72,000 presses in the country a per details given below:

1.	General commercial presses	71,150
2.	Newspaper presses	800
3.	Government presses	187
	Total	72,137

Practically 90% presses are letterpress units. Typesetting is done manually in 90% presses, by mono in 1.5%, by lino in 1.5% and by photo-typesetting 0.75%. These figures indicate the present state-of-the art of our printing industry. The annual growth rate of 62.5% in the case of photo-typesetting as can be seen from from the following table is a clear indicator that the industry's demand is for better and faster composing systems. It is also obvious that there was no other competing or better technology during that period as desktop publishing is a later introduction in India. Photo-typesetting is by and large a typesetting mechanism and not a total pre-press technology package. Moreover it is an expensive system to instal and operate even though it gives high resolution output on photo-sensitive paper/film.

TABLE 1

Number of Presses in India

Type of facility	*No. of presses*		*Annual growth rate*
	1977	*1986*	%
Hand composing	37,886	65,170	6.2
Mechanical composing	2,043	2,500	2.2
Letterpress printing	39,432	65,810	5.9
Offset printing	3,740	9,315	10.7
Photo-typesetting	10	790	62.5

The above figures clearly indicate that the pre-press industry has always remained handicapped for want of a suitable low-cost technology with a low turnaround time.

Pressure on Publishing and Printing Industries

The growth of educational institutions in India and the rate of increase in enrolments at various levels is presented in Tables 2 and 3.

TABLE 2

Growth of Recognised Educational Institutions in India

Class	*1950-51*	*1984-85*
Primary/Junior Basic Schools	209,671	519,701
Middle/Senior Middle Schools	13,596	129,879
High/Higher Secondary Schools	7,288	58,854
Universities	27	119
Board of Secondary/Intermediate Education	7	30
Colleges for General Education — Pre-degree level	128	4,060
Graduate and above	370	4,005
Colleges for Professional Education — Graduate and above	208	682

Source: *A Handbook of Educational and Allied Statistics*, Ministry of Human Resource Development Government of India (April 1987)

The responsibility for producing adequate reading material, both curricular and supplementary, is on a rapid increase. The pressure on the printing and publishing industries, is, therefore, mounting to adopt latest technologies to meet the national requirements.

TABLE 3

Growth of Enrolement at Different Levels of Education in India

Class	1950-51		1984-85	
Primary Classes (I-V)	19.154,457		83,932,704	
Middle classes (VI-VIII)	3,119,958		25,703,660	
High-Higher Secondary (Classes X-XI & 10 Plus 2)	1,219,917		13,820,039	
	Boys	*Girls*	*Boys*	*Girls*
Pre-Universiry Course/ Intermediate	194,921	26,416	1,660,085	590,992
Graduate	75,032	16,636	1,787,427	789,288
Postgraduate	14,401	2,127	215,646	102,556
Doctorate	1,051	139	19,729	8,893

Source: *A Handbook of Educational and Allied Statistics*, Ministry of Human Resource Development Government of India (April 1987).

Against the above background, desktop publishing had practically no difficulty in finding a ready market in the pre-press industry as well as by other users. Educational publishers, in particular, found it very useful to meet the increasing demand for education literature.

A Revolutionary Technology

Desktop publishing, popularly known as DTP, has come to be regarded as a revolutionary technology option for the generation of professional quality low-cost camera ready copy (CRC) mostly on plain paper, both graphics and text, using a system that fits on a desktop. It has liberated publishers and other users from having to run, often feverishly, for highly specialised services of typesetters, artists, camera operators, retouchers, make-up man etc.

The main reason for this revolution is that it has brought 'what you see is what you get' (WYSIWYG) environment to the pre-press industry and has transferred pre-press operations from the dingy workshop/factory atmosphere to the executive table with arm chair comfort. We shall no longer say that 'I have printer/s ink in my blood' to express our trade experience. The new technology has given a sense of pride to the trade which itself is a great motivating force for its acceptance, apart from the technological advantages.

The tools of production provide total control to the user over the content and form of the output. In general pre-requisite skills include a working knowledge of word processing, the ability to create and position graphics and an aesthetic sense for what constitutes acceptable layout and design.

In the field of typesetting alone, which is one of the major areas in the pre-press operations, it is considered to be a fourth revolution after the invention of movable types, linecaster and photo-typesetting. It is in this area, that is has found the maximum use. In Delhi alone about 300 DTP establishments with multistation configurations have come up during the last five years, commanding a sizable business from publishers/printers. This new technology has tremendous capability for providing full made-up pages electronically without cut and paste. It also provides facilities for quick editing, single or multiple column formatting, incorporation of graphics into text, selection and interchangeability of type fonts, proof-reading with spell checks, transfer of charts, graphs and illustrations from data bases, spread sheets and graphic programmes etc. in a WYISWYG environment. However, the best part is the low-cost professionally acceptable camera ready copy (CRC) output on plain paper which comes out of the laser printer instantaneously.

DTP software is now available for setting most of the Indian language scripts which can be merged to produce bilingual or multilingual publications.

Another area in which desktop publishing has found good use is the production of newsletters, inhouse magazines, periodicals and medium size newspapers. Some well established newspapers are also using this technology for the generation of text except that output is taken through dedicated photo typesetters for enhanced resolution of the printed image.

It is also very striking to note that the desktop publishing phenomenon has made practically every desktop with a personal computer a launching pad for turning out typeset output even in matters of routine correspondence and business communication.

Another major contribution of desktop publishing which has largely remained unexploited is that it has provided the necessary wherewithal for converting print from a static to a dynamic resource to provide customised print-services on demand. This flexibility was totally unknown to conventional printing technologies. In other words, repackaging of information say from 100-page book to a 10-page summary document was unthinkable earlier without going through the complicated procedures *ab initio* once again. Various front-end and back-end peripherals also provide it additional facilities to support output to other devices for photo-typesetting, slide making etc. Table 4 gives the manipulations possible in desktop publishing and other information delivery systems.

TABLE 4

Possibilities for Various Manipulations

Delivery System	*Content*	*Process*	*Format*
Handwritten Manuscript	0	0	0
Printed Book	0	+	0
Audio-Visual	0	+	+
Desktop Publishing	+	+	+

0 = Unchangeable + = Changing or enhancement of components possible

Advantages of Desktop Publishing

There art six general advantages which account for the extraordinary popularity of the desktop publishing. These are:

1. Cost benefits
2. Time savings
3. Better control
4. Increased productivity
5. Image/profile
6. Instant results.

Cost Benefits

Financial returns from investment on desktop publishing, hardware, software and training, could be quite high. Any printing/publishing establishment or business venture where there is enough work, the system should normally pay for itself within six months to a year. Savings are also made on form-production and designing or logo's, artwork and other graphics etc. Overall economy in typesetting expenditure through desktop publishing works out to be very considerable in case of jobs having large number of pages as compared to the expenditure on the same job by phototypesetting or even by hot-metal composing.

Time Savings

Time savings are enormous. The vendors of the desktop publishing systems very proudly estimate a reduction of 40-50% in time by desktop publishing over the time taken by the conventional typesetting process. In traditional printing, cycle of operations from galleys to made-up pages is very complicated and time-consuming. For example, typesetting is slow, authors corrections and changes take long time for correction, and worse, if they have to be carried out repeatedly, and page make-up is tedious and slow. On the other hand desktop publishing is a much speedier option for typesetting, formatting, corrections and editorial changes which can be carried out even at the final page stage. Use of spell checks minimises proof-reading errors.

Better-Control

Doing things in-house means much better control on production procedures and schedules to meet the targets, elimination of dependence on external services, protection against leakage of confidential information and minimisation of human errors in job execution at various stages because of the WYSIWYG environment.

Increased Productivity

Neat, clean and noiseless environment is very much conducive to greater productivity. User-friendliness of the system, time savings and better control mentioned above also contribute significantly to increased productivity.

Image/Profile

Credibility of companies especially those engaged in sales, marketing, public relations etc depends to a great extent on the presentation of their document. A good document inspires you to read it. It is said that printed words are seen and not heard. Therefore, most companies pay special attention to this aspect. This is precisely the reason why desktop publishing has penetrated into most areas of document production within business, industry, government and education.

Instant Results

All small jobs are almost done instantly in the presence of the customers. Laser printer is a very speedy device, the average speed being 8 pages per minute. Therefore, it can give an output of about 500 pages in A-4 size in one hour. Corrections, revisions and editorial changes hardly take any time. Commands for uniformity and stylisation run through the text in no time. Possibilities for editing are infinite and changes take place practically instantly.

What Makes Desktop Publishing System Work?

A stand-alone desktop publishing system consists of three components: a personal computer, a page layout software and a laser printer. A brief description of each of these three components is given below for a broad technological understanding of the system and its working.

Personal Computer

Personal computer is the front end through which the text and/or graphics are entered or into which these are transferred from other sources including micros, minis and mainframes.

Page Layout Software

Page layout or typesetting software allows screen based cut-and-paste from a variety of software sources and lends full support to page description language (PDL) resident in the output device, typically a laser printer.

The page layout software is what really makes the system work. It allows a user to set up, view and change page layout as many times as is necessary to achieve the desired design. It offers a range of fonts and characters sizes, handles text justification, hypenisation, merges graphics with text, provides powerful editing features which permit changes even at the page layout stage. The facility to zoom any part of page and to enlarge the same on the screen is available in most systems. These are some of the select features of a page layout software. A much better idea of a large number of functions which it performs can be had from the features given in Appendix 1.

Laser Printer

Laser printer is a fast and quiet output device. A desktop publishing system normally supports a laser printer with a minimum resolution of 300 dpi for giving an output directly on plain paper. A page description language (PDL) resident in the laser printer gives it the ability to print graphics and text together on the same page and to control the style and size of fonts used.

It is desirable that any complete desktop publishing system should support outputs to a variety of other devices in addition to the laser printer and should have the capability of sending complete camera ready copy (CRC) to a professional phototypesetter for producing an output of 1200 dpi or more on light-sensitive paper.

The figure 1 shows important constituents of a single-user desktop publishing system. Scanner and forge screen are add-ons.

A SINGLE-USER DTP SYSTEM

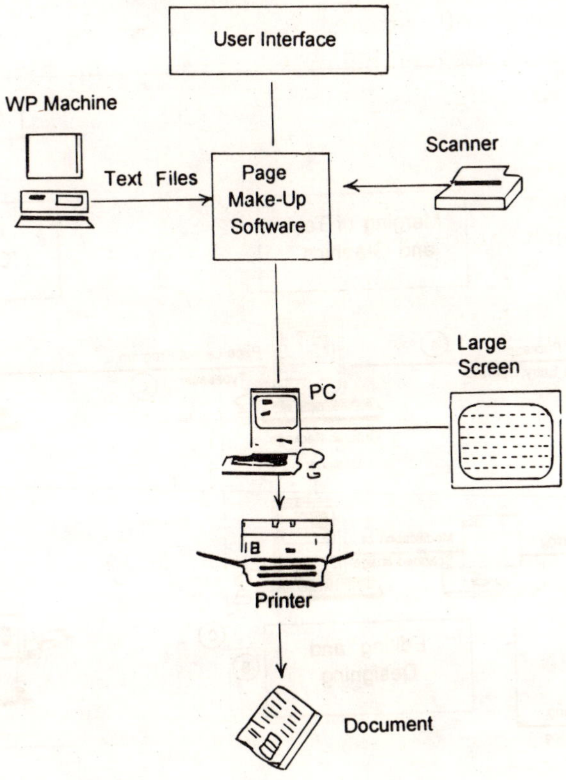

Fig. 1: Constituents of a desktop publishing system.

Add-on Peripherals

Depending upon the user's requirements all these components have plenty of add-on and function-enhancement capabilities with the help of front-end and back-end peripherals. Some important front-end peripherals are digitisers, tablets and optical scanner. Digitisers can read signals from video camera and change the signals into digital forms to be stored and manipulated by the computer. Tablets and light pens allow a person to draw free hand images that can be read by the computer and stored as digital information. Optical scanners scan a flat image, be it a photograph, drawing or text and digitise the information read from it. All these devices enhance the capability of the desktop publishing but may not be necessary for the common run of print jobs.

FLOW CHART OF THE PROCESS

Courtesy: **Apple Computers**

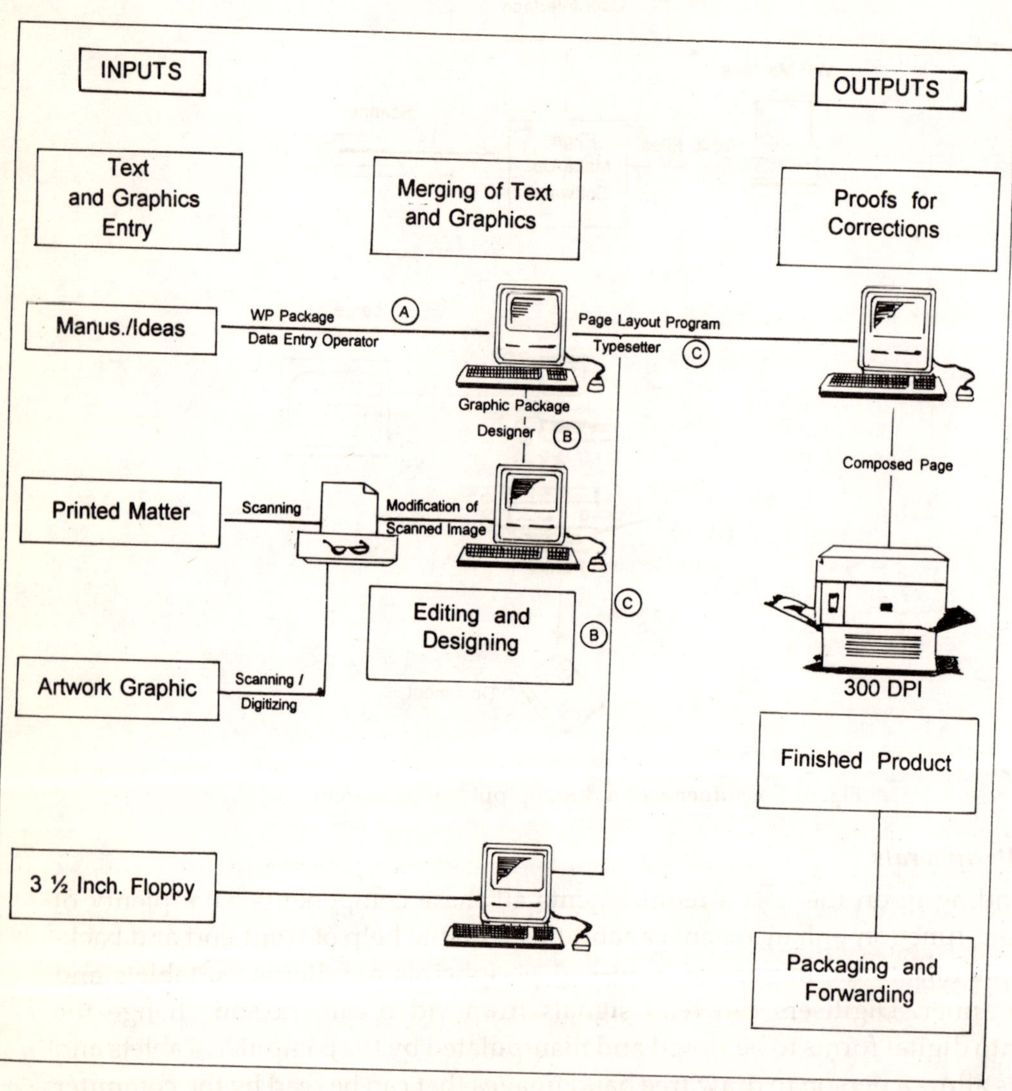

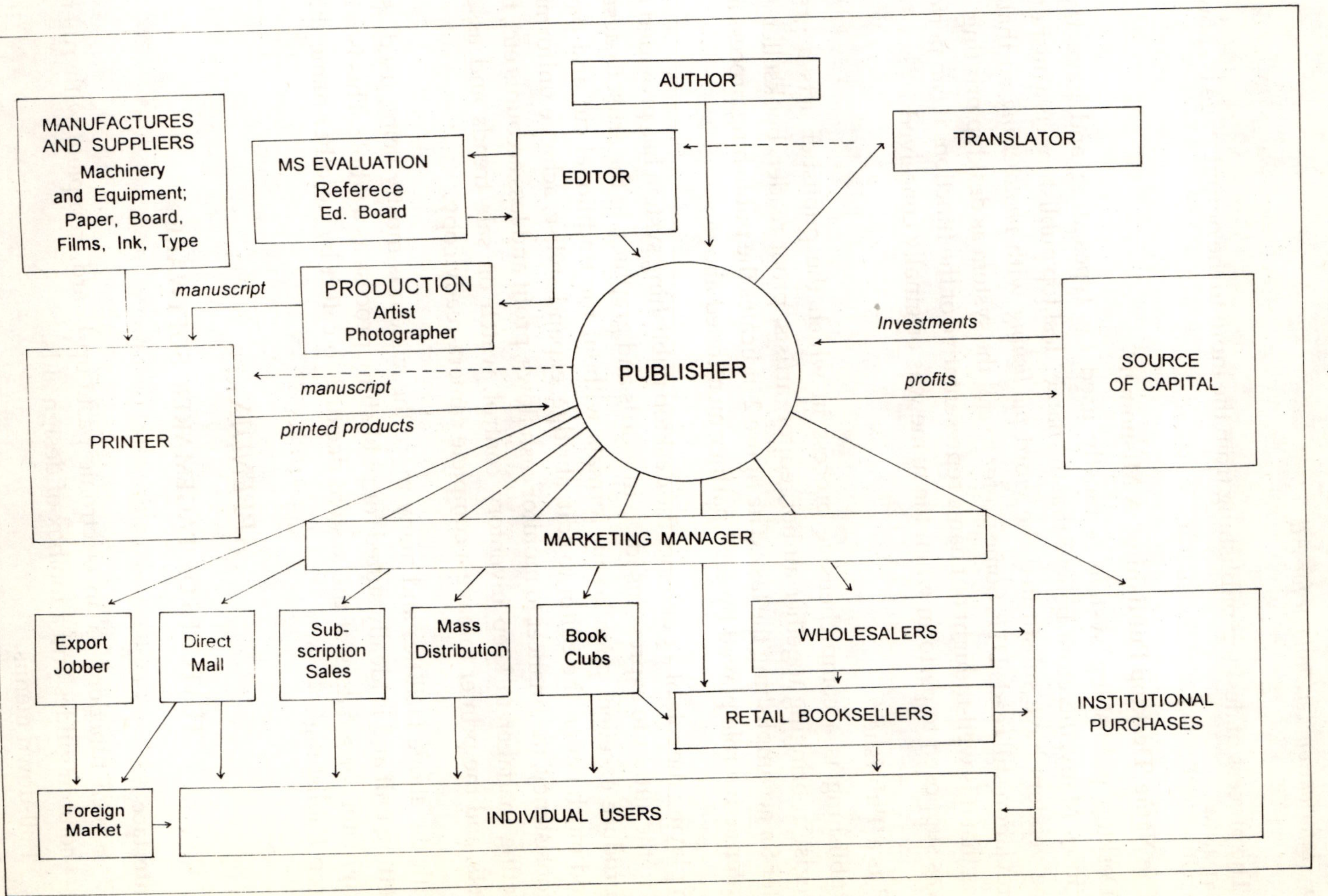

Fig. 2: Publishing Process

The process of desktop publishing from the input to the output stage is shown in the flow chart.

Is The Name 'Desktop Publishing' A Misnomer?

Desktop publishing system is mostly used for typesetting and page layout purposes. Many, therefore, believe that the name 'desktop publishing' is a misnomer. Some vendors have substituted the word *publishing* with *photosetting* so that the abbreviation still reads DTP. Some prefer to call the system as desktop printing. The fact is that it is well-thought out name representative of the functions it can perform or was supposed to perform when the name was originally conceived.

DTP as a 'Publisher'

Publishing is a comprehensive process in which the publisher acts a grand strategist in bringing together author, editor, artists, proof reader, bookseller and printer for accomplishing the task. The figure 2 indicates the publishing process and the inter-active role played by each partner mentioned above.

In playing the role of a publisher the desktop publishing system has provided the tools to the author to express his ideas in words and graphics, to the artist to design and produce excellent page layout formats without the traditional cut and paste method much better, the editor to edit, abridge, expand stylise, achieve uniformity and consistency, the financer to monitor cash flows, profit and loss accounts etc., the marketing manager to keep inventory control, watch on sale trends and assess markets, and the printer to have a complete camera-ready copy.

With the above facilities and many more the system is mostly being used as a typesetting unit and is ideally suited for publishing process as a whole. This is why the originator/originators of the system decided to call it by no other name than 'Desktop Publishing'.

APPENDIX

FEATURES OF 'PAGEMAKER' SOFTWARE

User Interface

1. Screen functions as an electronic paste-up board, complete with rulers column guides and a toolbox of design aids.
2. Pull-down menus.
3. Mouse-based selection and manipulation of text, graphics and menu commands.

4. Many keyboard shortcuts.
5. Five page views: full page, actual size, 200% enlargement, and 50% and 75% reductions.
6. WYSIWYG (what-you-see-is-what-you-get) screen display.
7. A highly intutive & interactive environment for electronic page composition.

Document Formatting

1. Up to 128 pages per file, 9, 999 pages per document.
2. Up to 20 columns per page.
3. Page sizes up to 17 inches by 22 inches.
4. Master pages for recurring design elements and page numbers.
5. Automatic page numbering.
6. Independent formatting of left-and right-hand pages.
7. Ability to override master page formats at any point in the document.
8. Ability to insert or delete pages.

Page Composition

1. Complete control over page composition.
2. Ability to integrate text and graphics from many sources.
3. Ability to change the number of columns, column widths (both regular and irregular) and column positions page by page.
4. Ability to resise and re-position graphic elements.
5. Ability to see and work on facing pages simultaneously.

Text Handling

1. Powerful built-in text editor for inserting, deleting, cutting pasting or creating new text.
2. Ability to change the length, width or position of text blocks on a page or between pages.
3. Automatic text threading from column and page to page so that changes ripple through the entire document.
4. Ability to present text flush left, flush right, centred or justified and to change such specifications at any time.
5. Ability to wrap text around both regular and irregularly shaped graphics.
6. Ability to change type specifications i.e. type size, face and style-for any increment of text, including a word, line, paragraph, column, page or entire story.

Typography

1. Type sizes from 4 to 127 points.
2. Type styles including plain, bold, italic, small caps, all caps, Strikethru, subscript, and superscript.
3. Support for a wide range of typefaces (depending on the printer capabilities).
4. Support for reversed type.
5. Complete control over leading (line spacing) in half-point increments.
6. Control over word spacing, letter spacing and paragraph spacing.
7. Kerning, both automatic and manual.
8. Automatic hyphenation and justification, based on a 110,000-word Houghton-Mifflin dictionary and user-specified entries of up to 1,000 words.
9. Prompted an manual hyphenation.
10. The ability to fill the space between tabbed columns with dots, dashes, underlines or user-specified characters (Leadered tabs).
11. Em-space, En-space and thin-space characters.

Graphics

1. Cropping.
2. Proportional re-sizing (reducing and enlarging).
3. Non-proportional re-sizing.
4. Ability to draw lines, squares, rectangles, circles and elipses in widths from 25 25-point (hairline) to 12-point.
5. Rapid re-positioning ("fast move" feature).
6. Ability to create screens in Page Maker at 10%, 20%, 30%, 40% 60% and 80%.
7. Ability to fill in Page Maker-created shapes with 10 patterns.
8. Ability to place Post Script graphics files (on Post Script-compatible printers).

'Page Maker' is a page composition program that can read both text as well as graphics files produced with MacWrite, Word, MacPaint, MacDraw, SuperPoint or any other word processing or graphics package.